Shipwrecks
of the
Isle of Man

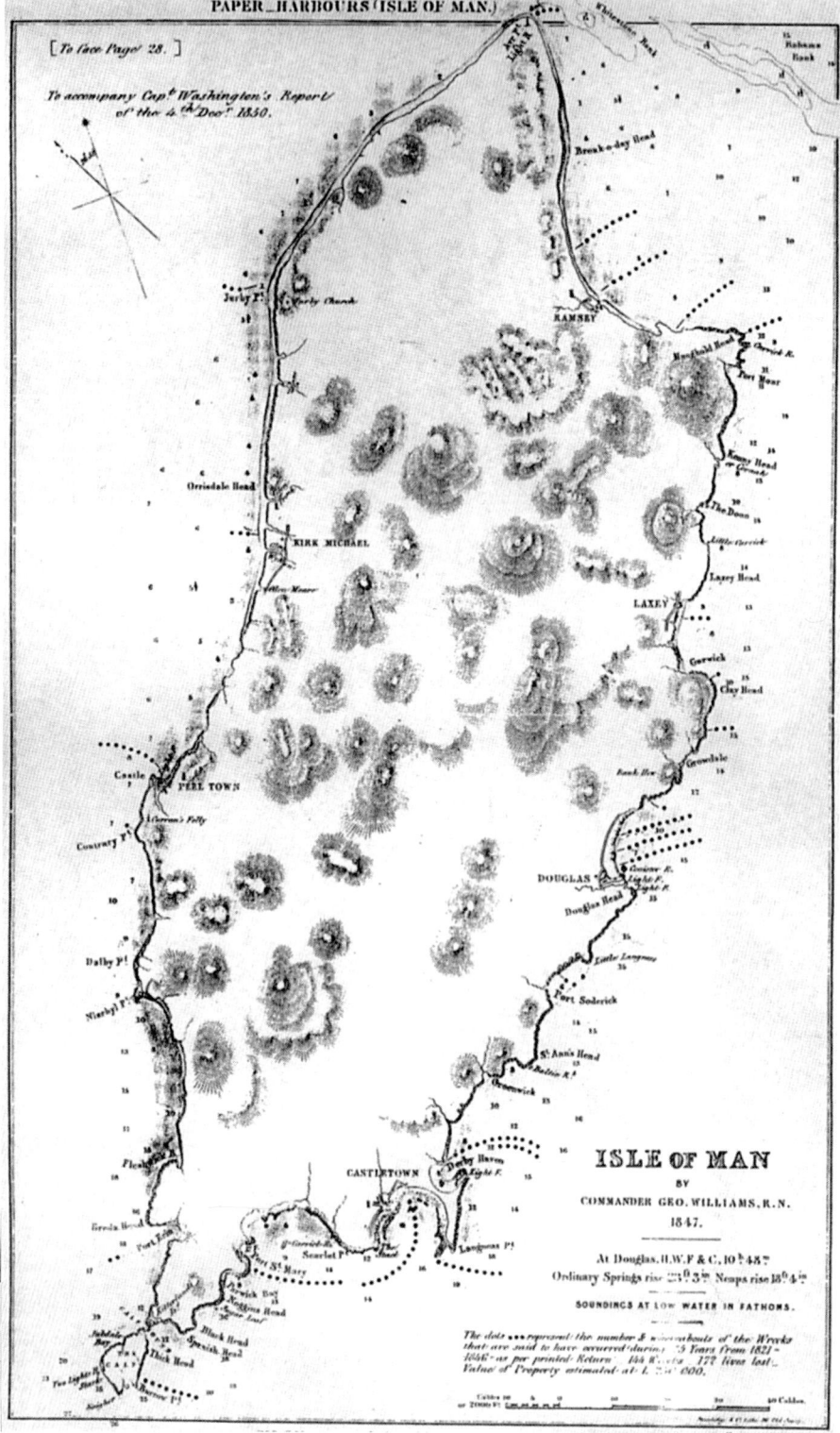

Shipwrecks
of the
Isle of Man

Adrian Corkill

TEMPUS

*This book is dedicated to the memory of my father,
Paul Corkill, who died on 27 November 2002.*

First published 2004

Tempus Publishing Ltd
The Mill, Brimscombe Port
Stroud, Gloucestershire GL5 2QG
www.tempus-publishing.com

© Adrian Corkill, 2004

The right of Adrian Corkill to be identified as the Author
of this work has been asserted by him in accordance with the
Copyrights, Designs and Patents Act 1988.

All rights reserved. No part of this book may be reprinted
or reproduced or utilised in any form or by any electronic,
mechanical or other means, now known or hereafter invented,
including photocopying and recording, or in any information
storage or retrieval system, without the permission in writing
from the Publishers.

British Library Cataloguing in Publication Data.
A catalogue record for this book is available from the British Library.

ISBN 0 7524 2698 2

Typesetting and origination by Tempus Publishing.
Printed and bound in Great Britain.

Contents

Acknowledgements 6

Introduction 8

Diving in the Isle of Man 11

How to Use this Book 20

    1 Wrecks in Open Water 25

    2 Wrecks on the Coast 159

    3 Wrecks on the Shore 217

Index of Wrecks 254

Acknowledgements

The author would like to thank the following people for their invaluable help in the compilation of this book.

Harold Appleyard, David Asprey, Martin Benn, Dr Ian Buxton, the late James Colledge, Bernard Lawley, Kevin O'Donoghue, Graeme Somner and Philip Thomas of the World Ship Society, for their patient help over the years with technical information on vessels. Manx National Heritage for permission to reproduce many of their photographs on local shipwrecks. The staff at the Manx Museum Library, Douglas, Isle of Man, for the help received from them by myself over the hundreds of hours that I have spent researching shipwrecks on rainy and windy winter days over the last fifteen years. Michael Craine, of Onchan, for his invaluable help with fishing vessels both in terms of technical data on the vessels and the numerous photographs of his used in this book. William H. Sleigh, for information on three wrecks of steamships in the 1940s around the southeast of the Isle of Man and for the loan of his superb collection of photographs of the wrecks which he took as a boy while attending King William's College. Roy Fenton, of London, for help in tracking down information on several of the ships. John Cook, for his work on the steamship *Empress Eugenie*. The staff at the Guildhall Library, London. Michael Corlett, of Laxey, for his assistance with the wreck of the *Ballina*. Tony Kennish, managing director of the Ramsey Steamship Co. for providing information on the two *Ben* boats featured. John Qualtrough, of Port St Mary, for his invaluable local knowledge and loan of some unique photographs. Captain Frank Devaney, of Dublin, and formerly of Sligo, for assistance with the wreck of the steamship *Liverpool*. Nancy Hughes, of Dublin, whose father, Captain John Hughes, was master of the steamship *Ringwall*. The staff at the UK's Public Record Office at Kew, in London. Alan Kelly at Mannin Collections of Peel for permission to use his photograph of the wreck of the steamship *Manx Maid*. The National Maritime Museum in Greenwich, for allowing me to use several of their photographs. Andrew Denholm for his photograph of the motor vessel *Polarlight*. Jim Porter, of Fleetwood, for his photograph of the steam trawler *Merisia*. John Clarkson, of Preston, for his permission to use photographs of the steamships *Ben Veg* and *Ringwall*. Hull Maritime Museum for allowing me to use the photographs of the steam trawler *Octavia* and the steamship *Romeo*. David Leece, of Peel, skipper of the fishing vessel *Two Sisters* and formerly the *Cardea*, with

Acknowldegements

information which has led to the discovery of several wrecks, including the steam tug *Grinder*.

I would also like to thank the following divers for their input: Maura Mitchell, of Ballasalla, for information on several of the coastal wreck sites and who also provided several photographs; Steve Taggart, of Laxey, for his local knowledge on wrecks and help with gathering additional information; Steve Lace, of Laxey, for his help over the years in diving the wrecks; Phil Hutchinson, of Whitehaven, for allowing me to use some of his underwater photographs and for additional information on the wrecks of the motor vessels *Teasel* and *Polarlight*, and the steamships *Fire King* and *Ben Veg*, and Dave Copley for information on several wrecks, including the steamship *Ringwall*.

And finally, thanks to my wife Lorna, for understanding the effort and many hours at the computer required to complete a book such as this one.

Introduction

My interest in shipwrecks began not by the usual route of learning to dive, but by my love of sea angling. I had fished from the local rocks and piers since I was very young, but had always watched as boats headed out from the harbours to the fishing grounds and returned with greater numbers of fish and larger fish than I could possibly catch from the shore. I was determined to own a boat as soon as I could afford to buy one. By the time I was in full-time employment at the age of nineteen in 1985, one of the first major purchases I made was a 14ft-long fibreglass dinghy complete with 10hp outboard motor. By 1987 I owned a locally built boat known as a 'Peel Inshore', an 18ft-long fibreglass boat with an inboard engine. I could therefore achieve greater distances in search of fish. By this time I had also acquired a Navstar 2000D Decca navigation set and a video echo sounder.

I had read about large catches of fish on wrecks in the southwest of England, so when one day I was told about a wreck off Laxey known as the *Four and Forty* by local trawler men, I was keen to give it a go. The name was not the ship's real name, but the Decca lane intersection on which she lay. On one calm August day in 1987 I set off, together with a friend, Paul Woods, from Douglas harbour in *Janie*. Apart from the name of the wreck we had no coordinates, so headed for the *Four and Forty* lane intersection. Arriving an hour or so later, we began searching the seabed with the sounder. After about half an hour, we passed over a section of the wreck, but were unable to relocate it on turning the helm around. Our first attempt at wreck fishing was not proving very successful! Paul then spotted a *mollag* (Manx for a marker buoy) about one hundred yards off to the port. We motored over to the spot and immediately the shape of an object on the seabed appeared on the screen of the video-sounder. The wreck was about 50m in length and about 4m proud of the seabed.

Looking back on that day, the fishing was poor compared to wreck fishing trips of today, but the fish appeared big to a couple of anglers used to working inshore waters. Eventually, it was time to make the eight mile journey back to Douglas, a daunting distance to a still inexperienced boat angler.

I later tried to find out the name of the vessel that lay on the seabed. Initially, I thought it was a small coaster. Subsequently, I was told her name was the *Ballin-I*, a strange sounding name. My curiosity had been aroused and I was determined to find out some of her history; when she sank and what had caused her to sink. What story did the wreckage lying off Laxey have to tell?

Introduction

My search commenced at the Manx Museum Library at the top of Crellin's Hill in Douglas. I started a search in the local newspapers during the period in which I thought the vessel had most likely foundered, about 1880 to 1920. Starting in 1890, I quickly came across wrecks other than the one for which I was searching, and made a note of the date and circumstances of their loss. I carried on through the years in sequential order until I reached 1920, but without finding any reference to the *Ballin-I*. I had, however, built a database of over one hundred shipwrecks. I decided that the *Ballin-I* must have foundered prior to 1890, so I started on the 1880s.

I was looking at the microfilm copy of the *Isle of Man Examiner* for the year 1882 when suddenly a headline caught my eye:

> **THE LOSS OF THE BALLINA.**
>
> SEVERE CENSURE ON THE OWNER.
>
> On Wednesday morning, in the St. George's Hall Liverpool, the inquiry instituted by the Board of Trade into the circumstances attending the

The name seemed very close to the one for which I was searching and, as I read on, I quickly deduced it to be the wreck off Laxey that I had fished the previous summer. My curiosity over the wreck had finally been satisfied, but I remained inquisitive about the other wrecks I had found in the records. I already realised the abundance of fish that could be caught on wrecks, and now that my research had led me to believe there must be more wrecks lying off the Manx coast, I hoped that many of them might yield better fishing than the *Ballina*. By this time it had also become evident that no comprehensive list of wrecks around the Isle of Man had been produced. It was at this point in 1988 that I decided to research all wrecks either on the coast of the Isle of Man or in surrounding waters, to as far back in time as I could reliably go. This, I later realised, was around the mid-seventeenth century. Today, after fifteen years of research, I have amassed a database of over 1200 wrecks, the first dating back to 1644. This forms the basis of my *Dictionary of Shipwrecks off the Isle of Man,* first published in 1995 and then again in 2001 on CD-ROM.

In the years 1993 and 1994 I made contact with a group of divers, including Steve Taggart and Steve Lace. During these two years I was able to show them the locations of several not previously dived wrecks, which I had been fishing. These included the *Lucy*, *Hibernian* and *Grinder*. The discoveries they made, and the encouragement they gave, led me to take up scuba diving as a sport during 1995. In the eight years since then I have been fortunate enough to have dived on more 'virgin' wrecks and was, with Steve Lace, part of the first pair of divers to search the wreck of the steamship *Liverpool* off Langness.

My fascination with shipwrecks continues in terms of their history, of diving on them, and of catching fish from around them. The historical record for many shipwrecks is less than accurate, with many ships having sunk many miles from where the records would lead you to believe. Piecing together the shipwreck sites around the Isle of Man is therefore akin to completing a jigsaw; the historical information forms the pieces and the available spaces that they can fill are the shipwreck sites. Now, in 2003, the jigsaw is substantially complete. There are still a couple of pieces that could be reversed and new sites are being discovered each year, but on the whole, the puzzle is now complete enough to publish.

This book gives details of fifty-seven shipwreck sites in open water, that is, sites located away from the coast. These sites are by no means all shipwreck sites, as those of little interest or that lie in deep water have been excluded. This section of the book will be of great interest to both divers and anglers. There are twenty-five sites located on the coast of the Isle of Man. These will be of interest to divers, but less so to anglers. Finally, a section contains fifteen shipwreck sites on the shore, which can be visited on foot at low water. All ninety-seven shipwreck sites will be of interest to local and maritime historians.

The story does not end here. I am still working on several shipwreck sites, and more still lie undiscovered, particularly those of wooden ships which leave less for the modern shipwreck hunter to find than steel or iron wrecks, but nonetheless could prove to be important discoveries. You can keep abreast of all the latest news on wreck diving around the Isle of Man at my website: www.iomshipwrecks.com.

Adrian Corkill
November 2003

Diving in the Isle of Man

The waters around the Isle of Man offer some of the best wreck diving available anywhere around the British Isles. Visibility is generally good at around 10-12m in summer and sometimes in excess of 20m. Most of the wrecks are relatively unexplored and certainly not crowded. Indeed, you would be very unlucky to dive a wreck and encounter any other divers there. Wildlife abounds, both above and below the water, and there is a very varied selection of scenic dives around the coast all the way from Maughold Head in the north-east of the Island to Peel in the west. Some of the scenic coastal dives around the south-west, including the Calf of Man, are probably among the best in the British Isles. Having such good scenic diving offers opportunities for second dives, or substitutes for wreck dives on days when the weather prevents access to the offshore wrecks.

There are two main drawbacks for the visiting diver. Firstly, diving facilities are not as well developed as in the United Kingdom. Don't always expect to be able to get a fill of tri-mix or nitrox, for instance. Secondly, the cost of transporting divers, vehicle and RIB across on the ferry is high. Despite this, every year divers from the United Kingdom make the journey to the Isle of Man and experience some of their best diving, both wreck and scenic, from around the British Isles.

Diving Facilities

Diving Air Services, The Old Boathouse, South Quay, Douglas, IM1 5BT (Tel. 01624 628123; e-mail. mail@aecdas.com; website. www.aecdas.com) provide air fills, maintenance services and retail a reasonable stock of equipment, mainly from the Scuba Pro range. They are open from 8.30 a.m. to 5.30 p.m. on weekdays and from 9.00 a.m. to 1.00 p.m. on Saturdays. Out of hours, air fills can be arranged by appointment. The staff are knowledgeable and always ready to help.

Air fills can also be obtained from the Hyperbaric Centre, The Fire Station, Peel Road, Douglas (Tel. 01624 626394). The Centre is open from 9.00 a.m. to 5.00 p.m. every weekday. The Centre is also able to fill oxygen cylinders.

The sole dedicated boat equipment chandler is Manx Marine Ltd, The Tongue, Douglas (Tel. 01624 674842), who stock an extensive range of both boat equipment and clothing.

Charter Boats

Manx Sea Charter Services Ltd operates the charter boat *Castaway* from either Douglas or Port St Mary, depending upon requirements. She is an Offshore 32 and is designed to carry ten divers. Contact Dean at The Old Boathouse, South Quay, Douglas, Isle of Man, IM1 5BT (Tel. 01624 628123, castaway@aecdas.com).

Weather Forecasts

As the Isle of Man is located in the middle of the North Irish Sea, the weather tends to be very changeable and it is essential to obtain an accurate weather forecast before proceeding to sea. The meteorological office based at Ronaldsway Airport provides weather forecast services for the Isle of Man and the North Irish Sea. The shipping forecast can be accessed on the web on Manx Radio's website (www.manxradio.com) or a pre-recorded version is available by telephone (Tel. 0900 624 3322). A forecaster can be also contacted (Tel. 0900 624 3200). Calls to both lines are charged.

Tides

The tidal range around the Isle of Man is quite large, being about 5m on neap tides and 7m on spring tides. The times of high water correspond closely (to within five minutes) to when they occur at Liverpool. Obviously, slack water periods at various wreck sites differ quite considerably from the actual times of low or high water. Guidance on slack water periods is given with each wreck site. Laver's *Liverpool & Irish Sea Tide Table* gives the times of low and high water at a very reasonable cost. Contact: Laver Publishing, PO Box 7, Liverpool L19 9EN (Tel. 0151 475 7649, www.laverpublishing.com).

Launch Sites

All the launch sites detailed below are publicly owned and available free of charge. More details are on the Isle of Man Harbours website: www.gov.im/harbours/Ports_Home.asp.

Douglas

The main slipway in Douglas is located within the harbour and is accessed by the South Quay. Parking is available on the road, except during the day on weekdays when commuters' cars can take up much of the space close to the slipway. Diving Air Services is also located less than 50m from the slipway.

The slipway itself gives all tide access. Caution should be exercised at very low water spring tides, as the slip ends in a step. Lighting is poor for recovery of boats in the hours of darkness. The slip is also quite long in length and it is only wide enough for one vehicle at a time, so there can be delays, especially during busy

Douglas slipway.

Castletown slipway.

times at weekends. The slipway is protected from all wind directions except the north-east. Anything above a moderate north-easterly wind can create problems with recovery.

Douglas harbour supports much of the commercial boat traffic to the Isle of Man. All boats launching into the harbour from the slipway should therefore contact Douglas Harbour Control on VHF Channel 12 in order to seek permission to either

The main slipway at Port St Mary.

The original slipway next to the Lifeboat House at Port St Mary.

exit the harbour or re-enter the harbour after a dive. Contact Douglas harbourmaster (01624 686628) for further information.

Castletown

The slipway at Castletown is located in the outer harbour opposite the Old Lifeboat House. The slipway is wide enough for two vehicles at a time, and parking is available at the top of the slipway. The slipway can only be used for approximately three hours either side of high water, however. The slipway is exposed when the wind is in the south or south-west. Contact Castletown harbourmaster (01624 823549) for further information.

Port St Mary

Port St Mary has two slipways that can be used to launch small boats. The original one next to the Lifeboat House is quite narrow and slopes at a very gentle angle so can make launching difficult. The newer slipway is the one most commonly used today. It is located in the main boat park and gives all-tide access. Being only a few years old, the slipway has been designed and built with the launching of modern boats in mind. This makes the slipway very popular so, unfortunately, it can get congested in the summer months, particularly at weekends. There is plenty of parking near to the slipway. Contact Port St Mary harbourmaster (01624 833205) for further information.

Port Erin

The slipway at Port Erin is situated next to the harbour and leads down to the sandy beach. Boats are launched from the beach, which is composed of firm sand. Boats can be loaded with diving equipment using the jetty between the Raglan Pier and the Lifeboat House or from the steps at the Pier itself. Contact Port Erin harbourmaster (01624 833206) for further information.

Port Erin harbour showing the slipway onto the beach.

Peel slipway.

Peel

The slipway at Peel is located next to the outer breakwater and offers all-tide access. The slipway is very wide, allowing several boats to launch at the same tide, but is quite steep. The slipway is also used by the Peel Lifeboat, so consideration must be given not to block access on the slipway, nor to park vehicles anywhere near the Lifeboat House where they may impede the lifeboat personnel in effecting a launch. Parking can be limited on busy weekends at peak times. Contact Peel harbourmaster (01624 842338) for further information.

Ramsey

There are two ways of launching a boat at Ramsey. The first is to use the slipway located on the northern side of the inner harbour. The slipway is limited in its use by being only usable two hours either side of high water. The more favoured alternative is to use the slipway in front of the Lifeboat House at the northern end of the South Promenade near to the harbour entrance. The slipway leads onto the beach. The sand is reasonably firm, but a four-wheel drive vehicle is recommended. Care should be taken not to impede lifeboat access. Contact Ramsey harbourmaster (01624 812245) for further information.

Ramsey slipway in the inner harbour.

Beach in front of the Lifeboat House in Ramsey.

Laxey

Laxey slipway is located in the inner harbour and is accessed via the boat park. The slipway is sheltered and gives access three hours either side of high water. Contact Laxey harbourmaster (01624 861633) for further information.

Laxey slipway.

Local Wreck Laws

The Isle of Man operates a twelve mile limit of its territorial waters. It is a legal requirement that all recovered wreck is reported to the Receiver of Wreck for the Isle of Man, whether recovered from within or outside Manx waters, and even if the finder is the owner. The Receiver of Wreck is responsible for the administration of the Isle of Man's Wreck and Salvage (Ships and Aircraft) Act 1979. Operating on behalf of the Department of Transport, the Receiver of Wreck is located within the Director of Harbours Office. Forms for reporting items of wreck are available from the Receiver of Wreck, Harbour Offices and Coastguard Stations.

The Receiver of Wreck will investigate ownership of the wreck items. The owner has one year in which to come forward and prove title to the property.

The Receiver of Wreck can be contacted at Director of Harbours Office, Department of Transport, Sea Terminal Building, Douglas, Isle of Man, IM1 2RF (Tel. 01624 686626, enquiries@harbours.dot.gov.im). Additionally, items of wreck recovered that might have historical or archaeological importance will be reported by the Receiver of Wreck to Manx National Heritage. Manx National Heritage can be contacted direct at the Manx Museum, Douglas, Isle of Man, IM1 3LY (Tel. 01624 648000, enquiries@mnh.gov.im).

Recompression Facilities

The Isle of Man has recompression facilities located next to the fire station in Douglas. Contact Dave Downie at the Department of Hyperbaric Medicine,

Peel Road, Douglas, Isle of Man, IM1 5ED (Tel. 01624 626394, hyperbaric@enterprise.net). If contacting the chamber in an emergency, phone the Coastguard on 999.

Diving Safety

When embarking on a dive trip to the various wreck sites around the Isle of Man, it is prudent to contact Liverpool Coastguard on VHF Channel 16 (or Tel. 0151 9313 343) with details of the dive plan together with the number of persons on board the vessel and estimated time of return. Don't forget to contact the Coastguard again upon safe arrival back from the launch site.

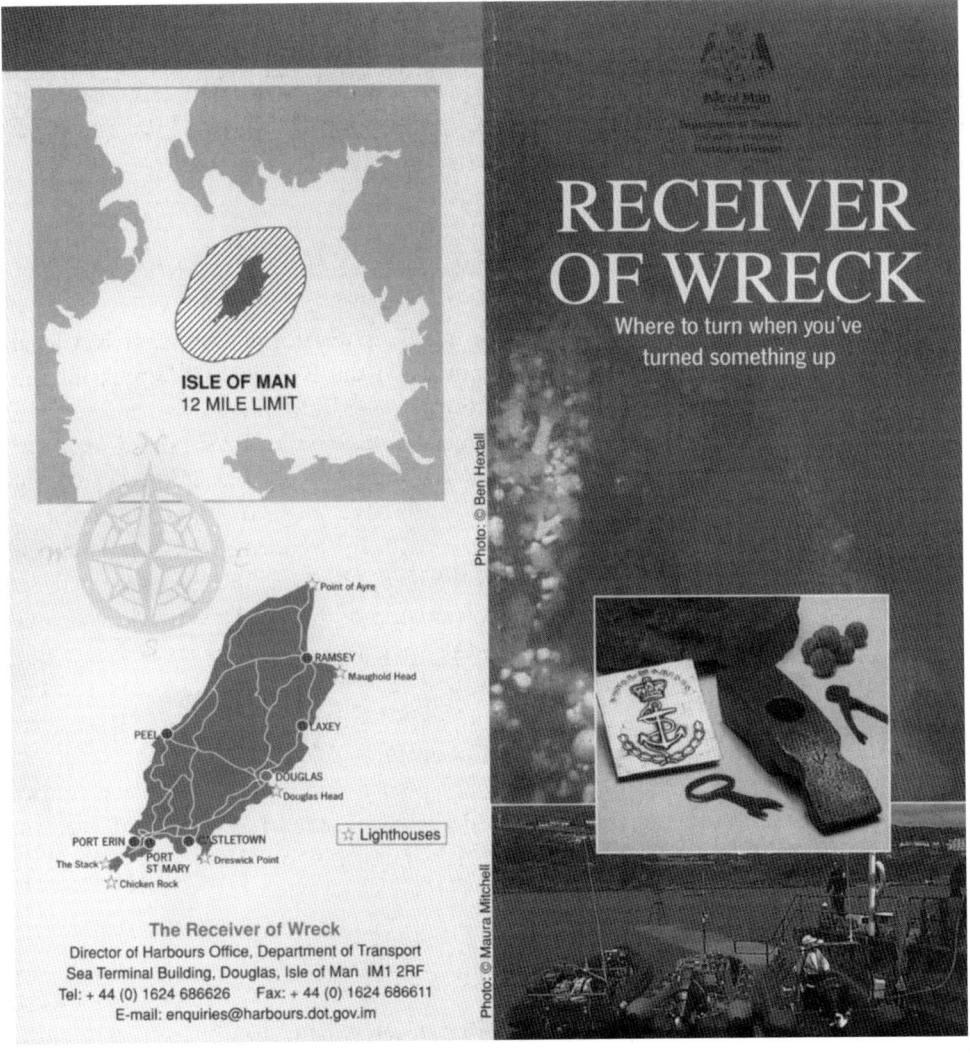

The Isle of Man has its own wreck laws and Receiver of Wreck. (DOT)

How to Use the Book

This book is split into three main parts. The first part details fifty-seven wrecks located in open water around the Isle of Man that lie in 60m or less of water. Some of the wrecks lie outside the Isle of Man's territorial waters limit of twelve miles with the most distant wrecks located approximately midway across the North Irish Sea toward neighbouring countries. All wrecks can however be described as being accessible from launch sites in the Isle of Man.

The second part details twenty-five wrecks that lie directly on the coast of the Isle of Man. These are wrecks that can be still dived and are quite often close to the Isle of Man's many scenic coastal dive sites.

Finally, the third section details fifteen wrecks that can be found on the shore and are accessible by walking to the site.

Wrecks in Open Water

For ease of quick reference, each wreck site listed in **Wrecks in Open Water** has the following information under the name of the vessel:

Wreck: ★★★
Scenery: ★★★★★
Angling: ★★
Depth: 38m
Position: 54 00.361 N, 04 33.403 W
Datum: WGS84
Location: 3.9n.m. south-east of Langness
Access: Douglas (9.0n.m.) and Port St Mary (7.5n.m.) slipways at all stages of the tide. Castletown (5.5n.m.) slipway three hours either side of high water.

The star rating after Wreck gives an indication of the condition of the wreck site:

★★★★★ Hull intact or virtually intact.
★★★★ Some deterioration in the hull.
★★★ Hull collapsed but the outline of the vessel is still discernible.

How to Use the Book

★★ Large amount of broken wreckage but vessel's form is indiscernible.
★ Only some scattered wreckage remains.

The star rating after Scenery gives an indication of quality of the wreck from a diving perspective:

★★★★★ Excellent dive, generally intact with plenty to see, generally good viz.
★★★★ Enjoyable dive, wreck has deteriorated to some degree, generally good viz.
★★★ Pleasant dive, but viz may be poor on occasions or there may be less to see.
★★ Very broken wreck, but worth a dive for a search through the debris.
★ Enthusiasts only.

The star rating after Angling gives an indication of species and size of fish encountered on the wreck:

★★★★★ Consistent angling where fish are both large and numerous.
★★★★ Generally excellent fishing, but perhaps certain species missing.
★★★ Fish numerous and mainly small, but with occasional larger fish.
★★ Moderate numbers of small fish.
★ Poor, generally not worth fishing.

The data under Depth gives the median low water general depth level that can be found around the wreck. As a general rule for high waters around the Isle of Man add a further 5m to the depth for neap tides and 7m to the depth for spring tides.

The Position section covers the latitude and longitude of the wreck site given in degrees, minutes and decimals of a minute. Positions have been gathered over the last few years using a GPS navigator (if the datum is WGS84 then the reading is from a GPS set, otherwise the position is an older reading derived from a Decca set). Due to the differences that exist between different manufacturers and models of GPS sets and even between individual sets of the same model, the positions may not match exactly with your set, although differences should be small. Great care should nonetheless be exercised when approaching the coordinates of wrecks lying on the coast, especially in limited visibility as quoted positions may lie within metres of the rocks.

Datum refers to the set of parameters, which defines the coordinate system and states its position with respect to the Earth's surface. Since the introduction of GPS, the most commonly used datum is World Geostatic Survey 1984 or WGS84 for short. Previously, Ordinance Great Britain (OGB) was commonly used in waters around the British Isles, especially in conjunction with Decca sets. The significance of datum to wreck locating is that the difference between WGS84 and OGB positions can be as much as 80m. Using a datum of OGB in a navigator set with a WGS84 derived position from this book could therefore result in delay or failure to locate the wreck. The datum in a GPS set is usually defined by the user in the navigation set-up function.

The Location gives an approximate position for the wreck by means of both a distance in nautical miles (n.m.) and a compass bearing from a significant landmark, which is usually the closest point on land to the wreck.

The nearest launch sites on the Isle of Man to the wreck are covered under Access. Those with all-tide access to slipways are given first, followed by sites with more limited access, even though they may be closer to the wreck.

Wrecks on the Coast

The same information is given for each vessel as for **Wrecks in Open Water** except that the star ratings for Wreck, Scenery and Angling are not used. The figure given for Depth is generally the maximum depth that will be attained at the site. Much of the wreckage may in fact lie at a shallower depth, especially where it is located in gullies on a rocky coastline.

Wrecks on the Shore

For quick reference, each wreck site listed in **Wrecks on the Shore** has the following information under the name of the vessel:

Position: 54 19.835 N, 04 33.914 W
Datum: WGS84
Map Reference: SC 332 958
Location: Ballakeig, half a mile south of the Cronk, Ballaugh
Access: From the car park at the Cronk, Ballaugh, turn left and head in a southerly direction for about 500m.

Position and Datum have the same definitions as for **Wrecks in Open Water**. Map references are based on the National Grid Reference System. The combination of the easting and northing positions defines a box 100 square metres. All references are derived from the Isle of Man *Public Rights of Way and Outdoor Leisure Map (Seventh Edition)* published by the Department of Local Government and the Environment.

Under Location, a general description of where the site lies is given, whilst Access provides an indication of how to get to the site by using public rights of way.

For All Wrecks

The Vessel section gives the technical details for each vessel, including (where known) the type, construction, port of registry, both gross and net tonnage, year built, builder, owners, dimensions in feet and metres, type and power of engine and engine builder, as well as any other relevant details.

An account of the events leading up to the vessel's loss is documented under History, and References gives the source of all technical and historical references and replaces the standard bibliography. Under this, MNH refers to Manx National Heritage's library at the Manx Museum in Douglas.

For **Wrecks in Open Water**, Wreck Site is divided into two sub-sections. Under Diving, confirmation on how the wreck has been identified is given, along with dimensions of the wreck, orientation, a general description of the wreck together with any notable features, expectations of the visibility and information on the tidal flow and slack water periods. Angling gives information on the species and size of fish likely to be encountered. For **Wrecks on the Coast**, only diving information is given. For **Wrecks on the Shore**, details of what to see are given.

Wrecks in Open Water

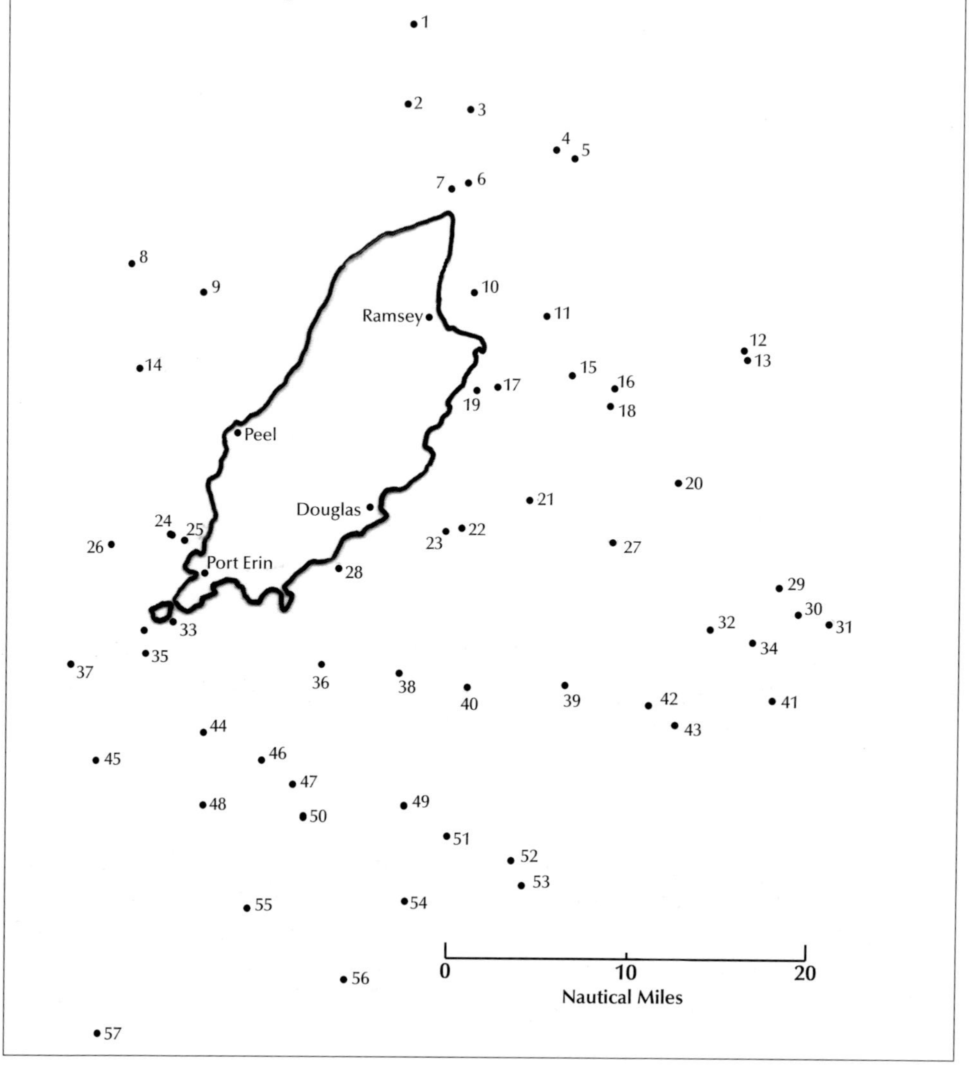

1	Inkosi	16	Queen of the	29	Glenmaroon	44	Vivid
2	Ben Veg		Isles	30	Adgillus	45	Carmelite
3	Sustain	17	Float	31	Ardbeg	46	Florence
4	Lembas	18	Lady Louisa	32	Limesfield	47	Grinder
5	Teasel		Pennant	33	Fenella Ann	48	PT1
6	Polarlight	19	Robert Dee	34	Ben Rein	49	Rostrevor
7	Fireking	20	Octavia	35	Amber Rose	50	Manchester
8	Romeo	21	Ballina	36	Liverpool	51	Skerries
9	Blue Star	22	Paddle Wheel	37	Tuskar	52	Mhari-L
10	Rian	23	Lady Louisa	38	Briar	53	Empress Eugenie
11	Joseph Hodgkins	24	Don Bosco	39	Peveril	54	Opal
12	Westburn	25	Thracian	40	Cardea	55	Dundalk
13	Girl May	26	Ringwall	41	Flying Meteor	56	Clwyd
14	Oona Hall	27	Dawn Waters	42	Lucy	57	U246
15	Albatross	28	Afton	43	Hibernian		

Wrecks in Open Water

Adgillus

Wreck: ★★★
Scenery: ★★
Angling: ★
Depth: 36m
Position: 54 02.833 N, 03 48.458 W
Datum: WGS84
Location: 24.2n.m. east-south-east of Douglas Head
Access: Douglas (24.2n.m.) slipway at all stages of the tide. Laxey (23.7n.m.) slipway three hours either side of high water.

Vessel

The wooden barque *Adgillus*, of Liverpool, (Official Number: 69,587), 415 tons register, was built by Oliver of Quebec in 1873 for the West African trading company, Messrs Thomas Harrison & Co., of Liverpool. She was 142.2ft in length, had a beam of 29ft and a draught of 13.2ft (43.4m x 8.8m x 4.0m). The *Adgillus* cost £6,560 to build and was insured for £6,000. She was classed in March 1874 as A1 for ten years at Lloyd's, London.

History

On 14 October 1874, the *Adgillus* commenced her second voyage from Liverpool for Brass River, Old Calabar, West Africa (now part of modern-day Nigeria) in a gale, but was forced to sit at anchor in the Mersey until the gale blew itself out. She had a crew of seventeen hands and was commanded by Martin Thompson. Her cargo consisted of various supplies, including salt, gunpowder and rifle ammunition, together with many household goods ranging from brass and glass oil lamps to plates, glassware and clay smoking pipes.

At 6.00 a.m. on 20 October, she finally sailed from the Mersey in charge of Mr Parry, a first class pilot, and in tow of a tug. The tug was cast off between the Bell Buoy

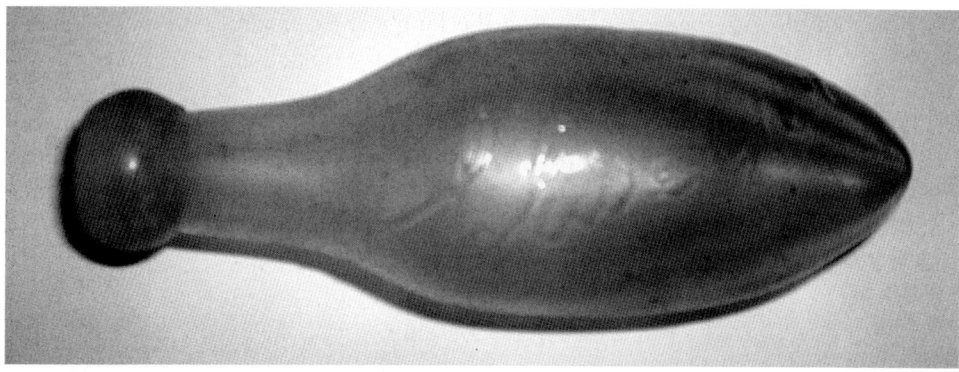

Schweppes bottle from the wreck of the *Adgillus*.

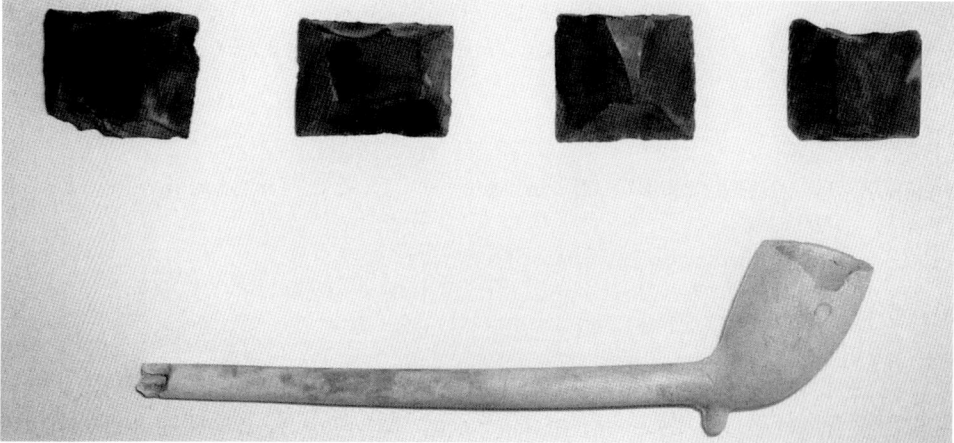

Smoking pipe and gunflints from the wreck of the *Adgillus*.

and the North West Lightship. The pilot remained on board, being engaged to take the ship as far as Point Lynas on the north coast of Anglesey. Sail was set on the port tack, the wind being a fresh westerly breeze at the time. At 8.00 p.m., the North West Lightship bore north-west four miles from the *Adgillus*. After midnight the wind increased further to a full gale. At about 3.00 a.m. on 21 October, the wind shifted to the north-west and a heavy squall split several of her sails. Heavy seas washed over her starting water casks and other items on deck, as well as washing away the ports.

Soon after 6.00 a.m. the master wore the ship to the south-west, but when she came to the wind she plunged so heavily that he found it necessary to wear around again immediately on the port tack. All hands had been on the deck since 3.00 a.m. and the ship had been pumped dry at 4.00 a.m. Subsequently, half hands had been kept busy at the pumps. Finding the ship making more water and labouring heavily, they began, at 11.00 a.m., to throw cargo over the side to lighten the ship and were so engaged when, at 2.00 p.m., the alarm was given that the ship was foundering. The crew barely had time to get into the longboat, which had previously been got ready, when the *Adgillus* lurched over, floating the longboat off her deck. The first mate, who was clearing some of the gear attached to the longboat, and a man called Antonio Natal, who was clinging to the backstays and apparently too frightened to move, both perished with the barque as she bodily went down in a few minutes. Her position, subsequently ascertained by Martin Thompson, was declared to be eighteen miles north-west of the Morecambe Bay Lightship. The longboat, containing the survivors, drifted towards the Lightship and eventually they managed to reach the safety of it after a gruelling journey lasting nine hours. They were kindly received by the crew of the Lightship. Afterwards, the surviving crewmen from the barque were forwarded to Fleetwood and then on to Liverpool.

It was thought by the Court of Inquiry that the starting of one of the *Adgillus*'s butts (the joining of two timbers or planks endways) had caused the leak that led to her eventual foundering. Mr T.S. Raffles, stipendiary magistrate, found that no blame for the loss of the *Adgillus* could be attributed either to the master, Martin Thompson, or the crew, and he renewed the master's certificate with no hesitation.

References

Manx Radio News, 03.09.1992; Parliamentary Papers, 1880, Volume 66; *Lloyd's Registers 1873 & 1874*.

Wreck Site

Diving

The ship's bell was recovered in August 1991 and was used to positively identify the wreck as the *Adgillus,* as it was inscribed '*Adgillus 1874*'. There then followed a period during the summer of 1992 when the cargo was salvaged on a commercial basis by Anglo-American Marine using their vessel, *Recovery 2*. They salvaged approximately 15,000 ceramic plates, but it is thought that large amounts of intact pottery still remain buried in the mud. The pottery is of a type known as Sponge Ware, and is colourful in its decoration with floral patterns in bold shades of green, blue and red. It is believed that the wreck is still owned by Lever Brothers.

With such a varied cargo on board, the finds from the *Adgillus* are of an exciting and intriguing nature. The fairly intact stern area is fascinating; it is rare to be able to see the remains of a substantial part of a wooden sailing ship so well preserved on the seabed. Rods of iron can be found everywhere in the stern area and are presumably part of the cargo. Further forward in the main hold area, which is fairly flush to the seabed, lies a jumble of timbers and the majority of the remnants of her cargo. This mainly consists of broken shards of pottery, clay pipes, glass bottles and rifle ammunition.

The wreck sits upright in a general depth of 36m of water and rises to about 3.0m from the seabed, the highest point being the stern section. The wreck extends for a length of about 45m and is about 15m at its widest point. The stern rises about 2-3m above the seabed, but the main sections of hold and bow areas are generally only about 1m high. The wreck is orientated on a north-north-east/south-south-west axis, with the stern at the southern end. The outline of the hull timbers can be followed, in many areas indicating that large sections of the hull below deck level remain well preserved in the mud.

As the seabed is composed of fine silt and mud, it is easily kicked up by careless fining and visibility is quickly reduced to zero when searching through the debris. Laying off a line as you swim away from the shot line is often a good idea in anything but ideal conditions. On a flood tide, expect there to be a current flowing from the south-west. Slack water occurs at the predicted high and low waters. It is often a good idea to dive the site when there is a small amount of tidal flow, as any mud suspended in the water is swept away and reasonable visibility is preserved.

Angling

As only a comparatively small amount of wreck protrudes from the seabed, not much protection is available to fish from tidal flow and nets of trawlers. Expect only pouting from this wreck, but lobsters are abundant amongst her remaining timbers.

Afton

Wreck: ★★★
Scenery: ★★★★
Angling: ★★
Depth: 22m
Position: 54 05.626 N, 04 32.230 W
Datum: WGS84
Location: 0.7n.m. south-east of Santon Head
Access: Douglas (4.1n.m.) slipway at all stages of the tide. Castletown (5.5n.m.) slipway three hours either side of high water.

Vessel

The iron steamship *Afton*, of Glasgow, 287 tons gross, 121 tons net, was built in 1877 by Hanna, of Glasgow. She was 140.4ft in length, had a beam of 23.2ft and a draught of 10.5ft (42.8m x 7.1m x 3.2m). She was equipped with a compound steam engine developing 60hp, which had been built by D. Rowan, of Glasgow. At the time of her loss, she was owned by the Ayr Steam Shipping Co. of Ayr.

History

At about 9.00 a.m. on Sunday 18 October 1896, a group of people on Douglas Head observed a steamer founder about a mile and a half off St Ann's Head (Santon Head). A surmise that the crew had been rescued by a nearby steamer proved correct.

The steamer immediately sailed towards Douglas Bay, where she anchored at about 10.30 a.m. She proved to be the *Onyx*, of Glasgow, Captain Stewart, master, bound from Llandulas in North Wales for Glasgow, laden with a cargo of limestone. From information given by those on board, it transpired that the foundered steamer was the *Afton*, of Glasgow, Roan, master. She had left Llandulas on Saturday afternoon, in company with the *Onyx* and was similarly laden with limestone, but bound for Ardrossan. Both vessels kept close company and were caught in the severe storm that came in at midnight.

Between 4.00 a.m. and 5.00 a.m., a very heavy sea was experienced off the Calf of Man and the *Afton* shipped so much water that the fires in her boiler were extinguished. Seas continued to pour over her until eventually she became much waterlogged. The *Onyx* was signalled, and returned, taking the *Afton* in tow. When off Santon Head, the rope parted and the crew of the *Afton*, ten in number, seeing she was settling down, took to the small boat and boarded the Onyx. Very shortly afterwards the *Afton* went down. The crew of the *Afton* was safely landed at Douglas.

References

Lloyd's Register of Shipping; *Isle of Man Examiner* spool EX7 MNH; *Isle of Man Times*, spool N19 MNH; *Mona's Herald*, spool N113 MNH.

Wreck Site

Diving

The identity of the wreck is assumed to be that of the steamship *Afton*, although no positive identification has been made. As the only steamship to have foundered close in to Santon Head however, the wreck must be hers. The size and construction of the wreck conforms furthermore to that of the *Afton*.

The wreck of the *Afton* can be quite difficult to locate on the echo sounder as the stern section, which includes the engine and boiler, lies on an outcrop of bedrock, which stands between 1-3m proud of the surrounding seabed. The wreck is well broken up and there is evidence that it has been extensively salvaged in the past before its recent rediscovery in 1999. The boiler and engine stand about 4m proud of the seabed in a general depth of 22m, but generally the wreckage is less than 2m high. Wreckage covers an area about 40m long by 8m wide. The wreck lies on a general axis of north-east/south-west, with the stern at the south-western end.

The remains of the *Afton*'s cargo, blocks of limestone, are scattered everywhere. A large steam winch lies forward of the boiler and bridge area. The hold section is largely buried in coarse shell grit, but the tip of the bow, complete with one anchor, remains and points towards the surface. Areas of wreckage, especially hull plating, lie away from the main wreck. Sections of her stern lie to the rear of the wreck amongst the outcrops of bedrock.

The *Afton* makes for a pleasant dive as visibility is usually at least 8m and often excellent in the range of 15m or more during summer (apart from the plankton bloom in May and early June, when it is generally more limited). The relatively shallow depth makes the wreck suitable for less experienced wreck divers. Care should be taken in pinpointing slack water; the tide circulating around nearby Port Soderick causes it to occur generally one to one and a half hours before the predicted high or low waters. The flood tide flows from the south-west and the ebb tide from the north-east.

Angling

The *Afton*'s close proximity to the coast at under 1n.m. does not lend herself to be a good angling wreck. Small pollack up to 5lb are usually present, however, together with cod and small ling up to 6lb on occasions in the summer months.

Albatross

Wreck: ★★★
Scenery: ★★★
Angling: ★★★
Depth: 23m
Position: 54 16.105 N, 04 10.380 W
Datum: WGS84
Location: 5.3n.m. south-east of Maughold Head
Access: Douglas (13.1n.m.) slipway at all stages of the tide. Laxey (8.1n.m.) slipway three hours either side of high water. Ramsey (8.5n.m.) slipway two hours either side of high water and beach launch possible in from of the Lifeboat House.

Vessel

The iron steam trawler *Albatross*, of Douglas, 123 tons gross, 84 tons net, was completed during November 1882 by W Walker & Co., of London. She was 101ft in length, had a beam of 19ft and a draught of 10.3ft (30.8m x 5.8m x 3.1m). The *Albatross* was equipped with a 50hp compound steam engine, built by W. Lockhead & Co. of Glasgow, which gave her a maximum speed of eleven knots. She was acquired in 1893 from the Albatross Steamship Co. Ltd, of Liverpool, (H.H. Grayson, manager), by Mr Robert Knox, of Douglas.

History

The *Albatross* left Douglas shortly after 3.00 p.m. on Monday afternoon on 5 November 1894, for the fishing grounds in the neighbourhood of the Bahama Bank Lightship. She was in the charge of Captain Albert E. Shimmin, an experienced seaman and fisherman. The other members of the crew were William Dougherty, mate; Henry Hudson, first engineer; Robert Kelly, second engineer; James Leadbeater, seaman; Charles Shimmin, trimmer; Thomas Turner, seaman, and Robert Gregg, seaman.

On arrival at the fishing ground, the trawl net of the *Albatross* was lowered and the steamer commenced to drag for fish. At about 1.00 a.m. on Tuesday 6 November, Captain Shimmin was in charge of the watch and standing in the wheelhouse. Also on watch were James Leadbeater and Charles Shimmin, on the deck close to the wheelhouse, and Robert Kelly, who was in the engine room. Captain Shimmin was just about to make preparations for getting in the net when he saw a large steamer, which later turned out to be the *Duke of Clarence*, owned by both the London and North-Western Railway Co. and the Lancashire and Yorkshire Railway Co. She was employed in carrying passengers and goods between Belfast and Fleetwood and was on a voyage from Belfast to Fleetwood. The *Duke of Clarence* was about a mile and a half off and steaming directly towards the *Albatross*. Captain Shimmin remarked to Leadbeater, 'This fellow is coming right on us' and at once blew the steam whistle and then kept blowing it in a vain attempt to attract the attention of those on the bridge of the *Duke of Clarence*. He also took a flare out of the flare box, but it failed to work. The whistle, however, was kept going until the *Duke of Clarence* struck the *Albatross*.

The *Albatross* was struck right amidships, parallel to the wheelhouse and, as the *Duke of Clarence* was going at full speed ahead at the time, the steam trawler was cut right down between the boiler and the fish hold and was only within a foot or two of being cut completely in two. Captain Shimmin called to Kelly to come up on deck and he did so, but immediately turned around and went back to shut off the steam in order to prevent the boiler from exploding. Kelly then regained the deck after successfully shutting off the steam. The *Albatross* foundered almost immediately. Captain Shimmin made for the funnel stays and climbed up one of them, from where he managed to get onto the deck of the *Duke of Clarence*. Charles Shimmin also climbed a stay, but, before he could get on board the *Duke of Clarence*, she rebounded off the *Albatross*. Shimmin and Leadbeater were thrown into the water and both men were drowned. Dougherty, Hudson, Turner and Gregg formed the watch below. Turner and Gregg, hearing the steam whistle, came on deck, but Dougherty and Hudson remained in their bunks and were probably drowned in them. Turner and Kelly, still on the sinking *Albatross*, managed to get hold of some fish boxes, which kept them afloat until they were rescued by boats lowered from the *Duke of Clarence*. Gregg was also unfortunately drowned. In all, five men from the *Albatross* perished.

How the loss of the *Albatross* was headlined in the local press. (Copyright: Manx National Heritage)

At the time of the disaster, the night was fine and clear. The steam trawler *Lady Loch*, also of Douglas, was fishing about half a mile from the *Albatross* and two miles from the Bahama Lightship. As soon as her master, Captain William Shimmin, saw what had befallen his brother's vessel, he hauled in his nets and made for the scene of the collision, which was reached in about twenty minutes. He intended in rendering assistance, but his efforts were in vain, for the unfortunate men had disappeared and nothing could be seen of them. The Barrow Steam Navigation Co.'s steamer *Manx Queen* also appeared shortly after the collision, as well as another large passenger steamer, the *Duke of York*, bound from Fleetwood for Belfast. All these steamers turned on their searchlights and remained in the vicinity for some time. Nothing, however, could be seen save some fish boxes and other wreckage. The *Lady Loch* remained at the scene of the disaster for two or three hours before she returned to Douglas at about 6.00 a.m. later that morning.

The three survivors remained on board the *Duke of Clarence* and were landed at Fleetwood, where they made dispositions at the Custom House. The next day they were given tickets to take the Isle of Man Steam Packet steamship *Fenella* to Douglas, arriving home on Wednesday evening.

References

Isle of Man Examiner, spool EX6 MNH; *Isle of Man Times*, spool N17 MNH; World Ship Society, G.H. Somner; Board of Trade Casualty Returns, Guildhall Library.

Wreck Site

Diving

The wreck of the *Albatross* was first discovered by commercial divers Mike Howard and Trevor Parker in 1975. They estimated that there was between 2 and 3 tons of brass and copper present on the wreck for them to salvage and applied to the authorities for an explosives licence. They then sought permission from the owner, Miss Anni Knox, daughter of Mr Robert Knox, who had been the owner of the *Albatross* at the time of her loss. The commercial salvage activity in the 1970s explains the broken nature of the wreck today.

The wreck still makes an interesting dive and is shallow enough at 23m for it to be suitable for relatively inexperienced wreck divers. The boiler is the highest point of the wreck at 4m. The wreck extends for about 35m in length and is about 8m wide. It is orientated on a south-east/north-west axis. Some of the wooden decking survives.

The *Albatross* lies on a sandy seabed, so visibility is generally good at 8m or so in the summer and sometimes excellent at 15m or more in calm weather and small tides (apart from the plankton bloom in May and early June, when it is generally more limited). Marine life can be abundant, with plenty of lobsters and conger eels to be observed. Shoals of fish swarm around the wreck during the spring, summer and autumn months.

Expect the slack waters to occur more or less at the predicted low and high water times and beginning about an hour or more before, to an hour and a half after. On

Wrecks in Open Water

The boiler on the wreck of the *Albatross* with a shoal of pouting. (Copyright: Phil Hutchinson)

spring tides, however, expect this window of slack to be of a shorter duration. In common with other wrecks in the vicinity, the slack water periods are lengthy compared to the rest of Manx Waters. The flood tide flows from the south-west and the ebb from the north-east.

Angling
Being relatively close to the shore, the wreck is quite heavily fished, so don't expect many large fish. The *Albatross* can, however, attract huge shoals of coalfish on occasion, although the average size is unlikely to exceed 5lb. Pollack are common, but again seldom exceed 5lb. Larger fish can be caught by anchoring ahead of the wreck and working a real or artificial sand eel close to the wreck. Cod are a possibility when the shoals are inshore. Pouting are prolific and a nuisance. Anchoring for conger eels should produce good results as there are many conger eels hiding amongst the broken wreckage.

Amber Rose

Wreck: *****
Scenery: ****
Angling: ***
Depth: 47m
Position: 54 00.855 N, 04 50.077 W
Datum: WGS84
Location: 1.5n.m. south-south-west of Chicken Rock
Access: Port St Mary (5.1n.m.) slipway at all stages of the tide. Port Erin (5.6n.m.) beach launch possible. Castletown (7.9n.m.) slipway three hours either side of high water.

Vessel

The wooden trawler *Amber Rose*, of Belfast (B417), 90.44 tons gross, was built at Fraserburgh in 1979. She was 79.2ft in length, had a beam of 24.6ft and a draught of 11.0ft (24.1m x 7.5m x 3.4m). Her engine was a Hedemora diesel developing 850hp. The *Amber Rose*'s owner was Thomas Hughes, of Portavogie, County Down.

History

The *Amber Rose*, skippered by her owner, Thomas Hughes, departed Portavogie, County Down on the evening of 15 October 1998 to fish for herring in the waters to the east of the Isle of Man. Pair trawling with the trawler *Quiet Waters III*, the six-man crew of the *Amber Rose* had a successful night's fishing and after hauling her nets all three of her refrigerated seawater tanks were full of fish, officially with a capacity of sixty-five tonnes, with the excess catch thrown over the side.

At 8.00 a.m. on 16 October, the *Amber Rose* was ready to motor back to Portavogie to land her catch, with John Young at the wheel. The rest of the crew went below to sleep after a hard night's work. She made good headway despite force 5-6 south-westerly winds, but on approaching the Chicken Rock, lying about half a mile off the Calf of Man on the Isle of Man's south-western coast, she would not answer to the wheel and suddenly began listing to starboard. John Young slowed the engine and immediately raised the alarm by the intercom. Thomas Hughes then ordered the engine to be cut into neutral to bring her to a halt. The vessel was foundering quickly by the head however, and within thirty seconds was on her way beneath the waves in a position about one and a half miles south of the Chicken Rock. Unbeknown to the crew, water had been pouring into the forward sections of the hull and the bilge alarms had not functioned to warn the crewman at the wheel, John Young, of the impending disaster.

John Young escaped through a wheelhouse window as soon as he realised the *Amber Rose* was capsizing. The first thing he saw when he got out of the wheelhouse was the boat's keel in the air with the propeller still turning. Noel McMaster, James Gibson and Thomas Hughes were below decks in a passageway near the galley, when a surge of water slammed shut an inner door, leaving them trapped. Noel McMaster found himself in an air pocket in the galley, while James Gibson, kicking with all his might against the door, managed to force it open and make his way to the surface. As soon as he broke through, Noel McMaster, still in the air pocket, was flushed out of the ship by the force of the incoming water and luckily suffered no injury. Thomas Hughes did not escape from his vessel and went down with her.

Meanwhile, Mark Hughes, the skipper's son, had a miraculous escape. As soon as the crew were alerted of impending disaster, he made for a ladder up to the deck. He waited, holding the door open for other crewmen. He was suddenly covered with water and became caught up in a cable and was being pulled down with the trawler. He just managed to extricate himself in time to avoid being drowned, but surfaced a quarter of a mile from James Hughes, John Young and Noel McMaster, who after clinging to a life-ring, had all clambered aboard a life raft and set off emergency flares to alert others to their peril. Fortunately for Mark Hughes, James Gibson, who was in only his third week at fishing, surfaced in the same area and helped the exhausted sixteen-year-old in to the raft.

Scottish Fishing News reporter Michael Craine, from Onchan, in the Isle of Man, who had been watching the vessel from a vantage point near Port St Mary, alerted emergency services at 10.15 a.m. He had seen the *Amber Rose* heeling over and sinking. Liverpool Coastguard decided to launch Port St Mary Lifeboat and very shortly afterwards Michael Craine phoned them back and said he had seen a red flare. Immediately, an RAF Valley rescue helicopter was scrambled and the Coastguard issued a mayday relay in order to alert other vessels in the area that might have been able to render assistance. The Royal Naval vessel HMS *Invincible* responded and deployed a helicopter. The Northern Irish fisheries protection vessel *Ken Vickers* and several other fishing vessels responded and a search area was determined.

The Port St Mary Lifeboat picked up the five survivors, who were airlifted to hospital. They were all suffering from hypothermia and James Hughes was in a critical condition, after inhaling engine oil from the *Amber Rose*. Thomas Hughes lost his life and left a wife, Patricia, together with three sons, Tom, Gary and Mark, and a daughter, Lauren.

Several efforts were made to recover the body of Thomas Hughes, but were hindered by bad weather and strong tides, which are common to the area where the trawler foundered. Eventually, in February 1999, a team of divers operating from the *Ken Vickers*, including Samuel McKeown and Mark McKee, recovered the body from the wreck, which lies at a depth of 47m.

The report into the sinking of the *Amber Rose* was published by the UK Marine Accident Investigation Branch on 19 July 2000 and was written by Captain Clifford Brand. The report arrived at twenty-three conclusions and made three recommendations to the Maritime and Coastguard Agency.

The cause of the sinking of the *Amber Rose* was given as undetected flooding of the forward spaces. The contributory causes of this were listed as the failure of the

The *Amber Rose* after her refit. (Copyright: Michael Craine)

Divers preparing aboard the *Ken Vickers*. (Copyright: Michael Craine)

bilge alarm in the refrigerated seawater tank space, allowing the flooding to go undetected; the overloading of the vessel reducing her freeboard and stability; the failure to have the vessel's stability recalculated after increasing the capacity of the refrigerated tanks and her refit and not having the vessel re-inclined.

The *Amber Rose* was overloaded by 31 tonnes above her maximum displacement of 323.7 tonnes, meaning that she didn't meet statutory stability criteria. The trawler had taken on board about 69 tonnes of water from the flooding and this was the most probable cause of her loss.

Just weeks before her loss, the *Amber Rose* had been in a Buckie shipyard for a £200,000 refit. The company's refit and repair director, James Farquhar, advised Thomas Hughes to have the vessel re-inclined following the overhaul and any adjustments to be made following the test to ensure her seaworthiness. The recommendation was also made by a Marine and Coastguard Agency inspector who carried out a spot check on the vessel in the shipyard. Their Belfast office was also notified. Two years previously, Thomas Hughes had also had work done by a different yard to extend two of the three refrigerated seawater tanks. He had no re-inclination done then and had not informed the Marine and Coastguard Agency of the change. The change had increased the tanks' capacity from 80.4 cubic metres to 87.3 cubic metres. This meant she was able to carry seven more cubic metres of fish of which inspectors would be unaware.

At the inquest of the death of Thomas Hughes held at Douglas by coroner Michael Moyle, he commented that, 'At least twice Mr Hughes had the opportunity to mention this. In this example Mr Hughes would have had every reason not to have it re-inclined.'

References

Border News, 15.10.1998; *ITV Oracle,* 15.10.98; *Manx Independent,* 16.10.98, 28.07.2000. & 01.12.2000; *Fishing Vessels of Britain and Ireland,* Peter Brady;

Notice to Mariners Number Five of 1998, issued by the Isle of Man Department of Transport Harbours Division; *Fishing News,* 23.10.1998; *Isle of Man Examiner,* 20.10.1998; Michael Craine.

Wreck Site

Diving

The wreck of the *Amber Rose* now sits in a general depth of 47m of water and rises to about 9m from the seabed. The wreck is about 25m in length and about 8m in width. It is orientated on a north-east/south-west axis. The wreck is still intact and is reported to lie on its keel with a forty-five degree list to port. I have not dived this wreck so a more comprehensive report is unavailable.

Being located on a sandy seabed should ensure visibility at 8m or so in the summer months, and visibility should sometimes be excellent, at 15m or more in calm weather and small tides (apart from the plankton bloom in May and early June, when it is generally more limited).

Expect the slack waters to occur more or less at the predicted low and high water times and beginning about half an hour before to three quarters of an hour after. On spring tides, expect this window of slack to be of a shorter duration. The flood tide flows from the north-west and the ebb from the south-east.

Angling

The predominant species on this wreck is pollack. Large shoals patrol around and feed best when the tide is flowing at its strongest. Most fish are in the 3lb to 7lb range and are prolific on occasions. The occasional coalfish is also taken, but as yet no other species frequent this wreck.

Ardbeg

Wreck: ★★★★
Scenery: ★★★★
Angling: ★★★
Depth: 36m
Position: 54 02.217 N, 03 45.828 W
Datum: WGS84
Location: 26.2n.m. east-south-cast of Douglas Head
Access: Douglas (26.2n.m.) slipway at all stages of the tide.

Vessel

The steel steamship *Ardbeg*, of Glasgow, (Official Number: 111,260), 227 tons gross, 85 tons net, was completed in June 1900 by Scott & Sons, of Bowling. She was 117ft in length, had a beam of 21.5ft and a draught of 9.4ft (35.7m x 6.6m x 2.9m). The *Ardbeg* was a steamer of the well deck type with machinery aft and was equipped with a compound steam engine developing 35rhp built by Muir and Houston Ltd, of Glasgow. Her owners were the Glasgow Steam Coasters Co. Ltd (Hendry, McCallum & Co., managers).

History

The *Ardbeg*, Captain William Hugh McCoffey, master, left Warrington for Larne with a cargo of 160 tons of soda ash on 7 February 1918. The cargo was being shipped by agents Brunner Mond & Co., of Winnington, for the Aluminium Co., of Larne.

At 2.30 p.m., the tide being about half flood, the weather hazy, wind blowing fresh from the west-south-west and with a heavy sea from the west, the *Ardbeg* was about thirty-two miles N ½ E (magnetic) from the Bar Light Vessel off the River Mersey in Liverpool Bay, when the master, who was on the bridge, observed two German submarines ahead about two and a half miles and about one and a half miles apart. One submarine was then seen to submerge and the other to circle around as if to ascertain if the *Ardbeg* was armed and then fired a shell, which missed the *Ardbeg*. A second shell was fired which struck the starboard boat and also carried away the steering gear. The submarine fired three more shots, with one striking the steamer aft and then fired a further six shots as the *Ardbeg*'s crew clambered in to the remaining lifeboat. A few more shots were fired before the boat was ordered alongside the submarine. Questions were asked by the commander of the submarine concerning the name of the ship and nature of her cargo. The *Ardbeg*'s crew were then told to leave their ship and the submarine continued to fire at the steamer until she sank at 4.00 p.m.

The *Ardbeg*'s crew reached the Selker Light Vessel at 9.15 p.m. and were taken off by HMS *Touchwood* at 8.15 a.m. the following morning and landed at Fleetwood.

References

Lloyd's War Losses, The First World War; British Vessels Lost at Sea, 1914-1918; World Ship Society, H. Appleyard; *Lloyd's Register*; UK Public Records Office Enemy Submarines Irish Sea, January/February 1918 ADM 137/1514.

Wreck Site

Diving

The author is not aware of any positive identification of this wreck having been made by a diver, but would welcome any further information on any dives which may have revealed its identity. The evidence concludes, however, that the wreck is almost certainly that of the steamship *Ardbeg*.

The wreck sits upright and fairly intact in a general depth of 36m of water and rises about 4m from the seabed at the highest point. The wreck is about 37m in length and about 8m in width. It is orientated on a north-west/south-east axis with the bow to the south-east.

In 1992 the stump of the foremast was reported to extend for a further 4m above the deck level. Some scour exists around the wreck. A large trawl net was reported to be attached to the bow area, so care should be exercised when descending to the wreck, especially at slack water as the net might well rise above the wreck.

The *Ardbeg* lies on a muddy seabed so visibility can be poor and is easily stirred up by careless fining. If the mud is not disturbed then visibility to 8m may be achieved from July to September. Expect the slack waters to occur more or less at the predicted low and high water times and beginning about half of an hour before to three quarters of an hour after. On spring tides expect this window of slack to be of a shorter duration. The flood tide flows from the west and the ebb from the east.

Angling
The author has no information on fishing this wreck, but it would seem likely that the muddy nature of the seabed will limit the numbers of fish present.

Ballina

Wreck: ★★★
Scenery: ★★★
Angling: ★★★
Depth: 29m
Position: 54 09.477 N, 04 14.675 W
Datum: WGS84
Location: 5.5n.m. south-east of Clay Head
Access: Douglas (8n.m.) slipway at all stages of the tide. Laxey (6.7n.m.) slipway three hours either side of high water.

Vessel

At the beginning of 1878, the iron steamship *Ballina*, of Liverpool, (Official Number: 78,780), was launched by the Barrow Shipbuilding Co., of Barrow-in-Furness, Cumbria, in accordance with plans submitted by her owner, Mr George Pollexfen.

Before work commenced, however, Mr Humphries, the manager of the Barrow Shipbuilding Co., wrote to George Pollexfen stating that the ship, in his opinion, was not stable enough to enable her to carry cattle on her main deck and he suggested that she should be strengthened by a number of modifications, including increasing the beam. An interview followed, when George Pollexfen stated his determination to adhere to his original plans. The *Ballina* was duly completed to the original specification and delivered to Mr Pollexfen's ownership on 5 January 1878.

For reasons not made clear in contemporary accounts, George Pollexfen suddenly had a change of heart and before the *Ballina* was put into service she was taken to Liverpool. She was lengthened to the extent of an extra 25ft amidships and a double-bottomed ballast tank with a capacity of 40 tons was fitted. Her gross tonnage was increased to 341 tons and her net tonnage to 210 tons. She was 170.5ft in length, had a beam of 23.2ft and a draught of 11.5ft (52m x 7.1m x 3.5m). The *Ballina* was equipped with a compound steam engine built by the Barrow Shipbuilding Co. developing 121hp.

From contemporary accounts she appears to have had a well deck, between the bridge and the forecastle head a flying bridge or cat walk, and another shorter one abaft the mainmast.

A Board of Trade official then surveyed her and a certificate was issued permitting the *Ballina* to carry 242 third-class passengers, fifteen passengers in the aftercabin, forty-one on deck and sixteen in the saloon. Oddly, George Pollexfen marked his own Plimsoll mark leaving only twelve inches of freeboard. The final cost of the *Ballina* was £10,000.

History

On 5 January 1882, the *Ballina* loaded a cargo of 370 sacks of wheat, 295 tons of coal and general cargo, 37 tons of chemicals as deck cargo and 10 tons of stone ballast, at the Clarence Half Tide Dock in Liverpool. As additional deck cargo she had greenheart piles for a new jetty, which was being built at the time at Larne, County Antrim and she was due to call in at Larne en route to Ballina.

When the *Ballina* began to leave the dock the official on duty noticed that she was deeply laden and said to her master, Captain Charles Lynn, 'You are deep this time'. The captain replied simply, 'Yes'. The *Ballina* then remained in the dock and for the next four hours the crew tinkered down below in the cargo hold, before the dock official saw her leave the dock and sail down the Mersey.

A short time after leaving the entrance of the Mersey, the *Ballina* encountered a severe westerly gale. Nobody knows what happened to her, but within a few hours she had foundered with the loss of all fifteen of her crew.

Artist's impression of how the *Ballina* may have looked. (Copyright: Michael Corlett)

On 10 January, the trawl boat *Desdemona*, John Moss, master, started trawling about one and a half miles off Maughold Head to the east of the Isle of Man and finished the tow about seven miles south-east of the prominent headland. On retrieving the net it was found to contain the body of a young man of about fifteen to sixteen years of age. The body appeared to have been in the water for only a short time. At a Coroner's inquest the body was identified as J. Flanagan, one of the crewmen of the *Ballina*.

On 11 January, the smack *Doddrell*, of Fleetwood, picked up the body of a man in her nets when off Ramsey, again off the east coast of the Isle of Man. The body was judged to be that of a fireman owing to the appearance and clothes. This body had also only been in the water a short time.

One of her lifeboats, marked '*Ballina*, of Liverpool' was washed ashore at Silecroft in Cumbria on 13 January. A third body was washed ashore and a quantity of wreckage was picked up from off the east coast of the Isle of Man. This evidence, together with reports of trawlers locating a new wreck in a position about ten miles to the south-east of Maughold Head, strongly suggested the *Ballina* had foundered off the east coast of the Isle of Man. The *Ballina* was posted as missing by Lloyd's on 1 February.

The reason for her loss can only be pure speculation as none of her crew survived and there were no eyewitnesses to her loss, but it seems that there was a fault in her design that made her unstable when fully loaded. On the day of her loss she was carrying 375 tons of cargo and ballast and had a freeboard of only 1ft 7ins. It is easy to see that in a violent storm she could have taken a large wave on the main deck, the weight of which would have caused her to capsize with a terrible suddenness. Mr Pollexfen, her owner, had stated that she had made over four hundred trips, including fifty with cargoes of wheat to Iceland and on some of these trips had been overloaded with no mishap, but even he had confessed to her unstableness on occasions. Alternatively, she may have experienced problems with her deck cargo becoming insecure causing her to list and then eventually capsize.

Why she ended up off the main shipping route, in close to the east of the Isle of Man, is also something of a mystery. It seems likely that she was following a course that would have taken her south of the Isle of Man, past the Chicken Rock, when she was caught by the full force of the gale. It was common for ships to run up the east coast of the Isle of Man to gain shelter in Ramsey Bay from westerly winds. Before she reached the safety of Ramsey Bay, however, she capsized off Laxey and sank, taking all fifteen hands with her.

The Wreck Commissioner found there was no evidence to show how the *Ballina* was lost, but she was not sufficiently stable and was overladen upon her last leaving Liverpool. He therefore fined Mr Pollexfen £150.

In early April 1904, fishermen from Ramsey reported sighting a steamboat's mast, which had apparently broken off near to the deck. The lower end of the mast was uppermost, the other end being apparently fast by the rigging on a sunken wreck as the mast stood in a perpendicular position. The break was noted to be fresh. The position of the wreckage was given as nine to ten miles south by east of Maughold Head. It seems likely by the position given that the wreck involved was that of the *Ballina*, lost twenty-two years previously.

References

Isle of Man Examiner, spool EX2 MNH; *Manx Sun*, spool N67A MNH; *Mona's Herald*, spool N104 MNH; *Sea Breezes*, Page 60, 1968; World Ship Society, G.H. Somner; *Ramsey Courier*, Friday, 15.04.1904. spool MN111 MNH.

Wreck Site

Diving

During the summer of 1967, a party of scuba divers led by Mr Michael Corlett, of Laxey, commenced diving operations at a particular spot, approximately seven miles south-east of Laxey Head, after complaints by various fishermen of loss of trawler gear. At a depth of 30m, the remains of a small steamer were found, her after end more or less covered with fishing nets. Means of identification were few, as after being so long under the water only the hull, boiler and main engine remained. Prior to the discovery of the ship's bell with the name *'Ballina'* inscribed on it, the wreck was thought to be that of the small steamer *Ben Seyr*, owned by the Ramsey Steamship Co. Ltd, which disappeared with all hands in 1938. In 1967, it was understood that the discovery of the *Ballina* was the first time a wreck had been found of a vessel that had been previously posted as missing by insurer Lloyd's, of London.

During 1994, the bell from the *Ballina*, which had been in the possession of Michael Corlett, was presented to the town of Ballina for public display.

The wreck of the *Ballina* still makes an enjoyable dive. Her remains are orientated on a north-east/south-west axis with the bows to the north-east. Even though the wreckage extends for 55m and is about 10m at the widest point, the most significant parts of the wreckage are the boiler, engine and stern area, the latter of which remains the most intact part of the actual hull structure. Generally, the wreckage stands up to 4m high, in a general depth of 29m. Forward of the boiler the wreck is flattened, but the hull plating protrudes out of the sand indicating the profile of her

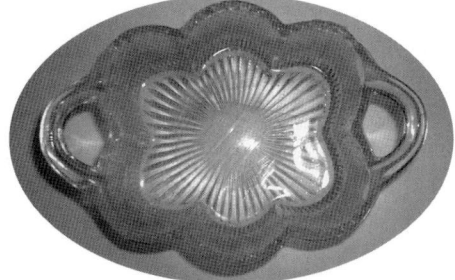

Above: Olive dish recovered from steamship *Ballina*.

Left: The *Ballina*'s bell recovered by Michael Corlett and now on public display in Ballina. (Copyright: Michael Corlett)

forward sections. During 1999 a trawl net was lost on her stern and the visiting diver, when first descending onto the wreck, should take care to avoid it.

Some interesting finds have come from the wreck over the years, including bottles, decanters, sealed jars complete with contents of the remains of cherries, glass olive dishes and various brass fittings.

The clean sandy seabed around the wreck normally means good visibility in the range of 8m or so in the summer and sometimes excellent visibility at 15m or more in calm weather and small tides (apart from the plankton bloom in May and early June, when it is more generally limited).

Expect the slack waters to occur more or less at the predicted low and high water times and beginning about half of an hour before to three quarters of an hour after. On spring tides expect this window of slack to be of a shorter duration. The tide flows from the south-west on a flood tide and from the north-east on an ebb tide.

Angling

There are always large shoals of fish around the *Ballina*, but quite often they are composed of small fish or unwanted species. May and June can see large shoals of coalfish, mostly to 5lb, though some years can produce bigger specimens to double figures. June also can see shoals of codling; more especially positioned several hundred metres away from the wreck. From June onwards there are plenty of pollack, but they are generally small and less than 6lb. When anchored directly over the wreck, the summer months of July and August yield ling to 15lb and conger eels to 30lb. Pouting are taken throughout the season along with the occasional ballan wrasse.

Ben Rein

Wreck: ★★★★
Scenery: ★★★★
Angling: ★★★★
Depth: 39m
Position: 54 01.627 N, 03 53.853 W
Datum: WGS84
Location: 21.5n.m. east-south-east of Douglas Head
Access: Douglas (21.5n.m.) slipway at all stages of the tide.

Vessel

The steel steamship *Ben Rein*, of Ramsey, (Official Number: 121,247), (ex *Starling*), 212 tons gross, 79 tons net, was built in 1905 by George Brown & Co., of Greenock (Yard Number 28). She was 110ft in length, had a beam of 22.1ft and a draught of 8.3ft (33.5m x 6.7m x 2.5m). She was equipped with a compound steam engine, developing 40nhp and built by Colin Houston & Co., of Glasgow. At the time of her loss, she was owned by the Ramsey Steamship Co. Ltd, of Ramsey, (J.B. McKee, managers).

History

On 7 February 1918, the *Ben Rein*, Captain John Cowley, master was on a journey from Liverpool to Belfast with a cargo of 150 tons of soap, when at 1.50 p.m. the crew heard firing in the distance. As the haze lifted they saw, about a mile distant, the three-masted steamer *Limesfield* being attacked by the German submarine UB57. The crew of the *Ben Rein* put on full steam to try to escape but the U-Boat soon finished with the other ship and turned its attention to the *Ben Rein*, firing a volley as a signal to stop. The *Ben Rein* duly stopped and the crew got the small boat out, whilst the submarine started firing at the steamer, but clear of the small boat. The first direct hit on the steamer went through the captain's room and the third shot got the boiler.

After this the submarine drew close to the small boat and the commander of the submarine put questions to the crew of the *Ben Rein* as to the nature of the cargo and her destination. The commander then ordered them, politely and in good English, to go back aboard the *Ben Rein* and to take off a portion of the cargo. At this point however, the steamer had caught fire and it was impossible to implement his command. The submarine then left and shortly afterwards the steamship rose vertically in the water and sank.

Two of the engine room crew had only dungarees as protection from the cold winter weather and so one of the other men gave his coat to fireman T. Corlett. In addition, a tarpaulin was cut up to form a lugsail and a piece of it was used to wrap engineer J. Lewin up in.

For the first four to five hours of their journey to safety there was a heavy sea running, but afterwards the sea was calm. During this time they heard more gunfire and this would seem to have been aimed at the third steamship sunk that day by UB57, the *Ardbeg*. Later, her crew of seven men was rescued by the steamer *Norman* and landed in Whitehaven at 2.00 a.m. on 8 February.

The crew of the *Ben Rein* was Captain John Cowley, master, of Port St Mary; J. Bridson, mate, of Peel; H. Corteen, engineer, of Douglas; J. Lewin, engineer, of Peel; T. Corlett, fireman, of St Jude's; H.J. Carran, seaman, of Port Erin; and J.W. Cowley, seaman, of Port St Mary.

References

Lloyd's War Losses, The First World War; British Vessels Lost at Sea, 1914-1918; *Isle of Man Times*, 10.02.1918. & 16.02.1918. spool N34 MNH; World Ship Society, H. Appleyard; Ramsey Steamship Co., Tony Kennish, 16.07.1992; War Casualty Book World War 1, Volume 3; *Lloyd's Register*; *Ninety Years of the Ramsey Steamship Co. Ltd*, Gray & Fenton.

Ben Rein. (Copyright: Manx National Heritage)

Wreck Site

Diving

The identity of the wreck was confirmed in 1997, following the recovery of the ship's bell inscribed *'Starling'*, the *Ben Rein*'s original name when launched.

The wreck sits upright in a general depth of 39m of water and rises to about 4.5m from the seabed for its entire length. The wreck is about 37m in length and about 8m in width. It is orientated on a north-east/south-west axis with the bow to the south-west. The superstructure, which was originally at the rear of the vessel, has collapsed to deck level. The long single hold still contains the cargo of soap in wooden crates. Even though the soap has long gone, the crates still contain the wrapping papers! Several large pieces of wreckage lie just off the bow. A large trawl net is attached to the stern area, so great care should be exercised when descending to the wreck, especially as, at slack water, the net rises above the wreck.

The *Ben Rein* makes an excellent wreck to dive, being largely intact and on a sandy seabed so that visibility is generally good at 8m or so in the summer months and sometimes excellent at 15m or more in calm weather and small tides (apart from the plankton bloom in May and early June, when it is generally more limited). Fish proliferate around the wreck and lobsters are large and numerous.

Expect the slack waters to occur more or less at the predicted low and high water times and beginning about half of an hour before to three quarters of an hour after. On spring tides, expect this window of slack to be of a shorter duration. The flood tide flows from the west-south-west and the ebb from the east-north-east.

Angling

The wreck of the *Ben Rein* produces some good angling for those prepared to motor the distance out to it. The wreck benefits from the three factors that seem to always indicate good wreck fishing: being in an offshore position, being surrounded by clear waters and being in the right depth range of 35m-50m. The primary species are pollack and cod, although the latter have been largely absent in the last few years. The pollack average 5lb-7lb with the occasional larger fish to double figures.

Ben Veg

Wreck: ★★★★
Scenery: ★★★★
Angling: ★★★★
Depth: 42m
Position: 54 32.392, N 04 25.773 W
Datum: WGS84
Location: 8n.m. north of the Point of Ayre
Access: Peel (21.5n.m.) slipway at all stages of the tide. Ramsey (14n.m.) slipway at two hours either side of high water and beach launch possible in front of the Lifeboat House.

Vessel

The steel steamship *Ben Veg*, of Ramsey, (Official Number: 87,583), 159 tons gross, 61 tons net, was built in 1914 at the Larne Shipbuilding Co., County Antrim. She was 100.5ft in length, had a beam of 19.1ft and a draught of 9.8ft (30.6m x 5.8m x 3m). The compound steam engine, developing 50nhp, was built by Messrs Gauldie, Gillespie & Co., of Glasgow. Her owner was the Ramsey Steamship Co. Ltd, of Ramsey.

History

At 2.00 a.m. on 22 May 1941, the *Ben Veg*, Captain H. Cregeen, master, was bound from Cairnlough to Whitehaven, in ballast, when she was in collision with another vessel, the motor vessel *Brittany*, in a position about six miles W by N of the Mull of Galloway. The *Brittany*, 4,772 tons gross and owned by the Royal Mail Lines Ltd, was part of an outward-bound convoy and she was heading for the River Plate, Uruguay, laden with a general cargo. The *Brittany*'s stem caught the *Ben Veg* on her starboard side and inflicted serious damage.

After some consultation it was decided to take the *Ben Veg* to the Isle of Man, with the possible chance of beaching her at Peel. At 6.00 a.m. that day, however, the pumps could no longer cope with the water gaining in the engine room and the steamer had to be abandoned.

From their lifeboat the crew of six men kept the *Ben Veg* under observation until she sank at noon eight miles north of the Point of Ayre. Wind and sea having risen, the lifeboat could not make the Isle of Man so ran instead for Burrow Head in south-west Scotland, where distress signals brought out an RAF launch to rescue the weary men.

Above: Ben Veg.
(Copyright: Manx National Heritage)

Right: Ben Veg.
(Copyright: John Clarkson)

The crew of *Ben Veg* was Captain H. Cregeen, Douglas, master; Mr H. MacDonald, Peel, mate; Mr A. Kneale, Laxey, chief engineer; Mr A. Corlett, Ramsey, second engineer; Mr W.A. Graham, Ramsey, able seaman; and Mr P. Kelly, Port St Mary, ordinary seaman.

References

Ramsey Steam Ship Co. Fleet List, Minute and Cargo Books; *Ramsey Courier*, Tuesday, 18.08.1914. spool MN481 MNH; *Sea Breezes*, Page 662, September 1965; World Ship Society, K. O'Donoghue; *Ramsey Courier*, 28.05.1941. spool MN531 MNH; *Ninety Years of the Ramsey Steamship Co. Ltd*, Gray & Fenton.

Wreck Site

Diving

The identity of the wreck was definitely confirmed in 2002, following the recovery of the ship's bell inscribed *'Ben Veg'*. When the wreck was first dived in July 1999, however, as the structure, shape and size of the hull conformed exactly to photographs of the vessel before she sank, it was assumed that this was the *Ben Veg*.

The wreck sits upright in a general depth of 42m of water and rises to about 4.5m from the seabed, the highest point being the forecastle at the bow. The wreck is about 30m in length and about 6m in width. It is orientated on an east-north-east/west-south-west axis with the bow to the east-north-east.

The wooden superstructure incorporating bridge, which was originally at the rear of the vessel, has collapsed to deck level and largely rotted away. Similarly, the wooden deck has gone, leaving just a network of steel girders covered in plum-rose anemones. The long single hold is empty, corresponding with the *Ben Veg* having been in ballast at the time of her loss. At the front of the ship, the lack of decking gives access to the forward accommodation area, together with the lantern and chain lockers all under the forecastle. Swimming down to the seabed gives the diver an appreciation of the lines of the steamer and at the stern the propeller can still be seen in place.

The wreck of the *Ben Veg*, being largely intact and on a shingle seabed, makes an excellent dive. Visibility is generally good at 8m or so in the summer months and sometimes an excellent 15m or more in calm weather and small tides (apart from the plankton bloom in May and early June, when it is generally more limited). Fish proliferate around the wreck, but lobsters and crabs are less than numerous.

Expect the slack waters to occur more or less at the predicted low and high water times and beginning about three quarters of an hour before to half an hour after. On spring tides, expect this window of slack to be of a shorter duration. The flood tide flows from the west-southwest and the ebb tide from the east-north-east.

Angling

The wreck holds large shoals of pollack during the summer and autumn months and the wreck is likely to attract other species, such as coalfish, cod and ling on occasions. Large conger eels occupy the darker regions of the wreckage.

Blue Star

Wreck: ★★★★★
Scenery: ★
Angling: ★
Depth: 41m
Position: 54 21.568 N, 04 45.068 W
Datum: WGS84
Location: 8.3n.m. north of Peel
Access: Peel (8.3n.m.) slipway at all stages of the tide.

Vessel

The steel barge *Blue Star*, measuring 90ft in length (27.4m), was owned by the Laxey Towing Co. in the Isle of Man.

History

At 11.00 p.m. on 25 November 1981, the *Blue Star*, laden with a cargo of 1,800 railway sleepers, bound from Ardrossan for Peel, was under tow by the motor tug *Salisbury*, owned by the Laxey Towing Co., when the *Blue Star* foundered in heavy weather about seven miles north-west of Peel.

References

Lloyd's List, 27.11.1981.

Wreck Site

Diving

The identity of the wreck was confirmed in May 2001, following a dive where the wreck was found to be that of a barge whose shape and size conformed to that of the *Blue Star*. As the *Blue Star* is the only barge to have been lost in the vicinity it is reasonable to assume that the wreck is indeed her.

The wreck sits upright in a general depth of 41m of water and it rises up to about 3m from the seabed. The wreck is about 30m in length and it is about 7m in width. It is orientated on a north-west/south-east axis, with the bow to the south-east.

Samson posts for attaching the towing hawsers can be seen at either end of the wreck, together with the steering tiller at the stern. It has a single hold and a few remnants of the cargo of railway sleepers remain.

The wreck of the *Blue Star* is not one of the premier wreck sites around the Isle of Man, but is intact and is reasonably accessible from Peel. It might prove a useful wreck site in a south-east wind when other sites are too exposed. The muddy seabed can easily be stirred up by careless fining and visibility reduced to 1m or 2m. There is little in the way of marine life to see, apart from a few small fish.

Expect the slack waters to occur more or less at the predicted low and high water times and beginning about half an hour before to three quarters of an hour after. On spring tides expect this window of slack to be of a shorter duration. The flood tide flows from the south-west and the ebb tide from the north-east.

Angling

Due to the muddy nature of the seabed the fishing is not as good as might be expected, given the wreck's distance from the shore and depth of water, but there are shoals of small pollack and coalfish, together with the ubiquitous pouting.

Briar

Wreck: ★
Scenery: ★
Angling: ★
Depth: 35m
Position: 53 59.490 N, 04 26.490 W
Datum: OGB
Location: 7.3n.m. south-east of Langness
Access: Douglas (9.1n.m.) and Port St Mary (11.5n.m.) slipways at all stages of the tide. Castletown (8.7n.m.) slipway three hours either side of high water.

Vessel

The wooden motor fishing vessel *Briar*, of Kilkeel (B630), 39 tons gross, was built in 1947 by Jones, of Buckie and equipped with a 152hp diesel engine. She was 61ft in length, had a beam of 18ft and a draught of 8ft (18.6m x 5.5m x 2.4m). She was owned by Mr Fred Annett, of Kilkeel.

History

On 18 September 1975, the *Briar* was pair trawling for herring with the motor fishing vessel *Wistaria*, when she was sunk following a collision with the motor fishing vessel *Mystic*, of 44 tons gross, in a position given as eight and a half miles, 124 degrees, from Douglas Head. The crew of the *Briar* was safely rescued.

References

Olsen's Fisherman's Nautical Almanac, 1975; Michael Craine, 14.02.1996. & 10.10.2002.

Wreck Site

Diving

The wreck of the *Briar* was dived in the years following her loss. The wreck, which was intact in those days, has deteriorated considerably over the years.

The wreck lies in a general depth of 35m of water and rises to barely 1m from the seabed. The remains are about 10m in length and about 5m in width. It is orientated on a north-east/south-west axis, but the wreckage is fairly indistinct.

The wreck will now compose of the more resilient parts of the vessel, such as the engine, fuel tank, propeller and propeller shaft. There may be some interesting metallic finds amongst the clutter.

The sandy seabed usually ensures that visibility is good at around 8m or so in the summer months and sometimes excellent at 15m or more in calm weather and small

Briar. (Copyright: Michael Craine)

tides (apart from the plankton bloom in May and early June, when it is generally more limited).

Expect the slack waters to occur more or less at the predicted low and high water times and beginning about half an hour before to three quarters of an hour after. On spring tides expect this window of slack to be of a shorter duration. The flood tide flows from the west-south-west and the ebb tide from the east-north-east.

Angling
Expect only pouting on this wreck.

Cardea

Wreck: *****
Scenery: ***
Angling: **
Depth: 54m
Position: 53 59.075 N, 04 20.040 W
Datum: WGS84
Location: 10.3n.m. S. of Douglas Head
Access: Douglas (10.3n.m.) and Port St Mary (15.3n.m.) slipways at all stages of the tide. Castletown (12.6n.m.) slipway three hours either side of high water.

Vessel

The wooden motor fishing vessel *Cardea*, of Peel (PL88), 22 tons gross, was built in 1954 in France. She was 52ft in length, had a beam of 16.6ft and a draught of 6ft (15.9m x 5.1m x 1.8m). The *Cardea* was powered by a 230hp Cummins diesel engine and was owned by Mr Ernie Leece, of Peel. She was chiefly employed in dredging scallops in season or dragging for queenies in the summer months.

History

On Sunday 18 February 2001 at 5.15 a.m., three Manx motor fishing vessels, *Cardea*, *Ocean Hunter* and *Venture Again*, left Douglas harbour for the fishing grounds 10n.m south-south-east of Douglas. The weather was good with calm seas, a light breeze and clear visibility. The *Cardea* was the leading vessel, slightly to port and ahead of the *Ocean Hunter*, of Peel (PL96), which was about 0.7 miles astern, and this vessel was followed by the *Venture Again*. All three vessels were cruising at nine knots and were in radio contact with each other.

At about 6.30 a.m., the *Cardea*, on reaching the fishing grounds 10n.m. south-south-east of Douglas Head, reduced speed, prepared her scallop dredgers and altered course about ninety degrees to the south-west. At this point the *Ocean Hunter* was about 0.75 miles away from the *Cardea*. The *Cardea* lowered her dredgers and began trawling at a speed of two to two and a half knots.

Skipper of the *Cardea*, David Leece, was at the wheel and noted the oncoming *Ocean Hunter*, but was not unduly concerned being of the opinion that the *Ocean Hunter* was aware of the *Cardea*'s position and that she was fishing. The *Ocean Hunter* approached the fishing ground at 6.25 a.m. and her skipper had started to identify and change the scale and area on the GPS navigational plotter to display the area of the fishing grounds, which took up to ten minutes. During this period the *Ocean Hunter*'s skipper, John Caley, was not aware that the *Cardea* had stopped, lowered her dredgers and was now trawling.

At about 6.40 a.m., when the *Cardea* had been towing for about five minutes, the skipper of the *Ocean Hunter* suddenly noticed *Cardea* towing closely across his vessel's bow from port to starboard. In an attempt to avoid a collision, he put the engine full astern, but the *Ocean Hunter*'s stem made contact heavily with the starboard side of the *Cardea*, just forward of midships. The two vessels ended up in contact with their port and starboard shoulders respectively.

The collision resulted in extensive damage to the *Cardea*'s starboard hull structure both above and below the waterline, bulwarks and deck. This resulted in the vessel beginning to flood with seawater, although there was no apparent damage to the *Ocean Hunter*.

David Leece immediately checked the midships fishroom for flooding, which was not evident, and then checked the engine room where he discovered 3-4ft of water. At this stage he was sure that the *Cardea* would sink as the pumps would not be able to cope. He therefore instructed crewman Steven Griffin to board the *Ocean Hunter*, which was still alongside the *Cardea*. David Leece followed him and shortly afterwards the *Cardea* foundered.

David Leece later commented:

It was a bit like a car crash. We were totally unaware what was going to happen. It was quite a substantial collision and we realised straight away that we would sink as when the engine hatch was lifted it was seen that there was already 4ft of water in the engine room. It took about three to five minutes for the boat to sink which gave us enough time to step over into the other vessel.

The *Ocean Hunter* then made contact with Liverpool Coastguard reporting the incident and that the crew of the *Cardea* were safe and his vessel was not taking in any water. John Caley also radioed the *Venture Again* to advise them of the situation.

David Leece, along with Steven Griffin, recovered debris, including the Emergency Position Indicating Radio Beacon (EPIRB) and a mooring rope, from where the vessel had gone down. The *Ocean Hunter* landed both men at Douglas at 8.30 a.m.

The incident was investigated by the Department of Trade and Industry's Marine Administration. It was concluded that the collision was a result of the *Ocean Hunter* failing to keep a proper lookout during the ten minute period leading up to the collision, failing to maintain a safe speed in view of her close proximity to another vessel and failing to take early and substantial action to keep well clear of a vessel being overtaken and subsequently engaged in fishing. It was also noted that the *Cardea* had failed to keep a proper lookout for the minute before the collision and had failed to take action as the 'stand-on' vessel when a collision could not be avoided by the action of the 'give-way' vessel alone. Both vessels were concluded to have failed to maintain effective communications with each other to establish each other's intentions when both vessels were operating in close proximity to each other.

References

Fishing Vessels of Britain and Ireland, 1993, Peter Brady; *Isle of Man Examiner*, 20.02.2001; The Maritime & Coastguard Agency, Press Releases; David Leece, MFV *The Two Girls*, trawler, 31.05.2001; Isle of Man Government Casualty Investigation Report CA67.

Wreck Site

Diving

The wreck of the *Cardea* now sits apparently upright on her keel in a general depth of 54m of water and the wreck rises to about 5m from the seabed. The wreck is

Cardea.
(Copyright: Michael Craine)

about 20m in length and about 5m in width. It is orientated on an east/west axis.

It is not thought that anyone has dived the *Cardea*, but lying intact and on a sandy or shingle seabed, the wreck should make a good dive. Expect visibility to be generally good at 8m or so in summer and sometimes excellent at 15m or more in calm weather and small tides (apart from the plankton bloom in May and early June, when it is generally more limited). Fish are just beginning to colonise the wreck.

Slack waters will occur more or less at the predicted low and high water times and will begin about half an hour before to three quarters of an hour after. On spring tides, expect this window of slack to be of a shorter duration. The flood tide flows from the west-south-west and the ebb tide from the east-north-east.

Angling

As the wreck is recent it is only just beginning to be colonised by fish. Pollack to 7lb have been taken and it is expected that numbers will increase rapidly each season until the wreck breaks up too much and so does not afford adequate shelter to the fish. Other fish such as coalfish, cod and ling should frequent the wreck in coming seasons.

Carmelite

Wreck: ★★★★★
Scenery: ★★★★
Angling: ★★★
Depth: 75m
Position: 53 55.341 N, 04 55.264 W
Datum: WGS84
Location: 8.1n.m. south-south-west of the Calf of Man
Access: Port St Mary (11.4n.m.) slipway at all stages of the tide. Castletown (13.6n.m.) slipway three hours either side of high water. Port Erin (11.5n.m.) beach launch possible.

Vessel

The steel steamship *Carmelite*, of London, (Official Number: 99,099), (ex *Clan Macrae* and ex *Shatt-El-Arab*), 2,583 tons gross, 1,617 tons net, was built in 1892 by J. Blumer & Co., of Sunderland. The *Carmelite* was 305.9ft in length, had a beam of 41.1ft and a draught of 18.8ft (93.3m x 12.5m x 5.7m). She was equipped with a triple-expansion steam engine developing 249nhp and built by the North East Marine Engineering Co. Ltd, of Sunderland.

At her time of loss she was owned by Page Shipping Co. Ltd (John I. Jacobs & Co. Ltd, of London, managers), but on charter to the British Government. During the First World War, she was fitted with a four-inch gun for her own protection against German U-boats.

History

The *Carmelite*, Captain Joseph Thomas Francis, master, departed Bilbao, in Spain, on 21 February 1918 bound for Glasgow, with a cargo of 3,300 tons of iron ore. She called in at Milford Haven on 1 March 1918 in order to receive instructions for the final leg of her journey through the Irish Sea. She was to zigzag north and pass within seven miles of the Calf of Man off the south-west tip of the Isle of Man.

At 5.20 a.m. on 2 March, in a fresh north-east wind and on a bright moonlit night, she was ten miles south-west by west of the Calf of Man on a course of north ½ east proceeding at eight and a half knots when she was torpedoed by the German submarine U105. The torpedo struck on the starboard side level with the engine room and boiler room bulkhead. The second engineer, Neil McCrae and a fireman, G.A. Turner, were both instantly killed by the explosion of the torpedo. The forepart of the starboard lifeboat was blown away in the explosion. The twenty-seven survivors escaped in the port lifeboat.

The master was the last to leave and was preparing to get into the port jolly boat when he heard cries emanating from the stoke-hole. He went back and found an injured porter jammed in the ventilator hoist. He lowered the hoist and pulled the porter up onto the deck. By this time the after well deck had 2ft of water on it. The master then cut away the after fall of the starboard boat and told the porter to jump in the water, but he refused so the master physically threw him overboard and then jumped into what remained of the boat and pulled the porter into the boat as well. Shortly afterwards, they were both rescued by the crewmen in the port lifeboat.

The *Carmelite* disappeared beneath the waves within eight minutes of the torpedo striking her. The survivors were subsequently picked up by the steamship *Pearlmoor* at 7.30 a.m. and were then transferred to a Royal Naval patrol vessel, which landed them at Holyhead.

The master, Captain Joseph Thomas Francis, of Bank House, Nenas Cross, Pembrokeshire, was awarded £100 by the Board of Trade for his bravery in saving the porter and his name was put forward for an Albert medal.

Both Captain Francis and the master of another steamship in the area, the *Idsa*, gave the position of loss of the *Carmelite* as ten miles south-west of the Calf of Man. The Royal Navy located a wreck in 1945 whilst hunting U-Boats in position 53 55.200 N, 04 56.200 W, which was undoubtedly the wreck of *Carmelite*.

References

British Vessels Lost At Sea, 1914-1918; *Lloyd's War Losses, The First World War*; *British Merchant Vessels Sunk by U-Boats in the 1914-1918 War*, Tennent; World Ship Society, H. Appleyard; *Lloyd's Register*; UK Public Records Office German Submarines March 1918 ADM 137/1515; UK Public Records Office ADM 137/2964.

Wreck Site

Diving

The identity of this wreck is assumed to be that of the *Carmelite* because of its size and location, but as far as is known, it has not been dived or positively identified.

The wreck of the *Carmelite* sits in a general depth of 75m of water and rises to about 9m from the seabed. The wreck is about 120m in length and about 15m in width. It is orientated on an east-north-east/west-south-west axis.

Due to the depth of water, the wreck of the *Carmelite* is only for the highly technical diver using tri-mix either in open circuit or in a rebreather. The *Carmelite* will certainly be an excellent dive, as the wreck appears largely intact on sonar. Being located on a sand or shingle seabed should ensure visibility at 8m or so in the summer months and sometimes excellent at 15m or more in calm weather and small tides (apart from the plankton bloom in May and early June, when it is generally more limited).

Expect the slack waters to occur more or less at the predicted low and high water times and beginning about half an hour before to three quarters of an hour after. On spring tides expect this window of slack to be of a shorter duration. The flood tide flows from the west-south-west and the ebb from the east-north-east.

Angling

The wreck of the *Carmelite* has been fished for at least fifteen years and yields reasonable numbers of pollack to 10lb or so. Due to the size of the wreck, it is often the case that the fish shoals will be on a specific part of the wreck so try different drifts until the fish are contacted. Good ling to 20lb have been taken and there is obvious potential for a good conger eel. There are sometimes coalfish and large pouting. Specimens of 2-3lb have been caught in the past.

Clwyd

Wreck: ★★★★★
Scenery: ★★★★★
Angling: ★★★★
Depth: 57m
Position: 53 43.197 N, 04 29.212 W
Datum: WGS84
Location: 21n.m. S. of Langness
Access: Douglas (25.7n.m.) and Port St Mary (23.2n.m.) slipways at all stages of the tide. Castletown (17.8n.m.) slipway three hours either side of high water.

Vessel

The steel steamship *Clwyd*, of Liverpool, (Official Number: 127,956), 289 tons gross, 123 tons net, was completed in November 1908 by J.P. Rennoldson & Sons, of

South Shields (Yard Number 256), for the Clwyd Steamship Co. She was powered by a compound steam engine. The *Clwyd* was 125.2ft in length, had a beam of 22.7ft and a draught of 9.5ft (38.1m x 6.9m x 2.9m). On 19 January 1916, she was sold to the Point of Ayr Collieries Ltd (George W Dishart and Alfred Stabback, of Liverpool, managers).

History

At about 5.00 p.m. on Wednesday 19 December 1917, the *Clwyd*, Captain John Jones, master, left Dublin, in ballast, bound for the Point of Ayr Colliery in Chester River. Notwithstanding the heavy sea, which was caused by a stiff easterly gale, all went well until about 11.00 p.m. when the vessel was off the Skerries. Another steamer, which later was proved to be the *Paragon*, of more or less the same size as the *Clwyd*, suddenly loomed out of the darkness and stuck her a tremendous blow on the starboard side close to the fore rigging.

The watch below, startled by the impact, rushed on deck, lightly clad, and joined the other members of the crew. Nothing could be seen of the vessel with which they had collided, she having disappeared in the darkness. *Clwyd*'s siren was sounded so as to alert attention and was kept going for half an hour whilst preparations were made to lower the ship's lifeboat. There was no response to the *Clwyd*'s distress signals.

One of the hatches was lifted and it was seen that water was pouring into the hold in a fashion that convinced the Captain Jones and his crew that their ship would soon founder. Accordingly the lifeboat was lowered into the sea and the crew, seven in number, got into it and pulled away from the doomed vessel. In their hurry the crew forgot to take any food with them and, to make matters worse, the keg of drinking water, which was part of the boat's equipment, had its bung stove in during the lowering operation and much of the water leaked away.

A dreary and awful experience for the men then commenced. A heavy and angry sea ran, the air was intensely cold and seawater constantly broke over their lifeboat. For thirty-six hours they rowed or drifted about the Irish Sea, the adverse weather conditions continuing throughout. Lights of other shipping were seen through the night and always the crew united in shouting with a view to attracting attention to their terrible plight, but in vain. Throughout Thursday 20 December they suffered dreadfully from cold, hunger and thirst. One man was clad in nothing more than his shirt, but a shipmate sacrificed his overcoat in order that he might have some better protection against the weather.

When daybreak came they scanned the sea anxiously in the hope of seeing a vessel, but no vessel was in sight. Fortunately, there was a can of oil in the boat and the contents were from time to time poured sparingly upon the sea with a view to calming the crests of the waves. Night again overtook the crew and, as the cold increased, their sufferings were intensified. Weak from hunger and thirst and numbed with cold, they allowed the boat to drift as it listed. They huddled together to conserve as much body heat as they could. A shower of rain came and some was caught on canvas, their thirst to some small degree quenched, but their relief remaining slight.

At about 2.00 a.m., William Owen Jones, the first engineer, a man of forty-seven years of age from Port Dinorwic, commenced to show signs of failing health and soon afterwards, died. It was not until between 10.00 a.m. and 11.00 a.m. on Friday 21 December that the steam trawler *Fly*, of Fleetwood, Captain Wignall, master, was observed some ten miles south-east of Maughold Head. The *Clwyd*'s crew used every last ounce of energy that they could muster to signal desperately to the *Fly* and eventually succeeded. There was still considerable delay in rescue owing to the fact that the trawler's net had to be taken in before they could come up to the boat. When she got alongside, the task of transferring the *Clwyd*'s men to the *Fly* was one of great danger and difficulty, as the exhausted men were unable to help themselves. Eventually, the six survivors and the body of the first engineer were taken on board the trawler.

The *Fly*'s master and crew did everything that lay in their power by way of affording relief to the shipwrecked crew. By early afternoon the *Fly* reached Douglas harbour and the six survivors were able to walk ashore.

The survivors were Captain John Jones, of Bangor, master; Llewellyn Griffiths, of Bangor, mate; William Griffiths, of Moelfre; William Williams, of Moelfre; William Jones, of Liverpool, second engineer; and Oscar Legg, of Belfast, fireman.

References

Mersey Rovers, Fenton; *Isle of Man Examiner*, Saturday, 29.12.1917. spool EX18, MNH; *Mona's Herald*, Wednesday, 26.12.1917. spool N124 MNH; Inquest File Index MNH.

Wreck Site

Diving

The identity of the wreck is assumed to be that of the steamship *Clwyd*, but as yet no positive identity has been achieved. Interestingly, in 2000 a diver recovered a telegraph made by J. Donkin & Co. They were a company based on Tyneside and this would perhaps match with a ship built in South Shields.

The wreck sits upright in a general depth of 57m of water and rises to about 8m from the seabed. The wreck is about 40m in length and about 7m in width. It is orientated on an east-south-east/west-north-west axis with the bow to the west-north-west.

The midships and stern sections of the wreck are reasonably intact, but the bow is greatly damaged. Debris lies off to the starboard side of the wreck. The seabed of shingle and mud means that visibility is limited at times.

Expect the slack waters to occur more or less at the predicted low and high water times and beginning about half an hour before to three quarters of an hour after. On spring tides expect this window of slack to be of a shorter duration. The flood tide flows from the west and the ebb from the east.

Angling

It is expected that the wreck holds good numbers of pollack and the occasional ling.

Dawn Waters

Wreck: *****
Scenery: ****
Angling: ***
Depth: 30m
Position: 54 06.905 N, 04 06.793 W
Datum: WGS84
Location: 12.7n.m. east-south-east of Douglas Head
Access: Douglas (12.9n.m.) slipway at all stages of the tide. Laxey (11.9n.m.) slipway three hours either side of high water.

Vessel

The steel beam trawler *Dawn Waters*, of Jersey (J472), but based at Newlyn in Cornwall, was built in Holland in 1967. A vessel of 99 tons gross, 35 tons net, she measured 82ft in length (25m). Her owner was A.M. Seafoods Ltd, of Fleetwood. She was equipped with a 500hp diesel engine.

History

The *Dawn Waters* left Fleetwood for the sole fishing grounds between the east coast of the Isle of Man and Morecambe Bay on Friday 14 March 1986. By Thursday 20 March, she was running low on fuel so her skipper, Anthony Leonard Ozard, radioed to order fuel for her from a company based at Douglas. On the radio he said that all was well and that it was a good trip. The weather worsened with force eleven north-west winds and huge seas, however, as the *Dawn Waters* made her way towards Douglas.

At 9.18 a.m. on 20 March, the diving support vessel, *British Enterprise V*, Captain Hector Thomson, master, which had been working in the area of the Morecambe Bay gas rigs, was heading towards the shelter of the east coast of the Isle of Man after having received a storm warning. At about fourteen miles off Douglas, Captain Thomson spotted an object in the water. The waves were now up to 30ft in height and it was only on drawing closer to the object that Captain Thomson could see that it was just 6ft of the bow of the *Dawn Waters* jutting out from the surface of the sea. No mayday message had been received from the *Dawn Waters*. Two fully inflated life rafts were floating near the submerged vessel, one of which was still attached to the *Dawn Waters*.

Captain Thomson then suddenly saw a man in the water with an arm through a lifebelt. The man was Gordon Coram, but a desperate fifteen minute battle to save him failed. The eight crewmen on the British Enterprise made four attempts to reach the man. He was seen to be very weak and, when finally a rope was passed to him, he was unable to hold onto it. The crewmen then saw Gordon Coram slump over and he unfortunately drowned. His body was later recovered by the Douglas Lifeboat, Robert Corran, coxswain, and taken to Douglas, being landed at 5.10 p.m. the same day.

Four merchant ships, two helicopters and two lifeboats, including the Douglas Lifeboat, searched unsuccessfully for possible survivors. Passing aircraft were also asked to reduce their height and search for any bodies, but none were located.

The search for the crew of the *Dawn Waters* was understood to have been hampered by no official crew list having been lodged with the owners prior to her departure from Fleetwood. Through ceaseless work by the police, Coastguards and the Royal National Mission to Deep Sea Fishermen at Newlyn and Fleetwood, a list was eventually released. It was Anthony Leonard Ozard, skipper, Newlyn; Christopher Dodd, Mousehole (28); Gordon Anthony Coram, Penzance (22); Jason Paul Ward, Plymouth (19); and David Norman Young, Paignton (36).

Later, the wreck of the *Dawn Waters* was found by the Trinity House search and salvage vessel, *Winston Churchill*, using her sonar equipment.

The official inquiry as to the cause of loss of the *Dawn Waters* was conducted by Captain Maurice Roberts, a principal nautical surveyor. The *Dawn Waters* had a stability booklet approved by the United Kingdom's Department of Trade in 1978. He was of the opinion that all hatches and port lights had been secured and that the cause of her loss was the severe weather conditions at the time.

References

Isle of Man Examiner; Olsen's Fishermen's Nautical Almanac, 1982; *Fishing News*, 08.03.1986.

Wreck Site

Diving

The wreck of the *Dawn Waters* lies on its starboard side in a general depth of 30m of water and rises to about 3m from the seabed. The wreck is about 30m in length and about 11m in width. It is orientated on a south-east/north-west axis.

There has still been relatively little deterioration in the vessel as yet. Despite being a modern wreck, the *Dawn Waters* makes an good dive as it is largely intact and sits on a sandy seabed so that visibility is generally good at 8m or so in the summer months and sometimes excellent at 15m or more in calm weather and small tides (apart from the plankton bloom in May and early June, when it is generally more limited). Fish proliferate around the wreck.

Expect the slack waters to occur more or less at the predicted low and high water times and beginning about half of an hour before to three quarters of an hour after. On spring tides expect this window of slack to be of a shorter duration. The flood tide flows from the south-west and the ebb from the north-east.

Angling

Fish are prolific, if not particularly large. Huge shoals of pollack and coalfish patrol the wreck and some considerable catches can be made of pollack in the 3lb to 6lb range and coalfish up to 5lb. There are also large amounts of pouting which can be

Dawn Waters. (Copyright: Michael Craine)

troublesome, taking baits intended for other species. Oddly, ling do not seem to frequent this wreck and cod are noted by their absence as well.

Don Bosco

Wreck: *****
Scenery: ***
Angling: *
Depth: 31m
Position: 54 07.437 N, 04 47.152 W
Datum: WGS84
Location: 2.2n.m. north of Bradda Head
Access: Port St Mary (7n.m.) and Peel (6.8n.m.) slipways at all stages of the tide. Port Erin (2.8n.m.) beach launch possible.

Vessel

The steel motor fishing vessel *Don Bosco*, of Peel (PL12), 24 tons gross, was built in 1969 by the Bideford Shipbuilding Co. She was 42ft in length, had a beam of 15ft and a draught of 6ft (12.8m x 4.6m x 1.8m). At the time of her loss she was owned by Reuban Reid, of Peel.

History

At approximately 4.00 a.m. on Thursday 8 November 1990, the motor fishing vessel *Don Bosco* left Peel to dredge for scallops off Bradda Head on the south-western coast of the Isle of Man, along with a substantial part of the Manx fishing fleet. There were strong easterly winds at the time forcing the fishing fleet to work a lee under the land. The wind was blowing down from the tops of the hills and formed wheels and walls of spray, making it fishable, but difficult. Conditions worsened, however; the *Don Bosco* took a wave over the stern and was in danger of sinking. It was 7.00 a.m. and skipper Reuban Reid radioed that his vessel was taking in water and was in danger of foundering.

It was understood that Liverpool Coastguards were alerted to the incident by a member of the public in Peel, who had been listening to a radio scanner. Peel Lifeboat secretary Allen Corlett was alerted to the incident by a telephone call from Liverpool Coastguard at 7.14 a.m. The lifeboat was launched immediately. At least thirty-five residents of Peel rushed to the breakwater to offer what help they could and Mr Corlett said, 'It was fortunate the drama happened in daylight, as the consequences of such an incident happening in darkness would have been far more serious.'

Meanwhile, a number of fishing boats headed for *Don Bosco*. The vessels *Our Lassie* (PL92) and *Acorn* (PL2) were close by and went to the aid of Reuban Reid and crewman Stephen Lester. While trying to rescue the crew of the *Don Bosco*, skipper Frank Windsor and crewman Martin Corkish in the wooden *Our Lassie* pulled up alongside and accidentally hit the steel hulled *Don Bosco*, resulting in the *Our Lassie* springing planks, taking in water and sinking. Geoff Gilbert, skipper of the *Acorn*, came onto the scene and safely rescued all four crewmen of both sunken vessels, who were in the icy sea for more than ten minutes. The Peel Lifeboat arrived on the scene immediately afterwards. It escorted the *Acorn*, complete with survivors, back to Peel. All men were soon discharged from hospital none the worse for their experience.

An inquiry into the accident, headed by Department of Highways, Ports and Properties marine surveyor Captain Geoff Davis, attached no blame to either of the two skippers. He said in an interview:

Don Bosco. (Copyright: Michael Craine)

Our Lassie. (Copyright: Michael Craine)

Inquiries were made and results from those inquiries arrived on my desk. I concluded from these that the sinkings were a complete accident and that no further action was necessary. We haven't necessarily got every detail – but there is enough evidence to satisfy ourselves it was effectively an accident.

Captain Davis said the second sinking resulted from the hazard of two boats working in close proximity in poor weather. 'They collided in their attempts to rescue the crew of the *Don Bosco*. There was not sufficient space for both to manipulate their vessels in the conditions,' he said.

Fisherman's Association secretary Eric Moore commented, 'It is the outcome we expected. We're completely satisfied that it was just an accident. No further action is being called for, but safety recommendations may be made in the department's report.'

Reuban Reid eventually received a full insurance payout of £40,000 after attempts to salvage the *Don Bosco* were called off. Sunderland Marine Insurance Co. had previously suspended payment pending the salvage attempt, but this was abandoned after Manx divers decided the financial gain from raising the vessel wouldn't merit continuing.

References

Scottish Fishing News, 16.11.1990; *Isle of Man Courier*, 08.11.1990; *Isle of Man Independent*, 09.11.1990; *Isle of Man Examiner*, 13.11.1990, 17.12.1990 & 12.02.1991; Michael Craine 14.02.1996.

Wreck Site

Diving

The wreck of the *Don Bosco* sits upright on its keel in a general depth of 31m of water and rises to about 6m from the seabed. The wreck is about 13m in length and about 5m in width. It is orientated on a south-west/north-east axis.

There has been relatively little deterioration in the vessel as yet, although its propeller has been salvaged and other items removed. Despite being a modern wreck, the *Don Bosco* is a favourite dive site for some divers as it lies close to land and is easily accessible from Port Erin or Port St Mary. In addition, the wreck is largely intact and sits on a sandy seabed so that visibility is generally good at 8m or so in the summer months and sometimes excellent at 15m or more in calm weather and small tides (apart from the plankton bloom in May and early June, when it is generally more limited).

Expect the slack waters to occur more or less at the predicted low and high water times and beginning about an hour before to an hour after. On spring tides expect this window of slack to be of a shorter duration. The flood tide flows from the south-west and the ebb from the north-east.

Please note that the wreck is in private ownership and the Diving Officer of the Port Erin Marine Biologists' Sub-Aqua Club (Tel. 01624 823027) should be contacted before making a dive on the wreck.

Angling

There are some pollack and coalfish around the *Don Bosco*, but they tend to be small.

Dundalk

Wreck: ****
Scenery: *****
Angling: ****
Depth: 56m
Position: 53 47.210 N, 04 40.610 W
Datum: WGS84
Location: 17.2n.m. south-south-west of Langness
Access: Douglas (22.8n.m.) and Port St Mary (17.4n.m.) slipways at all stages of the tide. Castletown (17.4n.m.) slipway three hours either side of high water.

Vessel

The steel steamship *Dundalk*, of Dundalk, (Official Number: 107,003), 794 tons gross, 327 tons net, was built in 1899 by A. & J. Inglis, of Glasgow. She was 236ft in length, had a beam of 32.1ft and a draught of 15.2ft (72m x 9.8m x 4.6m). She was owned by the Dundalk and Newry Steam Packet Co., (S.J. Cooks, managers). The *Dundalk* was fitted with a triple-expansion steam engine built by A. & J. Inglis of Glasgow, developing 283nhp and driving the *Dundalk* along at twelve knots at full speed.

During the First World War she was armed with a single 90mm gun for protection against German submarines.

History

On 6 December 1917, the *Dundalk*, when bound from Liverpool for Dundalk, was attacked by a German submarine, but survived the attack.

At 11.20 p.m. on Monday 14 October 1918, whilst on a voyage from Liverpool to *Dundalk* with 150 tons of general cargo, she was torpedoed in the port side of her engine room by the German submarines UB123 and U90 to the south of the Isle of Man. She had been zigzagging since leaving Liverpool Bar, but there was bright moonlight, clear visibility and calm seas at the time, enabling the submarines to see their target easily. The explosion was described by survivors to have practically blown her to pieces. The *Dundalk* sank immediately in only four minutes. The ship's company numbered thirty-two persons, consisting of twenty-seven crewmen (including three gunners), four cattlemen and one passenger. The two main lifeboats were destroyed by the explosion, but there were two life rafts on deck, which floated off as the vessel foundered. Most of the crew were left struggling in the water.

A collier steamer then appeared on the scene. Survivors from the *Dundalk* tried to hail the steamer, but she continued on her course without rescuing any of the men. One of the two submarines was seen close by and, without offering any assistance, headed south and went out of sight. One of the two small rafts contained five men who had to continually bale it out to keep it afloat. Though fortunate to still be alive, the men were starved with hunger, suffered greatly from exposure and were exhausted when picked up some sixteen hours later by the Isle of Man Steam Packet Co. steamship *Douglas*. The names of the five men were Francis Deery, William Tune, Patrick Kearney, John Higgins (first mate) and Mr Byrne.

Another six men in the other raft were rescued by the armed steam trawler *Stormcock* at 4.30 p.m. and landed at Holyhead after having been observed by an aeroplane. Those killed numbered twenty-one men and women and included the master, Captain Hugh O'Neill, the general manager of the company, Mr S.J. Cooks (who was the only passenger), the first engineer, the steward and stewardess.

There was some confusion over her position of loss. Official records list her position as five miles north-north-west of the Skerries, Anglesey and this was the position given by the survivors landed at Holyhead. The survivors who landed at Douglas however, estimated her position to be fifteen miles south of the Chicken Rock. Confirmation of the wreck's identity has proved the latter party to be correct. Indeed, in his statement, one of the gun crew who survived, Angus Ferguson (RNR 1987D), gave the position of loss as forty-six miles north-west x west ½ west from the Liverpool Bar Light Vessel, a position which tallies with the actual and not the official position of loss from the time.

The other two gunners were Timothy O'Connor (RNR 8223) and Harold Gray (RNVR).

References

Lloyd's War Losses, The First World War; British Merchant Ships Sunk by U-boats in the 1914-1918 War, Tennent; *Dictionary of Disasters at Sea During the Age of Steam*, Hocking; *British Vessels Lost at Sea, 1914-1918*; *Ramsey Courier*, Friday, 25.10.1918. spool MN487 MNH; *British Shipping Fleets*, Joseph Fisher & Sons, Fenton and Patterson; *Lloyd's Register*; UK Public Records Office ADM137/1517, ADM137/634 & ADM137/2964.

Wreck Site

Diving

The identity of the wreck was definitely confirmed in 1999 following the recovery of artefacts by divers.

The wreck of the *Dundalk* now sits upright in a general depth of 56m of water and rises to about 6m from the seabed. The wreck is about 80m in length and about 10m in width. The wreck is split into two pieces, the main section is orientated on an east-north-east/west-south-west axis, with the smaller second piece orientated on a south-east/north-west axis. The break exposes the vessel's boiler and engine room.

The wreck of the *Dundalk* is for the experienced diver only and makes an excellent dive, being a reasonably complete passenger/cargo steamer.

As it lies on a sandy seabed, visibility is generally good at 8m or so in the summer months and sometimes excellent at 15m or more in calm weather and small tides (apart from the plankton bloom in May and early June, when it is generally more limited). Fish proliferate around the wreck.

Expect the slack waters to occur more or less at the predicted low and high water times and beginning about half an hour before to three quarters of an hour after. On spring tides expect this window of slack to be of a shorter duration. The flood tide flows from the west-southwest and the ebb from the east-northeast.

Angling

As would be expected, the *Dundalk* produces some good pollack fishing with individual fish to double figures in the late summer months. There are also some coalfish and good potential for ling and conger eels. This is not a wreck known for its cod fishing.

Empress Eugenie

Wreck: ★★★
Scenery: ★★★
Angling: ★★
Depth: 50m
Position: 53 48.098 N, 04 15.348 W

Datum: WGS84
Location: 20.3n.m. south-east of Langness
Access: Douglas (22.1n.m.) and Port St Mary (23.5n.m.) slipways at all stages of the tide. Castletown (21.5n.m.) slipway three hours either side of high water.

Vessel

The iron screw steamer *Empress Eugenie*, of Liverpool, (Official Number: 1,353), 582 tons gross, 425 tons burthen, was built in 1855 by Rennie, Johnson and Rankin, of Liverpool. She was 186.7ft in length, had a beam of 25.7ft and a draught of 14ft (56.9m x 7.8m x 4.3m). The vessel was rigged as a brig, with a standing bowsprit and a figurehead of a woman. Later, in 1859, a deckhouse weighing 11.8 tons was erected.

The *Empress Eugenie* was owned by the trading partnership of Frederick Augustus Tamplin and Thomas McClune, both well-known Liverpool merchants and shipping agents. They originally traded as the West of France Steam Navigation Co. until that route proved unprofitable and they decided to switch to a more profitable route and subsequently trade as the London and Liverpool Steam Navigation Co. She was equipped with a direct acting steam engine rated nominally at 110hp driving a three-bladed propeller. Messrs James Jack & Co., of the Victoria Foundry built the engine.

History

The *Empress Eugenie* left the Trafalgar Dock, Liverpool at 10.30 p.m. on Thursday 24 January 1861, with a valuable general cargo, under the command of Captain Higgins. She was bound for London, stopping along the way at ports such as Falmouth and Penzance. In addition to twenty-seven crewmen, there were seven passengers on board.

Captain Higgins reported that after leaving dock he steamed down the North Channel and at midnight passed the Fairway Buoy, in the Queen's Channel. The next morning it blew a strong gale from the south-west and at 3.00 a.m. on Friday 25 January, the engineer reported that the steamer was making water, the engine room was filling and the pumps were unable to keep the water level down.

At 6.00 a.m. the engine stopped, the water having reached the fires in the boiler. The passengers and crew then took to the manual pumps in an attempt to prevent the steamer from foundering. The mainsail was set to keep the ship's head to sea as she was labouring heavily. By 3.00 p.m. on Friday, finding the water still increasing, the pumps were stopped and the lifeboats lowered, with nineteen people departing in one boat and fifteen in the other.

At 5.30 p.m., when the *Empress Eugenie* was thirty miles north-east of Point Lynas, Anglesey, they finally abandoned the steamer, which immediately settled and sank at 5.50 p.m. The crew and passengers then rowed the lifeboats in a north-easterly direction until 2.15 a.m. on Saturday 26 January, when the foremost boat fell in with the steamer *Countess of Galloway*, bound from Kirkcudbright for Liverpool. On being told of the existence of a second lifeboat, Captain Broadfoot, master of the *Countess of Galloway*, conducted a search lasting two hours before finally locating it and rescuing the occupants.

Certificate of Registry for the steamship *Empress Eugenie*. (Copyright: John Cook)

References

Manx Sun, Saturday, 02.02.1861. spool N60 MNH; World Ship Society, G.H. Somner; Parliamentary Papers 1860 Volume 60, Guildhall Library; John Cook, Centre for Maritime Historical Studies, University of Exeter.

Wreck Site

Diving

The first clue as to the identity of the wreck was recovered in 1990 in the net of a trawler. It was a gravy boat with the emblem of the shipping company on the side of it with the words, 'West of France Steam Navigation Co.'. No trace of this company could be found until 1999 when the historical proof surfaced to connect the shipping company name to the *Empress Eugenie* (see Vessel details on page 67).

The wreck sits upright in a general depth of 51m of water and rises to about 7m from the seabed, the highest point being at the bow. It is about 60m in length and about 8m in width. It is orientated on a south-east/north-west axis. The wreck is quite broken up and partly buried. On the sounder it appears more of a mound than a cleanly protruding wreck.

The *Empress Eugenie* makes an excellent dive, and many artefacts must still remain on the wreck. It is a deep dive and suitable only for the experienced wreck diver.

The wreck lies on a sand/shingle seabed, so visibility is generally good at 8m or so in the summer months and sometimes excellent at 15m or more in calm weather and small tides (apart from the plankton bloom in May and early June, when it is generally more limited). It can be a dark wreck, however, so a good torch is imperative.

Expect the slack waters to occur more or less at the predicted low and high water times and beginning about half an hour before to three quarters of an hour after. On spring tides, expect this window of slack to be of a shorter duration. The flood tide flows from the west and the ebb from the east.

Angling

The main species of fish on the wreck is the pollack. Fish in the 5lb-8lb range are the mainstay, but there is potential for larger fish as well as ling and cod.

Fenella Ann

Wreck: ★★★★★
Scenery: ★★★★
Angling: ★
Depth: 41m
Position: 54 02.640 N, 04 47.840 W
Datum: WGS84
Location: 0.4n.m. south-east of the Calf of Man
Access: Port St Mary (3n.m.) slipway at all stages of the tide. Castletown (5.7n.m.) slipway three hours only either side of high water. Port Erin (2.8n.m.) beach launch possible.

Vessel

The wooden motor fishing vessel *Fenella Ann*, of Castletown (CT27), 30 tons gross, 14 tons net, was built in 1960 at Girvan and was equipped with a 230bhp Gardner diesel engine. She was 50.2ft in length, had a beam of 17.5ft and a draught of 6.6ft (15.3m x 5.3m x 2m). The *Fenella Ann* was owned by Mr Gordon V. Challenor, of Port Erin.

She was chiefly employed in dredging scallops in winter or dragging for queenies in the summer months and operated out of Port St Mary.

History

On Saturday 9 November 2002 at about 4.10 a.m., the *Fenella Ann*, Vincent Lamont, skipper, of Port St Mary and crewman, Tony Watterson of Port Erin, left Port St Mary harbour for the fishing grounds between three and a half and four miles south-south-west of the Chicken Rock. She reached the fishing grounds at 5.10 a.m. and shortly afterwards commenced to dredge for scallops. For early winter the weather was excellent with clear skies, and a light force one to two southerly wind and calm seas. The *Fenella Ann* made six tows throughout the day and the fishing proved very successful. By 7.00 p.m. she had a large catch of scallops on board, some of which they had bagged.

At about 7.15 p.m., the *Fenella Ann* departed the fishing grounds and set an east-north-easterly course back to Port St Mary. Three other local vessels had already returned to Port St Mary. The fourth vessel, *Heather Maid*, a short distance south-east of the *Fenella Ann*, hauled her gear in at about the same time, and followed astern of the *Fenella Ann*.

As the *Fenella Ann* headed back towards Port St Mary, her skipper reduced the speed of his vessel in order to give more time for both men to sort the day's catch, with the intention of having all the scallops bagged and ready to unload as soon as they reached port. The wind had by now increased slightly to a force three to four south-south-easterly, and the tide was flowing from the south-east at a rate of more than two knots. This meant that the trawler had both wind and tide on her starboard side and was being pushed northwards of her intended course.

The vessel was not fitted with an autopilot, so skipper Lamont secured the steering wheel with starboard helm. He then returned to the wheelhouse on several occasions. On each visit he noticed that the vessel's course was too far to the north and he corrected this by applying more starboard helm. Both men kept a lookout from the deck area aft of the wheelhouse.

About eight or nine minutes after his last visit to the wheelhouse, skipper Lamont looked up and noticed his vessel was off course and too far to the north. He ran to the wheelhouse, but just as he got to the door he felt the *Fenella Ann* shudder heavily and saw Tony Watterson thrown to the deck.

It was shortly before low water, at 8.05 p.m. and the *Fenella Ann* had struck a rock about 10-12ft above the water, later surmised to be the outermost rock off the Burroo known as the Cleats, on the southern coast of the Calf of Man. It was a glancing blow and she did not sink immediately. The vessel was then about twenty minutes from Port St Mary, but with water gushing into the cabin and the bilge pumps failing to cope with the quantity of water entering the vessel, skipper Lamont radioed for help to the Manx trawlers *Heather Maid* and *De Bounty*. The *Heather Maid* was about two miles astern of the *Fenella Ann* and raced towards her to provide assistance.

Skipper Lamont then decided to try to get his vessel to the safety of Port St Mary some 3.5n.m. away. Unbeknown to him, however, she was taking in water fast, and after she had travelled only half a mile the engine stopped and she quickly began to settle by the head. The *Heather Maid* was now about half a mile astern and skipper Lamont radioed to her that the *Fenella Ann* was going down. The *Heather Maid* quickly closed the distance between the two vessels and went stern to stern with the sinking vessel and got off her two crewmen without injury. Just four minutes later, the *Fenella Ann* listed to starboard and foundered about half a mile off the south-east corner of the Calf of Man. There was about 800 gallons of diesel fuel on the *Fenella Ann*.

Shortly after the *Fenella Ann* sank, another fishing vessel, *De Bounty*, reached the scene, this vessel having previously alerted the emergency services of the incident, at the request of the skipper of the *Heather Maid*.

Port St Mary All Weather and Inshore Lifeboats arrived at the scene soon after and recovered the *Fenella Ann*'s EPIRB and other floating debris. The following day the lifeboat picked up the trawler's inflated but damaged life raft from the rocks on the Calf of Man.

During January 2003, an investigation into the sinking of the *Fenella Ann* was conducted by the Isle of Man's Marine Administration. The report said that it was clear that a safe navigational watch, both visual and by electronic means, had not been carried out, which was particularly important as the vessel was navigating close to land with a lee shore. The report went on to state that the skipper helping on deck was 'a well-established practice on fishing vessels' but that work 'should not be carried out at the expense of maintaining a safe navigational watch, which was clearly the case in this instance'.

Fenella Ann.
(Copyright: Michael Craine)

References

Isle of Man Online website, 10.01.2002; Port St Mary Lifeboat website, 10.11.2002; *Fishing Vessels of Britain and Ireland, 2001*; *Isle of Man Examiner*, Tuesday, 12.11.2002; Manx Radio Website, Monday, 11.11.2002: Mersey Shipping Website; Isle of Man Marine Administration Casualty Investigation Report CA81.

Wreck Site

Diving

Shortly after the *Fenella Ann* sank it was anticipated that she would be raised. At the time of writing in the autumn of 2003, this hope seems to have faded and therefore the *Fenella Ann* will provide divers with an excellent wreck close to the popular scenic dive sites of the Calf of Man. Care should be taken as despite lying close to the shore it is a fairly deep wreck.

The wreck presently sits on its keel with a list to starboard in 41m of water on a clean and sandy seabed. The bow faces to the north. The wreck is intact and suffered no impact damage with the seabed upon sinking. The damage caused by her hitting the rocks can be observed at the bow near to the seabed. The damage is more pronounced on the port side.

Being only 15m in length, the wreck is easily observed in a short time. Due to the *Fenella Ann*'s wooden construction, the wreck will not remain intact for many years, but its location outside of trawled grounds will prevent it from being broken up by scallop dredgers. As it lies on a sand/shingle seabed, visibility is generally good at 8m or so in summer, and sometimes excellent at 15m or more in calm weather and small tides (apart from the plankton bloom in May and early June, when it is generally more limited).

Slack waters occur about an hour and, sometimes an hour and a half, before the predicted low and high waters. The flooding tide comes from a south-westerly direction and the ebb from a north-easterly direction.

Angling

As the *Fenella Ann* only sank in 2002, it is only just being colonised by marine life. Over the coming years, the wreck will gradually be colonised more fully and it would be expected that it will eventually support shoals of small pollack and the occasional ballan wrasse. Lying as it does fairly close to shore, it cannot be expected that the wreck will yield the quality of fishing found on offshore wrecks, but it may prove to be a useful wreck to fish when the weather prevents access to wrecks further offshore.

Fire King

Wreck: ****
Scenery: ****
Angling: ***
Depth: 33m
Position: 54 26.080 N, 04 21.990 W
Datum: WGS84
Location: 1.1n.m. north of the Point of Ayre
Access: Ramsey (7n.m.) slipway two hours either side of high water and beach-launch possible in front of the Lifeboat House. Peel (17.5n.m.) slipway at all stages of the tide.

Vessel

The steel steamship *Fire King*, of Liverpool, 758 tons gross, 552 tons net, was launched on 29 October 1925 by John Duthie Torry Shipbuilding Co., of Aberdeen, (Yard number 468), for owners Robert Gilchrist & Co., of Liverpool. The *Fire King* was 190.3ft in length, had a beam of 32.1ft and a draught of 11.8ft (58m x 9.8m x 3.6m). She was powered by a triple-expansion steam engine developing 155nhp, which was built by A. Hall & Co. Ltd, of Aberdeen. During 1929, ownership of the *Fire King* was transferred to Gilchrist's Traders (Steamships) Ltd, (Robert Gilchrist & Co., managers).

History

The *Fire King*, bound from her home port of Liverpool for Glasgow with a general cargo, was approaching the Point of Ayre on the fine, clear morning of 10 December 1939, when the mail steamer *Duke of Lancaster* was observed ahead whilst on her passage from Belfast to Heysham with cargo and 180 passengers, having passed the Point of Ayre. The ships were converging on a collision course and for some reason the vessel giving way, the *Duke of Lancaster*, did not. At some time around 3.30 a.m., the bows of the *Duke of Lancaster* sliced right through the second hold of the *Fire King*. It was fortunate that this part of the *Fire King* received the full force of the impact, for had the impact occurred amidships or forward, it would have caused serious loss of life amongst the crew of the *Fire King*.

Describing how his ship was sunk, Captain Neil Kerr, who had skippered the *Fire King* for the previous fourteen years, said:

I was below when it happened. I looked out through a porthole and saw the large vessel heading for us. I thought she might miss us by going to our stern. I shouted, "Put her hard over", but the next moment there was a sickening crash. I saw her bows cutting through our boat and I knew we could not possibly stay afloat. So I immediately ordered all hands on deck.

The crew, seeing what had happened, grasped hold of ropes and swung themselves onto the *Duke of Lancaster*. However, an elderly fireman, James Stein, was badly crushed between the two ships. The *Fire King* sank minutes afterwards.

Meanwhile, the Ramsey Lifeboat, the *Lady Harrison* was launched, having been alerted to the accident by Portpatrick Radio Station, which had picked up the distress call direct from the mail steamer. The lifeboat, under coxswain John Comish and with a doctor aboard, made for the collision area originally given as six miles north-west from the Point of Ayre Lighthouse. Medical supplies were also taken and the *Lady Harrison* escorted the surviving ship back to a safe anchorage in Ramsey Bay. The *Fire King*'s survivors were then taken off the mail steamer and landed at Ramsey. The injured fireman, James Stein, died in Ramsey Cottage Hospital later in the day.

The crew of the *Fire King* was as follows: Captain Neil Kerr, master, of Bute, Isle of Bute; Archibald Downie, first mate, 36 Thurston Road, Liverpool; Neil McKinnon, second mate, 122 Stampland Gardens, Glasgow; G.A. Dudgeon, chief engineer, of 8 Rundle Road, Liverpool; Leslie Ormisher, 27 Scraly Grove, Liverpool; R. Roberts, 60 Vulverton Road, Liverpool; M. Martin, 28 Fiscavisy, Portree, Skye; B. McBride, Catacol, Loch Ranza, Arran; James McKinnon, Fairy Cottage, Arinagour, Isle of Coll; Michael Kelly, 7 Henderson Place, Cromner Street, Liverpool; Peter Gibbons, of Liverpool; and James Stein, 65 Tradeston Street, Glasgow.

In May 1940, the exact position of the wreck of the *Fire King* was located only a mile north of the Point of Ayre, not the six miles originally thought. Local fishing boats were engaged to take the salvage men out to the wreck. Divers went down, but it was a while before the identity of the vessel was confirmed. The salvage operations were carried out by a Liverpool firm and attempts were made to blow up the wreck so that it would not prove to be an obstruction to shipping.

On Monday 26 August 1940, Mr Justice Langton, in the Admiralty Court, limited to £27,088 the liability of the London, Midland and Scottish Railway Co. as owners of the *Duke of Lancaster*, whose vessel was to blame for the collision.

References

Isle of Man Examiner, spool EX34 MNH; World Ship Society, K. O'Donoghue; *Ramsey Courier*, Friday, 24.05.1940. & 30.08.1940. MNH; *The Ramsey Lifeboats*, Seybold; *Ramsey Courier*, 15.12.1939. MNH.

Wreck Site

Diving

The *Fire King* has been a well-known wreck dive around the Isle of Man for many years, but is mostly dived by visiting divers rather than locals nowadays.

The wreck sits on its keel, with a list to starboard of forty-five degrees, in a general depth of 26m of water. Over the years, however, the strong tidal currents have cut a huge scour around the wreck and it now lies at the bottom on the scour, which is 33m at its deepest point. The wreck rises to about 5m from the seabed, is about 60m in length and about 10m in width. It is orientated on a north/south axis with the bow pointing south towards the Point of Ayre Lighthouse.

The wreck of the *Fire King* makes an excellent dive, being still fairly intact and covered in plumrose anemones and other marine life. Large fish, lobsters and crabs abound. It has suffered some damage especially above deck level; a result of demolition charges exploded on it in the 1940s in an attempt to disperse the wreckage. A large quantity of debris and one of the two boilers have spilled out into the scour crater on the starboard side. At the stern, next to the intact rudder and propeller, lies a small cavern where monster lobster and conger eels fill the deep gap between wreck and the shingle seabed. Further up the port side, there is a large plum-rose anemone-covered tunnel where hull plates have popped off the wreck, before a small gap where the wreck is flat before the bow. The bow itself sits high with an anchor still in place, and can safely be entered and explored inside.

The *Fire King* lies on a shingle seabed so visibility is generally good at 8m or so in the summer months and sometimes excellent at 15m or more in calm weather and small tides (apart from the plankton bloom in May and early June, when it is more generally limited).

Expect the low water slack to occur about five and a half hours after high water and to last for about an hour or so. At high water the slack period starts at around one and a half hours before high water and lasts for less than half an hour. On spring

Rudder on the wreck of the *Fire King*. (Copyright: Phil Hutchinson)

tides, expect both windows of slack to be of a shorter duration. The flood tide flows from the west-north-west and the ebb from the east-south-east.

Angling

Large shoals of pollack patrol around the wreck, especially in the late summer and autumn months. Ballan wrasse is also large and common. Divers have observed many fine congers on the wreck, but the strong tidal currents at this wreck would make anchoring for congers difficult. Cod must be a possibility on occasions and ling cannot be ruled out.

Float

Wreck: ★★★★
Scenery: ★
Angling: ★
Depth: 25.5m
Position: 54 15.605 N, 04 17.765 W
Datum: WGS84
Location: 2.2n.m. south of Maughold Head
Access: Douglas (9.5n.m.) slipway at all stages of the tide. Laxey (4.2n.m.) slipway three hours either side of high water. Ramsey (4.9n.m.) slipway two hours either side of high water and beach launch possible in front of the Lifeboat House.

Vessel

The wreck is the remains of a light float, presumably originating from the River Mersey.

History

It is not known how or when the *Float* came to be sunk off Port Cornaa on the north-east coast of the Isle of Man. It is thought that the *Float* may date from the Second World War Blitz period on Liverpool and the ships in the River Mersey.

Wreck Site

Diving

The wreck of the *Float* sits upright in a general depth of 25.5m of water and rises to about 3m from the seabed. The wreck is about 11m in length and about 3m in width. It is orientated on an east-south-east/west-north-west axis.

The *Float* makes an excellent warm-up dive in the spring or a training dive for someone learning to wreck dive. It is intact, but now missing the light tower and easily covered in a short bottom time.

As it lies on a sand/shingle seabed, visibility is generally good at 8m or so in summer and sometimes excellent at 15m or more in calm weather and small tides (apart from the plankton bloom in May and early June, when it is generally more limited).

Expect the slack waters to occur more or less at the predicted low and high water times and beginning about half an hour before to three quarters of an hour after. On spring tides, expect this window of slack to be of a shorter duration. The flood tide flows from the south-west and the ebb from the north-east.

Angling

The main species are pouting and mackerel in the summer together with a few small pollack.

Florence

Wreck: *****
Scenery: ****
Angling: ****
Depth: 50m
Position: 53 54.997 N, 04 39.415 W
Datum: WGS84
Location: 8.3n.m. south-south-west of Langness
Access: Douglas (15.4n.m.) and Port St Mary (9.7n.m.) slipways at all stages of the tide. Castletown (9.1n.m.) slipway three hours either side of high water.

Vessel

The iron screw steamship *Florence*, of Liverpool, 268 tons gross, 115 tons net, was built in 1882 for £8,250 by T.B. Seath & Co., of Rutherglen. The *Florence* was 146.8ft in length, had a beam of 22.2ft and a draught of 10.7ft (44.8m x 6.8m x 3.3m). She was equipped with a compound steam engine developing 70hp built by W. King & Co., of Glasgow. Her owner was Messrs J. & J. Mack, of Water Street, Liverpool, trading under the name Florence Steamship Co. The *Florence* was insured for £6,500.

History

On Tuesday 17 September 1889 at 4.00 p.m., the *Florence* left Garston bound for Belfast with a cargo of coal. An extra wagon load of coal was put in the aft hold above the desired maximum with the effect that the hatch could not be fastened correctly and so a tarpaulin was used to keep out the elements. It was not certain whether the *Florence* was definitely overloaded, but she was witnessed in dock to be very low in the water. In any regard, the fitting of a tarpaulin over the insecurely fastened wooden hatch covers would seem to have been an unwise act.

All went well on the first part of the voyage with fine weather and calm seas. At about 8.00 p.m. the wind increased from the south-west and a heavy sea developed.

The *Florence* began to labour badly, with the seas continually sweeping over her. Captain A. Cameron, the master, turned in about 10.00 p.m. and the mate, J. Wilson, took over in command on deck. At the same time an able-bodied seaman, William O'Neill, took over at the wheel. No sail was set. At 1.00 a.m. on Wednesday 18 September, the *Florence* had passed Langness and was about ten miles off, but still in sight of the Chickens Light. The mate noticed one of the binnacle lamps was getting dim and so instructed O'Neill to go and get it trimmed. By this time, the weather was extremely dirty with heavy squalls of wind and rain. O'Neill, his oilskins on, went down to the engine room with the lamp. On his way down he noticed that the water was nearly to the top of the half-door of the engine room. The second engineer, J. Duncan, and a fireman were on duty, the watch consisting of four men. The second engineer pricked up the lamp for O'Neill. O'Neill had only got to the top of the stairs to go on deck again, when the second engineer came running after him and shouted, 'She is full of water aft.' O'Neill ran aft and saw some of the hatches had gone over the side of the ship. He rushed back to the mate, who asked O'Neill who was calling out to him. O'Neill told the mate that the ship was full of water aft and so the mate exclaimed, 'Call the captain!', who was in his cabin at the time. O'Neill tried to reach the captain's cabin, but was unable to get aft because so much water was coming on board. He then blew the steam whistle to attract the captain's attention and the captain came up to the wheelhouse immediately. Captain Cameron asked, 'What is the matter?' The mate replied that the *Florence* was full of water aft. The captain dismissed his assessment by saying, 'Not at all!' but the *Florence* was actually already settling down fast.

Captain Cameron then ordered those on deck to get the starboard lifeboat out. The *Florence* had two lifeboats, but the port boat was only a very small one and could not have survived in the heavy seas that were running. The gripes were cut, the shackles unhooked and the cover taken off, but before the starboard lifeboat could be swung out, the *Florence* went down.

O'Neill was thrown in the water. Another seaman, Michael Grace, was in his berth forward at the time the *Florence* foundered and he leapt in to the sea from the fore rigging. The remaining ten crew members and one passenger managed to reach the deck, but did not get far enough aft before the ship went down, taking them all with her.

O'Neill swam about for about a quarter of an hour before he came across the lifeboat which was floating keel up. Grace was already holding onto the lifeboat and the pair spent the night floating alongside the up-turned lifeboat. Several times it floated away from them and they had to swim back to it again. They saw nothing of the foundered steamer or the rest of the crew apart from a few hatches that were floating around.

All the next day Grace and O'Neill kept alongside the lifeboat and it was not until midnight, some twenty-three hours after the *Florence* had foundered, that a large wave knocked the lifeboat upright. O'Neill, a good swimmer, reached the lifeboat, but had to help Grace, who was struggling. Once in the boat they found two oars, a breaker and a lifebuoy. Their troubles were not over, for the boat was badly damaged. The sternpost was out of her, the bows broken and a couple of planks were gone at the bottom. The lifeboat floated level with the water, but only the airtight tanks kept it afloat.

During the first night they picked up a boat hook, which floated close enough to be retrieved and they used this as a signal post with firstly O'Neill's muffler, then his oilskin trousers, fixed to the top as a flag. The first day they spotted over forty vessels. They could plainly see men on the decks, but none saw them. At one point, a vessel nearly ran them down, coming within 10ft. They called out, but nobody on board the vessel heard them. At another stage they thought they were about to be rescued. A three-masted schooner approached on its way to the Isle of Man, passed close to them, but did not stop.

On Friday 20 September, a screw steamer with red funnels passed close by. About this time, Grace, who had pulled on the oars all night and had complained of thirst and hunger continually, let the oars fall out of his hands, so weak had he become. O'Neill had cut the bottom out of his trousers and stuffed this in his mouth in an attempt to overcome his terrible thirst.

At 1.00 p.m. the Isle of Man Steam Packet vessel *King Orry* left Liverpool for the journey to Douglas. A seaman, Joseph Kneale, was on deck, and two and a half hours after leaving Liverpool, when the vessel was about twenty miles off Douglas, a small boat was spotted flying a flag. The King Orry headed for the boat and, as she went close, Captain Ruthven, her master, ordered a boat to be put out. This was not needed. The mate of the *King Orry* threw O'Neill a rope and Kneale climbed down another rope and retrieved the body of the deceased Grace. Attempts were made to revive him, but these were in vain.

William O'Neill proved to be the only survivor of the foundering of the steamship *Florence*. This was probably attributable to the fact that he was on watch at the time of foundering, therefore on deck and equipped with warm and waterproof clothing and this undoubtedly delayed the onset of hypothermia. Grace, on the other hand, was not so lucky as he was in his bunk at the time of the disaster and so had only his bed clothes on, consequently making him very vulnerable to exposure and then hypothermia.

The crew of the *Florence* was Captain A. Cameron, master, of Liverpool; J. Wilson, chief officer, of Workington; J. Philipson, boatswain, of Workington; Michael Grace,

The loss the steamship *Florence* as reported in the *Ramsey Courier*. (Copyright: Manx National Heritage)

able seaman, of Dublin; William O'Neill, able seaman, of Cork; J. Law, able seaman, of Dublin; R. Williams, chief engineer, of Liverpool; J. Duncan, second engineer; J. Douglas, fireman; P. Cull, fireman; and an unknown labourer who was the sole passenger.

References

Dictionary of Disasters at Sea During the Age of Steam, Hocking; *Isle of Man Examiner*, spool MN38 MNH; *Manx Sun*, spool N68 MNH; *Isle of Man Times*, spool N12 MNH; Douglas Lifeboat House; World Ship Society, G.H. Somner; Board of Trade Casualty Returns, Guildhall Library.

Wreck Site

Diving

The identity of the wreck was confirmed in 1995, following the recovery of the ship's bell, inscribed '*Florence*'. The wreck of the *Florence* sits upright in a general depth of 50m of water and rises to about 5m from the seabed. The wreck is about 45m in length and about 6m in width. It is orientated on a south-west/north-east axis.

The wreck is intact and on an even keel. The wooden superstructure has rotten away. The boiler and engine are aft and the holds still contain the cargo of coal. The *Florence* remains intact and, owing to the few dives to it, retains many of its artefacts. This makes it an excellent dive. It is a deep dive and only for the experienced wreck diver.

It lies on a sand/shingle seabed, so visibility is generally good at 8m or so in the summer months and sometimes excellent at 15m or more in calm weather and small tides (apart from the plankton bloom in May and early June, when it is generally more limited). It can be a dark wreck, however, so a good torch is imperative.

Expect the slack waters to occur more or less at the predicted low and high water times and beginning about half an hour before to three quarters of an hour after. On spring tides, expect this window of slack to be of a shorter duration. The flood tide flows from the west-south-west and the ebb from the east-north-east.

Angling

Fishing on the *Florence* is usually productive, with a full range of species available. Pollack and coalfish to 10lb proliferate, but on occasions shoals of cod occupy the wreck. Ling are available and congers to 30lb have been caught. The usual jumbo mackerel and pouting add to the catches, together with gurnards and whiting.

Flying Meteor

Wreck: ★★
Scenery: ★★
Angling: ★★
Depth: 40m

Position: 53 58.580 N, 03 51.302 W
Datum: WGS84
Location: 23.7n.m. south-east of Douglas Head
Access: Douglas (23.7n.m.) slipway at all stages of the tide. Laxey (24.3n.m.) slipway three hours either side of high water.

Vessel

The iron steam paddle tug *Flying Meteor*, of Glasgow, (Official Number: 50,352), 127 tons gross, 28 tons net, was built in 1864 at Port Glasgow by Blackwood and Gordon. She was equipped with a 65hp side lever steam engine by the shipbuilder. The *Flying Meteor* was 111.5ft in length, had a beam of 18.6ft and a draught of 9.7ft (34m x 5.7m x 3m). She was owned by G.J. Kidston, of Glasgow, trading as the Clyde Shipping Co. and cost £4,200 to build.

History

On 13 March 1874, the *Flying Meteor*, Morrison, master, was engaged in towing the barque *Ravensbourne*, of Hartlepool, 397 tons gross, from Liverpool to Troon, when in a position given in the official records as fourteen miles from Douglas, she suddenly started taking in water. The strap of her connecting rod had broken, falling to the bottom of the hull, where the lever handle punctured one of her iron hull plates. Water gushed in and the *Flying Meteor* soon foundered, the weather conditions being fine at the time. The nine crewmen were able to make their way across to the barque, which returned to Liverpool.

References

Wreck Registers UK Volumes 22-24, Guildhall Library; *Lloyd's Register*; Parliamentary Papers, 1880, Volume 66, Guildhall Library; World Ship Society, PN Thomas; *Clyde Shipping Co.*, Harvey and Telford.

Wreck Site

Diving

The identity of the wreck was confirmed in the summer of 2001, following the recovery of the ship's wheel hub inscribed *'Flying Meteor'*. It lies as a very broken area of wreckage in a general depth of 40m of water and rises to about 2m from the seabed. The wreck is about 30m in length and about 15m in width.

The wreck of the *Flying Meteor* is very broken and largely buried into the seabed, and where it does protrude from the seabed it is substantially covered in lost trawl nets and marine growth. As it lies on a sandy and muddy area of seabed, visibility is generally moderate at 5m or so in summer (apart from the plankton bloom in May and early June, when it is generally more limited).

Expect the slack waters to occur more or less at the predicted low and high water times and beginning about half an hour before to three quarters of an hour after. On spring tides expect this window of slack to be of a shorter duration. The flood tide flows from the west-south-west and the ebb from the east-north-east.

Angling
I have not fished this wreck but few fish have been seen whilst diving apart from pouting and the occasional pollack.

Girl May

Wreck: ★★★
Scenery: ★★★
Angling: ★★
Depth: 30.5m
Position: 54 16.927 N, 03 54.475 W
Datum: WGS84
Location: 14.5n.m. east-south-east of Maughold Head
Access: Douglas (21.8n.m.) slipway at all stages of the tide. Laxey (17.6n.m.) slipway three hours either side of high water. Ramsey (17n.m.) slipwaytwo hours either side of high water and beach launch possible in front of the Lifeboat House.

Vessel

The steamship *Girl May*, of Ayr, 81 tons gross, 34 tons net, was built of wood on a steel frame at Fraserburgh in 1911. She was 82.9ft in length, had a beam of 19ft and a draught of 8.3ft (25.2m x 5.8m x 2.5m). Her owner was John Runcie, 8 Castle Terrace, Fraserburgh.

History

On 12 October 1932, the *Girl May*, Captain Morgan, master, was proceeding on her journey from Ayr for Salcombe in Devon, laden with a cargo of coal, when she sprang a leak in a position about seven miles south-east of Maughold Head off the north-east coast of the Isle of Man. The pumps were used, but the water level gained until the engineers were waist deep in water. Signals of distress were flown, but were ignored by other passing steamers. As darkness approached rockets were fired one after another until the supply was exhausted. Blazing blankets ignited with paraffin were then used and the signal was seen by the steam trawler *Peter Lovett*, of Fleetwood.

Despite the heavy seas, the trawler launched her small boat. 'When we abandoned the ship, the sea was on a level with the deck' said Captain Morgan. 'The trawler's small boat made three attempts to get near us, and finally, as a swell dashed her against our hull, we jumped for our lives one by one.' The only article saved from the *Girl May* before she sank was the captain's gramophone.

The skipper and crew of the *Peter Lovett* were presented with rewards from the Shipwrecked Fisherman's and Mariners' Association at Fleetwood for bravery. A cheque for an unknown amount of money from an anonymous donor was also presented to the men.

References

Ramsey Courier, Fridays, 21.10.1932. & 09.12.1932. MNH; World Ship Society, K. O'Donoghue; Lloyd's Casualty Book, 1932.

Wreck Site

Diving

The identity of the wreck was confirmed in 1998, following the recovery of the ship's bell, inscribed *'Girl May'*.

The wreck of the *Girl May* sits upright in a general depth of 31m of water and rises to about 3m from the seabed. The wreck is about 25m in length and about 8m in width. It is orientated on a south-south-west/north-north-east axis. The wreck is very broken as a consequence of having been a wooden hull laid on steel frames. The highest point is now at the boiler and engine, which lie in the middle of the wreckage.

As the seabed is composed of fine silt and mud, it is easily kicked up by careless fining and visibility is quickly reduced to zero when searching through the debris. Laying off a line as you swim away from the shot line is often a good idea in anything but ideal conditions. Visibility is generally poor at less than 5m or so in the summer months. The plankton bloom in May and early June can make the wreck very dark.

Expect the slack waters to occur more or less at the predicted low and high water times and beginning about half an hour before to an hour after. On spring tides, expect this window of slack to be of a shorter duration. The flood tide flows from the west-south-west and the ebb from the east-north-east.

Angling

The author has no experience of fishing on this wreck, but would expect it to be poor given the relatively small size of the wreck and the muddy seabed.

Glenmaroon

Wreck: *****
Scenery: ****
Angling: **
Depth: 56m
Position: 54 04.750 N, 03 50.858 W

Datum: WGS84
Location: 22.3n.m. east-south-east of Douglas Head
Access: Douglas (22.3n.m.) slipway at all stages of the tide. Laxey (21.2n.m.) slipway three hours either side of high water.

Vessel

The steel steamship *Glenmaroon*, of Belfast, 716 tons gross, 502 tons net, was completed in April 1917 by J. Fullerton & Co., of Paisley, (Yard Number 241). She was 190ft in length, had a beam of 29.6ft and a draught of 11.2ft (57.9m x 9m x 3.4m). Her owner was John Kelly Ltd, of Belfast. She was powered by a triple-expansion steam engine developing 144nhp, which was built by Ross and Duncan, of Glasgow.

History

On the night of 7 December 1944, the *Glenmaroon*, Captain Adair, master, was bound from Larne for Ellesmere Port, with a cargo of empty petrol cans. She was steaming about twenty-two miles east-south-east of Douglas Head, when through the darkness and snow squalls came the noise of an aircraft engine, approaching ever closer. Incredibly, the unidentified aircraft attacked the *Glenmaroon*, causing damage to the starboard side of the vessel, and started a fierce fire as well as holing the ship below the waterline. The *Glenmaroon* then began to settle.

A crew member (the lamp trimmer) was cut off on the foredeck by the fire, so climbed the port rigging of the foremast and slid down the preventer wire from near the masthead. He therefore managed to escape past the fire. Three crewmen were, however, lost when the ship foundered. Captain Adair and the survivors were picked up by the Royal Naval destroyer HMS *Clare*.

It has been subsequently discovered that the attacking aircraft was British and had attacked the *Glenmaroon* by incorrectly assuming that she was an enemy ship.

References

British Vessels Lost At Sea, 1939-1945; *Sea Breezes*, Page 558, 1980; World Ship Society, K. O'Donoghue.

Wreck Site

Diving

As far as is known, the wreck of the *Glenmaroon* has not been positively identified, but it is certain that this is her wreck as its position correlates closely to the historical position of loss and the wreck is the correct size for the *Glenmaroon*. In addition, no other vessels of this size have been lost in the vicinity.

The wreck sits upright in a general depth of 56m of water and rises to about 8m from the seabed. The wreck is about 60m in length and about 12m in width. It is orientated on a south-south-west/north-north-east axis. It is intact and on an even keel. The boiler and engine are aft and the holds are empty.

As the seabed is composed of fine silt and mud, it is easily kicked up by careless fining and visibility is quickly reduced. Visibility is generally poor at less than 5m or so, even in the summer months. The plankton bloom in May and early June can make the wreck even darker than normal. A good torch is recommended.

Expect the slack waters to occur more or less at the predicted low and high water times and beginning about half an hour before to three quarters of an hour after. On spring tides, expect this window of slack to be of a shorter duration. The flood tide flows from the west and the ebb from the east.

Angling

Fishing on the wreck of the *Glenmaroon* has not produced good results, probably due to the poor underwater visibility and dark conditions. It may well be that the muddy nature of the seabed also discourages fish from populating the wreck in any great numbers. However, pollack to 10lb and pouting have been taken by anglers.

Grinder

Wreck: ★★★
Scenery: ★★★★★
Angling: ★★★
Depth: 43m
Position: 53 53.657 N, 04 36.303 W
Datum: WGS84
Location: 9.7n.m. south of Langness
Access: Douglas (16n.m.) and Port St Mary (11.7n.m.) slipways at all stages of the tide. Castletown (10.9n.m.) slipway three hours either side of high water.

Vessel

The wooden paddle tug, *Grinder*, 505 tons displacement, was launched for the Admiralty on 21 March 1868 by Whites, of Cowes and was equipped with disconnecting steam engines developing 500ihp built by Rennie. She was 128ft in length, had a beam of 25.1ft and a draught of 10ft (39m x 7.7m x 3m).

History

After a long career serving the Admiralty, the *Grinder* was sold to the Multilocular Shipbreaking Co. on 28 October 1919 for £300. On 18 November, it was reported in *Lloyd's List* that the government tug *Grinder*, in tow from Sheerness for Stranraer, for breaking up purposes, drifted ashore during the night at Periel on the east side of Holyhead Bay. The government tug *Aid* was standing by to assist.

A day later, on 19 November, the *Grinder* was towed off at high water by the *Aid* and left in tow for Stranraer, apparently undamaged. Later the same day, when ten miles south of the Calf of Man, she broke adrift from the *Aid*. When last seen, the *Grinder* was waterlogged and heavy seas were washing over her forepart. It was thought by the crew of the *Aid* that the *Grinder* would shortly afterwards sink.

References

British Steam Tugs, Thomas; World Ship Society, P.N. Thomas; World Ship Society, H. Appleyard; World Ship Society, J.J. Colledge; World Ship Society, Dr I. Buxton; *Lloyd's List*, 19.11.1919, 20.11.1919. & 25.11.1919.

Wreck Site

Diving

The identity of the wreck was confirmed in 1995, following the recovery of the ship's bell inscribed '*Grinder* 1868'. The wreck sits upright in a general depth of 43m of water and rises to about 5.5m from the seabed. The wreck is about 40m in length and about 10m in width. It is orientated on a south-south-west/north-north-east axis.

The wreck of the *Grinder* is one of the Isle of Man's premier wreck dives for the relatively experienced diver and is a fairly unique opportunity to observe up-close

Grinder alongside *Imperieuse* in 1886. (Copyright: National Maritime Museum)

a wooden paddle tug built for the Admiralty and dating from the 1860s. It is relatively intact and lying upright on its keel. The boiler and engines are located amidships and overlain by the superstructure and bridge. The stern section to the rear of the superstructure is very broken and disappears into the seabed. The bow section ahead of the superstructure is fairly broken, but there is still plenty to see. The hull structure consists of massive beams of timber, and in places the copper sheathing is still in place on the hull and has helped preserve the wood from attack by marine creatures. The copper pins, which held her timbers together, are commonly found.

As the wreck lies on a sandy seabed, visibility is generally good at 8m or so in the summer months and sometimes excellent at 15m or more in calm weather and small tides (apart from the plankton bloom in May and early June, when it is generally more limited).

Expect the slack waters to occur more or less at the predicted low and high water times and beginning about half an hour before to three quarters of an hour after. On spring tides expect this window of slack to be of a shorter duration. The flood tide flows from the west-south-west and the ebb from the east-north-east.

Angling
Pollack and coalfish predominate on the *Grinder*. Expect both species to range from 4lb to 7lb on average with larger specimens to 10lb or so. There is the chance of a ling, and occasionally cod are present.

Hibernian

Wreck: ★★★
Scenery: ★★★★
Angling: ★★★★
Depth: 38m
Position: 53 57.126 N, 04 00.508 W
Datum: WGS84
Location: 20n.m. south-east of Douglas Head
Access: Douglas (20n.m.) slipway at all stages of the tide.

Vessel

The iron screw steamer *Hibernian*, of Glasgow, 334 tons gross, 204 tons net, was built at Port Glasgow in 1875 by H. Murray & Co. The compound steam engine, developing 47hp, was built by Kemp and Hume, of Glasgow. She measured 145.3ft in length, had a beam of 22.7ft and a draught of 11.8ft (44.3m x 6.9m x 3.6m). The *Hibernian* was rigged fore and aft and at the time of her sinking was owned by David MacBrayne, of Glasgow.

History

At 7.00 p.m. on 11 August 1894, the *Hibernian*, under the command of Captain Duncan Leech, left Garston bound for Glasgow. She was taking 400 tons of coal to Glasgow, which was short of coal owing to a Scottish miner's strike. It was high water at the time, the weather fine and the wind a fresh breeze from the west-north-west. The *Hibernian* sailed along at a steady eight knots and at midnight, with everything going fine, the master retired below, leaving the mate, Robert Leech (who was the master's brother) in command on the bridge at the wheel, with an able seaman acting as the lookout. At this time the *Hibernian* was on a north-north-west course by compass.

At about 11.45 p.m. the steamship *Prince of Wales*, Captain Keig, master, belonging to the Isle of Man Steam Packet Co. Ltd, left Liverpool for Douglas, where she was to take up the Monday morning sailing to Liverpool. The *Prince of Wales* was a schooner-rigged, steel paddle steamer of 1,568 gross tons. She was travelling light, in other words without passengers or mail, and was manned by a crew of sixty-eight. From leaving the Mersey until the Bar Lightship was passed, Captain Keig kept the bridge and looked after the navigation of his vessel. After passing the Lightship, Captain Keig retired to rest and the bridge watch was taken by Mr Stephen, the second officer. The night was fine and clear and the *Prince of Wales* proceeded towards Douglas at eighteen knots and on a course of north twenty-eight degrees west.

On Sunday 12 August at 2.40 a.m., Edwin Keig went on lookout at the forecastle head of the *Prince of Wales*. The last watchman reported a light on the starboard bow and Keig noticed it also. About nine minutes after he came on duty, Keig saw a black object a little off the starboard bow and immediately reported it. It was about two or three lengths off the *Prince of Wales* and Keig made it out to be the hull of a steamer. The *Prince of Wales*, going at eighteen knots, struck the unfortunate steamer with her starboard paddle.

On board the *Hibernian*, Captain Leech was asleep in his bunk when he heard a loud crash and, jumping up, tried to make his way on deck at once. Before reaching the staircase he found that the *Hibernian* was making water rapidly, and the water was up to his waist before he reached the deck. When he reached deck he found that the funnel and masts had been knocked down and everything swept from the deck.

Thomas McNaught, one of the firemen, was on watch in the stoke-hole with the second engineer William George McMillan at the time of the collision. McNaught afterwards gave a vivid account of the incident:

Suddenly there was a shock. The Hibernian *quivered violently, and then I heard a grinding noise. The bunkers fell in, and the coals they contained were thrown all around us. The skylight also went smash to the floor of the stoke-hole, and we were buried in a mass of timber, iron plates, and coal. I was imprisoned for a few minutes and had some difficulty getting away, as my ribs were hurt. The second engineer, however, gave me a helping hand, and somehow or other we reached the open air. Where we were we scarcely knew, and we could at that moment have hardly said whether we were on our head or heels or on deck or down at the keelson. We were on deck I suppose, but it would have been difficult to recognise it. The planking was all* torn up, leaving big yawning gulfs, scarcely distinguishable at that time of night. The funnel was lying over on the starboard side, and the masts were splintered to pieces. I made my way as best I could forward, and it was no easy matter I assure you. The whole port side of the vessel seemed to have been carried away, and a clean sweep of the deck also seemed to have been made. All who were able to get forward did so immediately, and then we yelled at the top of our lungs to attract the attention of the crew of the steamer, which we could see some distance ahead of us. All this time our engines were working, as we had no possible chance of stopping them before we left the engine room. It was fairly clear weather at the time, and we could make out the steamer in the vicinity without much difficulty. We were gradually settling down, and we were afraid it would be all over with us before any assistance could reach us. How long we waited I can scarcely form any estimation. It seemed an age to me. It was terrible. But I suppose it could not have been much more than half an hour, perhaps it was not that long. A lifeboat at last came close to our side. We were then nearly up to our necks in water. We could not have held our footing many more minutes, and had that boat not arrived just at that moment I would not have been giving this narrative. I'm sure we had no boats. The ones on the port side had been carried away, and the one on the starboard side was wedged in by the funnel, which had fallen over it. I let myself go and was caught by one of the men in the boat. The chief mate of the Prince of Wales was the man in charge of the boat, I afterwards discovered. I must give him a word of particular praise. We had been holding on during the whole of the time after the collision in dire dread of the boiler exploding through the rush of water in to the engine room. The first thing I did was shout to the boat, "Watch the boiler". The chief mate replied, "Never mind the boiler; we must look after the poor men." Notwithstanding the terrible danger he was running, he held on until he found that he had taken on board all the men there were to be seen, and then pulled off for the Prince of Wales. And it was not before time. I should judge it would only be two or three minutes after we were rescued that the Hibernian disappeared. When we reached the Prince of Wales it was found that there were only eight of us.

Of the *Hibernian*'s ten-man crew, two men lost their lives. Robert Leech, who was at the wheel at the time of the collision, stood no chance of survival and an ablebodied seaman, William Davie, was killed below decks.

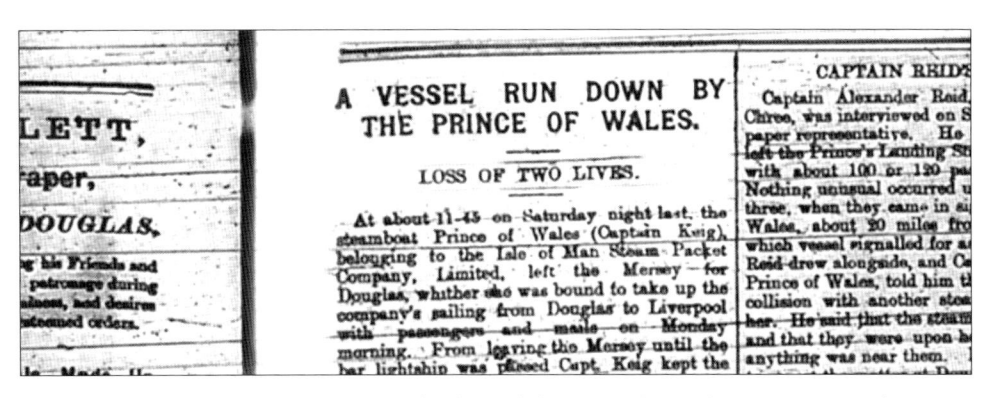

Contemporary newspaper headline of the loss of the steamship *Hibernian*. (Copyright: Manx National Heritage)

The Isle of Man Steam Packet Co. steamer *Ben-my-Chree* left the Prince's Landing Stage, Liverpool, at midnight, with about 120 passengers on board. Nothing unusual occurred until about 3.30 a.m., when they came in sight of the steamer *Prince of Wales* about twenty miles from the Manx coast, which signalled for assistance. Captain Reid, master of the *Ben-my-Chree*, drew alongside and Captain Keig, of the *Prince of Wales*, told him that he had been in collision with another steamer and had sunk her. He said that the steamer showed no light and that they were upon her before they knew anything was near them. He asked Captain Reid to report the matter at Douglas. The *Ben-my-Chree* was beginning to move away, when Captain Keig again spoke to Captain Reid and asked him to take on board two men who were injured. Captain Reid then brought his vessel to the port side of the *Prince of Wales* and put his gangway out, and got Neil Anderson and James Livingstone on board. They were both suffering from fractured legs and their clothing was drenched with water. At the same time Mr Tait, chief engineer of the *Ben-my-Chree*, made an inspection of the damage to the *Prince of Wales* to enable him to report her condition on his arrival at Douglas. After a delay of three quarters of an hour altogether, the *Ben-my-Chree* resumed her voyage to Douglas and arrived at the Victoria Pier at 6.10 a.m.

The directors of the Isle of Man Steam Packet then decided to send the steamer *Tynwald* to assist the *Prince of Wales* and a wire was sent to Liverpool requesting two tugs to be dispatched. The *Tynwald* left harbour shortly after 11.00 a.m. on Sunday morning and came upon the *Prince of Wales* at about 12.30 p.m. The *Prince of Wales* was anchored near to the spot where the accident happened. Nothing was to be seen of the sunken ship, but there were several caps floating around and other such wreckage. As soon as the *Tynwald* came within hailing distance of the *Prince of Wales*, Captain Keig informed the master of the *Tynwald*, Captain Pritchard, that he did not require any assistance and that in about fifteen minutes the Prince of Wales would be ready to sail under her own steam. The Captain's estimation proved to be correct and the *Prince of Wales* set sail for Liverpool, the *Tynwald* keeping in company with her. Good progress was made, and when near to the Mersey the tug *Challenger* was seen coming to aid the *Prince of Wales* and the captain of the *Tynwald,* seeing that his services were no longer required, turned his steamer's head for Douglas. The *Prince of Wales* was safely docked in Liverpool at 9.30 p.m.

The crew of the *Hibernian* was Captain Duncan Leech, master, Robert Leech, first officer; William J. Mowatt, first engineer; William George McMillan, second engineer; William Davie, seaman; James Livingstone, seaman; Neil Anderson; seaman; Alexander Stewart, fireman; Thomas McNaught, fireman; and Henry Burrows, fireman.

References

Isle of Man Weekly Times, 01.09.1894. & 14.08.1894. spool N17 MNH; *Manx Sun*, 13.08.1894. spool N71 MNH; *Isle of Man Examiner* 18.08.1894. spool EX6 MNH; *Island Lifeline*, Chappell; World Ship Society, G.H. Somner; Board of Trade Casualty Returns, Guildhall Library.

Wreck Site

Diving

The identity of the wreck was confirmed in August 1993, following the recovery of the ship's brass wheel hub, inscribed 'Shipbuilders H. Murray of Port Glasgow'. This was the company that built the *Hibernian*. This evidence, together with the location, size of wreck and the coal cargo, positively identifies it as the *Hibernian*.

The wreck sits upright in a general depth of 38m of water and rises to about 4m from the seabed. The wreck is about 40m in length and about 10m in width. It is orientated on more or less a north/south axis.

The wreck of the *Hibernian* has deteriorated to quite a large degree, but nonetheless makes for an interesting dive. The highest point of the wreck is the large boiler and engine situated towards the stern. The rest of the stern structure is very broken and rises to only a metre or two above the surrounding seabed. In front of the boiler, in the hold section amidships, the wreck appears to disappear into the seabed. Further forward it rises again to reveal a very broken forecastle and bow. Plenty of lobsters and crabs inhabit the wreckage. Large shoals of fish cruise around above the wreck.

As the wreck lies on a sandy seabed, visibility is generally good at 8m or so in summer and sometimes excellent at 15m or more in calm weather and small tides (apart from the plankton bloom in May and early June, when it is generally more limited).

Expect the slack waters to occur more or less at the predicted low and high water times and beginning about half an hour before to three quarters of an hour after. On spring tides, expect this window of slack to be of a shorter duration. The flood tide flows from the west-south-west and the ebb from the east-north-east.

Angling

The *Hibernian* produces large numbers of both pollack and coalfish. Mostly in the range of 5lb to 10lb, occasional double figure fish are also taken. The best months are from June to October. Cod are sometimes present on the wreck, as is the occasional ling. Conger eels also inhabit the wreck and troublesome pouting are present in large numbers.

Inkosi

Wreck: ★★★★★
Scenery: ★★★★★
Angling: ★★★★
Depth: 48m
Position: 54 35.448 N, 04 24.885 W
Datum: WGS84
Location: 10.7n.m. north of the Point of Ayre
Access: Peel (24.5n.m.) slipway at all stages of the tide. Ramsey (16.4n.m.) slipway two hours either side of high water and beach launch possible in front of the Lifeboat House.

Vessel

The steel steamship *Inkosi*, of Liverpool, (Official Number: 115,582), 3,575 tons gross, 2,261 tons net, was built at Aberdeen in 1902 by Hall, Russell & Co. Ltd. She measured 350.2ft in length, had a beam of 43.3ft and a draught of 28ft (106.8m x 13.2m x 8.5m). The *Inkosi* was equipped with a triple-expansion steam engine developing 484nhp, which was built by Hall, Russell & Co., of Aberdeen. She was owned by the Charente Steamship Co. Ltd, of Liverpool (Thomas and James Harrison, of Liverpool, managers).

History

The *Inkosi*, Captain John Arthur, master, left Liverpool at 6.00 p.m. on Wednesday 27 March 1918 bound for Lamlash and then Pernambuco, Brazil, with a cargo of 2,000 tons of coal and 300 tons of general cargo. At 7.18 a.m. on Thursday 28 March, she was zigzagging at full speed and on a course of N82W (magnetic) when a torpedo suddenly struck the vessel amidships on the port side between the engine room and stoke-hole. At this point she was about ten miles south-west of Burrow Head in south-west Scotland. The explosion stopped the steamer immediately and three firemen who were on duty were killed. The boats were then lowered on Captain Arthur's order, but the foremost boat had been rendered useless by the force of the explosion and in lowering the fall of the port after boat, the fall was carried away rendering that boat useless also. The remaining boats were safely lowered and most of the forty-seven surviving crewmen began to get into the boats.

The two gunners, Lieutenant Corporal W.N. Griffiths and Private S.A. Mahugh, RMLI meanwhile remained with the gun on the aft platform, ready should the submarine show herself on the surface. The captain then shouted to the gunners to abandon ship; he was about to do likewise after destroying confidential papers. The decks aft were now awash and the engine room was full of water. The remaining men then made their way to the boats, which quickly pulled off to a safe distance.

The *Inkosi* didn't appear to be settling as fast as originally anticipated, so Captain Arthur said that he would board her again. The two gunners agreed to go with him and manned the gun ready to fire it in order to attract attention from other ships in the area. The gun unfortunately misfired and, as the gunners tried to ready the gun again, Captain Arthur shouted to them to take to the boat immediately. The gunners depressed the gun in case it went off and joined Captain Arthur in the lifeboat again. As they pulled clear, a periscope appeared and shortly afterwards the German submarine U96 surfaced off the port bow of the steamship to finish off the *Inkosi* with her deck guns.

The U96 fired over a dozen rounds at the *Inkosi* and, eventually, at 8.18 a.m. the steamer sank about six miles south-west of Burrow Head. The submarine made no attempt to question the *Inkosi*'s crew, who set off in the direction of Burrow Head with the U96 still motoring around the spot where the *Inkosi* had gone down. Both of the *Inkosi*'s lifeboats landed at the Isle of Whithorn and it was only then that the three firemen were discovered to be missing and were presumed to have died in the attack on the steamer.

References

Galloway Wrecks, Miller; *British Merchant Ships Sunk by U-Boats in the 1914-1918 War*, Tennent; *Lloyd's War Losses, The First World War; British Vessels Lost At Sea 1914-1918*; World Ship Society, H. Appleyard; *British Shipping Fleets*, Joseph Fisher & Sons, Fenton and Patterson; UK Public Records Office, Enemy Submarines Irish Sea, March 1918 ADM 137/1515; UK Public Records Office ADM 137/2964.

Wreck Site

Diving

As far as it is known, the *Inkosi* has never been positively identified, but her sheer size means that this wreck has to be the *Inkosi*, being the only vessel of her size lost in this part of the Irish Sea between Burrow Head and the Point of Ayre.

The wreck lies on its side in a general depth of 48m of water and rises to about 16m from the seabed. It is about 110m in length and about 20m in width, and orientated on an east-south-east/west-north-west axis.

The wreck of the *Inkosi* is broken about halfway along its length and the two halves lie on a slightly different alignment. This is a wreck only for the experienced diver and the cavernous holds allow the diver access into the wreck. Great care should be exercised. It was reported several years ago that a diver had failed to surface from a dive on the *Inkosi* and his body was later found inside the wreck. He may well have become disorientated in limited visibility. A further risk can be found in the cases of shells lying in the wreckage. Recovery of these shells could potentially carry a risk, despite their years of immersion in seawater.

Inkosi. (Copyright: National Maritime Museum)

As the wreck lies quite close to the Solway Firth, visibility is generally not as good as it would be closer to the Isle of Man. Expect about 5m or so in the summer months and sometimes more at 10m or more in calm weather and small tides (apart from the plankton bloom in May and early June, when it is generally more limited).

Expect the slack waters to occur more or less at the predicted low and high water times and beginning about half an hour before to three quarters of an hour after. On spring tides, expect this window of slack to be of a shorter duration. The flood tide flows from the west-south-west and the ebb from the east-north-east.

Angling

The author has not fished the wreck of the *Inkosi*, but would expect pollack and cod to be present and possibly shoals of coalfish.

Joseph Hodgkins

Wreck: ★★★
Scenery: ★★★★
Angling: ★★★
Depth: 18.5m
Position: 54 19.407 N, 04 12.605 W
Datum: WGS84
Location: 3.9n.m. north-east of Maughold Head
Access: Douglas (14.2n.m.) slipway at all stages of the tide. Laxey (9.1n.m.) slipway three hours either side of high water. Ramsey (6.1n.m.) slipway two hours either side of high water and beach launch possible in front of the Lifeboat House.

Vessel

The steel steam trawler *Joseph Hodgkins*, of Aberdeen (A186), 276 tons gross, 120 tons net, was built in 1919 by Hepple & Co. Ltd, of South Shields as an Admiralty Castle-class trawler. She was 123ft in length, had a beam of 23.4ft and had a draught of 12.6ft (37.5m x 7.1m x 3.8m). Her compound steam engine, which developed 62hp, was built by Bellis and Morcom Ltd, of Birmingham.

She was completed too late for naval service in the First World War and was sold to Mr F.R. Samson, of London (S. and B. Trawling Co. Ltd). At the time of her loss she was owned by Messrs W. Morley & Co. Although registered in Aberdeen, it is doubtful whether she ever fished from the port and probably mostly operated out of Fleetwood.

History

The *Joseph Hodgkins*, Captain 'Jock' Tomlinson, master, left Fleetwood at 10.30 a.m. on 28 December 1921 bound for the fishing grounds, but the weather worsened so much that Captain Tomlinson decided to seek the shelter of Ramsey Bay from the west-north-west gale. At about 6.30 p.m., James Kemp, the mate, was at the wheel when in clear weather he saw the Grimsby registered steam trawler *Cuirasse* (GY436), belonging to Messrs Moody and Kelly and captained by George Elliott, heading on a collision course. The *Cuirasse* struck the *Joseph Hodgkins* a severe blow in the fish room with her stem. The *Joseph Hodgkins* immediately began to fill with water.

Jack Parker, a deckhand, later said in an interview:

I was in my bunk at the time, but was fortunately not asleep. I heard a cracking, grating noise, and knew that something had happened. I sprang out of my bunk when the bow of a trawler came through the ship's side. I climbed through the hole thus made on to the deck of the Joseph Hodgkins. It was a risky job, as all was darkness, and the sea was running heavily.

Captain Tomlinson hurried back on deck and saw the serious condition of his vessel. He ordered the lifeboat to be launched, which was done only after many valuable minutes had been wasted. The trawler was by now sinking rapidly so it was with horror that the crew watched as the painter holding the lifeboat to the trawler snapped and the lifeboat drifted away without them on board.

The Fleetwood steam trawler *Jacinta* (FD325), owned by Messrs J. Marr & Sons, suddenly appeared on the scene, pulling alongside the stricken vessel to within a few feet. This enabled the ten crewmen of the *Joseph Hodgkins* to jump over to safety, albeit without any of their personal belongings. Captain Tomlinson was the last man to jump. He tripped, injuring his back in the process, but still managed to get on the *Jacinta*.

Within fifteen minutes of the impact, the *Joseph Hodgkins* had foundered in the angry seas off Maughold Head in Ramsey Bay and the crew were safely aboard the *Jacinta*, which returned to Fleetwood. The *Cuirasse* was badly damaged and also returned to Fleetwood.

The *Joseph Hodgkins* was insured for the sum of £15,000 with the United Kingdom Indemnity Association. Her crew was as follows: Captain 'Jock' Tomlinson, master; James Kemp, mate; J. Tooley, bosun; W. Colgate, deck hand; Jack Parker, deck hand; J. Sutton, deck hand; W. Keenly, cook; G. Wright, chief engineer; Owen McNeill, second engineer; J. Wood, fireman; and W. Sale, fireman.

References

The Real Price of Fish, Aberdeen Steam Trawler Losses 1887-1961, Ritchie; *Isle of Man Examiner*, 07.01.1922. spool EX20 MNH; Lloyd's Register of Shipping; *Fleetwood Chronicle*, Friday, 30.12.1921.

Wreck Site

Diving

The identity of the wreck is assumed to be that of the *Joseph Hodgkins* in light of the circumstantial evidence that has been gathered. It lies in a general depth of 18.5m of water and rises to about 2.5m from the seabed, and is about 30m in length and generally about 7m in width. It is orientated on more or less a south-east/north-west axis.

The wreck of the *Joseph Hodgkins* is very broken and pieces of her lie only in their approximate position relative to each other. Indeed, the boiler is situated about 12m north of the main area of wreckage as if moved there by a great force. It can only be assumed that the wreck has been blown up either to prevent it being a danger to shipping or to enable it to be salvaged. The other notable feature of the wreck is the extent to which most of the wreckage is buried in the sand. Despite this the wreck makes for an interesting dive.

The wreck is ideal for inexperienced wreck divers, or as a second dive, perhaps. Visibility is usually good, slack water periods are long and the depth is less than 20m at low water. Add in the profusion of marine life that abounds around this wreck and an enjoyable dive is usually guaranteed. As it lies on a sandy seabed, visibility is generally good at 8m or so in the summer months and sometimes excellent at 15m or more in calm weather and small tides (apart from the plankton bloom in May and early June, when it is generally more limited).

Expect the slack waters to occur more or less at the predicted low and high water times and beginning about three quarters of an hour before to an hour or more after. On spring tides, expect this window of slack to be of a shorter duration. The flood tide flows from the south-west and the ebb from the north-east.

Angling

The wreck holds a large number of fish in the summer months. Don't expect anything large, but the numbers and variety of species present make a trip to the wreck worthwhile. Large shoals of pollack, coalfish and mackerel patrol over the wreck, whilst in amongst the wreckage can be found conger eels to 20lb, ling to 10lb and plenty of pouting. Codling, gurnards, whiting and tope are all present on occasions.

Lady Louisa

Wreck: ★★
Scenery: ★★
Angling: ★★
Depth: 29m
Position: 54 07.792 N, 04 22.463 W
Datum: WGS84
Location: 3.4n.m. east-south-east of Douglas Head
Access: Douglas (3.4n.m.) and slipway at all stages of the tide. Laxey (5.7n.m.) slipway three hours either side of high water.

Vessel

The steamship *Lady Louisa*, of Larne, (Official Number: 74,760), 161 tons gross, 61 tons net, was built by W. Thomas & Co., of Milo, Cumbria in 1882. She was a steamer of wooden construction with a single deck and was schooner-rigged. The compound steam engine, built by J. and T. Young, of Ayr, developed 32nhp. The *Lady Louisa* was 105ft in length, had a beam of 21.5ft and a draught of 9.3ft (32m x 6.6m x 2.8m). At the time of her loss, she was owned by Captain Robert Hall, of Larne, County Antrim.

History

At 5.00 p.m. on Saturday 25 February 1905, the *Lady Louisa* left Garston bound for Belfast, laden with a cargo of 160 tons of coal. At 10.00 p.m., the steamer was about eighteen miles north-west of the Bar Lightship when a strong south-westerly wind began to rise. As it threatened to increase still further into a full gale, her master, Captain William O'Neill, who had been steering a course to take her around the Calf of Man at the southern end of the Isle of Man, decided to alter her course and run for the shelter of Ramsey Bay.

By 3.15 a.m. on 26 February, the *Lady Louisa* was about fifteen miles from Douglas Head, battling through the heavy seas towards Maughold Head, when Captain O'Neill, who was on the bridge at the time, was informed by the assistant engineer that there was seawater in the engine room and that its level was rising. Captain O'Neill went down to the engine room and found a depth of eighteen inches of seawater. He gave orders for the pumps to be worked, but then, to the dismay of all on board, water was discovered in the hold as well. It was now evident that the *Lady Louisa* had sprung a serious leak.

The water continued to gain rapidly as Captain O'Neill headed the gradually sinking steamer for Douglas. By 6.00 a.m. her decks were nearly awash and Captain O'Neill decided their task was hopeless, so gave the order to launch the small boat, their only means of escape. Some difficulty was encountered, but eventually the task was accomplished. Shortly afterwards the *Lady Louisa* foundered in a position, thought by the master, to be about five or six miles south-east of Douglas Head at 6.30 a.m. on 26 February.

The crew found it impossible to row towards Douglas because of the heavy seas, and so they headed for the relative shelter of Laxey Bay. On reaching Laxey harbour, they found that, owing to the rough sea and the low tide, they could not land, but they managed a safe landing at Gatwick on the far more sheltered southern side of Laxey Bay.

References

Lloyd's Register of Shipping; *Isle of Man Examiner*, 04.03.1905. spool EX12 MNH; *Manx Sun*, 04.03.1905. spool N78 MNH; UK Public Records Office CUST104/297.

Wreck Site

Diving

The identity of the wreck of the *Lady Louisa* has been known to fishermen and divers for many years.

The wreck lies in a general depth of 29m of water and rises to about 3.5m from the seabed. It is about 20m in length and about 15m in width.

The wreck of the *Lady Louisa* would not be the diver's first choice on a day of calm weather, but is a useful dive when the weather prevents journeys further offshore.

As the hull of the *Lady Louisa* was constructed of wood, her wreck has completely broken up and it is only the metal parts of the wreck that remain. The boiler is the single largest piece of the wreck and now lies at right angles to the axis of the vessel, after having been caught by a trawler some years ago. Large amounts of the cargo of steam coal still abound despite the exertions of divers lifting large quantities over the years. Fairly close to the boiler lies the engine and a real jumble of other metal parts from the ship. Bollards and fairleads lying in the sand about 20m ahead of the main wreckage area give an indication of where the bow once stood.

As the wreck lies on a sandy seabed, visibility is generally good at 8m or so in the summer months and sometimes excellent at 15m or more in calm weather and small tides (apart from the plankton bloom in May and early June, when it is generally more limited).

Expect the slack waters to occur more or less at the predicted low and high water times and beginning about half an hour before to three quarters of an hour after. On spring tides expect this window of slack to be of a shorter duration. The flood tide flows from the south-west and the ebb from the north-east.

NB: Great care should be taken when diving this wreck, as it lies on the track taken by the passenger ferries into and out of Douglas harbour when they are operating on the Heysham route. A careful watch should therefore be maintained, especially when divers are below.

Angling

Pollack to 5lb can usually be caught on this wreck. Shoals of coalfish sometimes take up residence and there is the usual pouting. One or two congers can be seen in the wreckage while diving.

Lady Louisa Pennant

Wreck: **
Scenery: **
Angling: *
Depth: 18m
Position: 54 15.525 N, 04 05.950 W
Datum: WGS84

Location: 7.9n.m. east-south-east of Maughold Head
Access: Douglas (14.8n.m.) slipway at all stages of the tide. Laxey (10.6n.m.) slipway three hours either side of high water. Ramsey (10.9n.m.) slipway two hours either side of high water and beach launch possible in front of the Lifeboat House.

Vessel

The wooden schooner *Lady Louisa Pennant*, of Caernarfon, 73 tons net, was built in Bangor, North Wales in 1847 by J. Parry. She was 62.3ft in length, had a beam of 16.5ft and a draught of 8.9ft (19m x 5m x 2.7m).

History

On 14 October 1902, the *Lady Louisa Pennant* left the Menai Straits bound for Ayr, with a cargo of slates, in company with the schooner *Fomalhaut*. Both vessels subsequently disappeared, the *Lady Louisa Pennant* with all three hands. Both the lifeboat personnel and the Bahama Lightship crew noticed a schooner disappear off Ramsey Bay at the time. The only part of the schooner found was her small boat, washed up at St Bee's Head.

About a month later, the master of the Ramsey trawler *Nerbudda*, Richard Leadbetter, reported a sunken vessel, three to four miles east of the Bahama Lightship. One of the vessel's masts was above the water with the end of one spar being held down by rigging. Later, in December, fisherman still reported the wreck to be a danger to navigation. It was presumed that the wreck was that of the *Lady Louisa Pennant*.

References

Ramsey Courier, 14.11.1902. & 12.12.1902. spool MN109 MNH; *Manx Sun*, Saturday, 15.11.1902. spool N76 MNH; World Ship Society, M. Benn; *Bangor – Port of Beaumaris*, Elis-Williams.

Wreck Site

Diving

The identity of this wreck has never been established but is assumed to be that of the *Lady Louisa Pennant*. Lost at the same time, was the schooner *Fomalhaut*, which was in company with the *Lady Louisa Pennant* and also carrying a cargo of slates. This wreck has not been found. Analysis of a piece of slate from the wreck by the Welsh Slate Museum at Llanberis revealed that it originated at one of the quarries at Penrhyn and is of late nineteenth-century or early twentieth-century production. This is consistent with the wreck being the *Lady Louisa Pennant*.

The wreck lies in a general depth of 18m of water and rises to about 1m from the seabed. It is about 10m in length and about 4m in width.

As the hull of the *Lady Louisa Pennant* was constructed of wood it has virtually all rotted away and all that remains on the seabed are her cargo of Welsh roofing slates. Metal objects from her hull may well be present, but are buried in the sand. The slates still lie stacked on edge as they were packed into the hold of the schooner. Every so-many slates, the stacking changes through ninety degrees, a method used to prevent the cargo from moving around in the hold. The slates are all machine cut and several sizes are represented.

As the wreck lies on a sandy seabed, visibility is generally good at 8m or so in the summer months and sometimes excellent at 15m or more in calm weather and small tides (apart from the plankton bloom in May and early June, when it is generally more limited).

Expect the slack waters to occur more or less at the predicted low and high water times and beginning about three quarters of an hour before to an hour after. On spring tides, expect this window of slack to be of a shorter duration. The flood tide flows from the south-west and the ebb from the north-east.

Angling
Just a few pouting inhabit this wreck.

Lembas

Wreck: ****
Scenery: **
Angling: *
Depth: 51m
Position: 54 28.673 N, 04 12.185 W
Datum: WGS84
Location: 6.8n.m. north-east of the Point of Ayre
Access: Douglas (22.2n.m.) and Peel (23.4n.m.) slipways at all stages of the tide. Ramsey (11.3n.m.) slipway at two hours either side of high water and beach launch possible in front of the Lifeboat House.

Vessel

The motor fishing vessel *Lembas*, of Peel (PL3), 25 tons gross, 11 tons net, was built of wood in Norway in 1956 and was equipped with a 133hp diesel engine. She was owned by Geoffrey R. Comber and John M. Campbell, of Peel. The *Lembas* was 49ft in length (14.9m).

History

At 4.50 p.m. on 14 August 1983, the Coastguards contacted the Ramsey Lifeboat Deputy Launching Authority, Captain Michael Brew, to inform him that the motor fishing vessel *Lembas*, M. Campbell, skipper, was making water in a position to the

Lembas. (Copyright: Michael Craine)

east of the Point of Ayre. The Ramsey Lifeboat, *James Ball Ritchie*, was launched at 5.03 p.m. and made her way north-east.

The lifeboat was informed that a helicopter had located the casualty and remained on hand until she was sighted from the lifeboat. Whilst Coxswain Gawne was speaking to the crew of the *Lembas* whilst drawing alongside, the fishing vessel took another sea aboard and began to sink. The crew's attempt to save their vessel had failed after water entered the electrical system and her pumps failed. Her three crewmen immediately jumped into their life raft, which was made fast to the bow of the boat, and frantically tried to let go the painter. They succeeded, but only just, with one minute to spare before the *Lembas* foundered. The weather was fine, but the sea was rough with a force five southerly wind. The survivors were landed in Ramsey at 7.18 p.m.

References

Olsen's Fisherman's Almanac, 1982; *The Ramsey Lifeboats*, Seybold; *Manx Star*, Friday, 26.04.1983. spool MN11 MNH.

Wreck Site

Diving

It is assumed that this wreck is that of the *Lembas*, as it lies very close to the position where the *Lembas* sank and is of the correct dimensions.

The wreck lies in a general depth of 51m of water and rises to about 4m from the seabed. The wreck is about 20m in length and generally about 8m in width. It is orientated on more or less a south-east/north-west axis. Little information is available about the wreck; as yet, it is not known that anyone has dived on it.

Expect the slack waters to occur more or less at the predicted low water times and beginning about an hour before to an hour or about low water. On spring tides, expect this window of slack to be of a shorter duration. The flood tide flows from the north-west and the ebb from the south-east.

Angling
No information is available, but it should produce fish.

Limesfield

Wreck: *****
Scenery: ****
Angling: ***
Depth: 41m
Position: 54 01.875 N, 03 56.790 W
Datum: WGS84
Location: 18.9n.m. south-east of Clay Head
Access: Douglas (19.9n.m.) slipway at all stages of the tide.

Vessel

The steel, single screw steamship *Limesfield*, of Liverpool, (Official Number: 137,527), 427 tons gross, was built in 1916 by the Lytham Steam Boat and Engineering Co. Ltd, of Lytham. She was 142.2ft in length, had a beam of 26ft and a draught of 11.5ft (43.4m x 7.9m x 3.5m). The *Limesfield* was launched on 4 March 1916 and was equipped with a triple-expansion steam engine developing 88rhp, constructed by the shipbuilder. At the time of her loss she was owned by Zillah Shipping and Carrying Co. Ltd, of Liverpool (G.A. Savage Ltd, managers).

History

On Thursday 7 February 1918 at 11.45 a.m., the tide being fours on the ebb, the weather hazy, the wind from the west-south-west blowing fresh and a rough sea from the west, the *Limesfield* was proceeding on her voyage from Belfast to Preston, laden with cotton waste, when, in a position about twenty miles south-east of Maughold Head, a shell suddenly burst above the bridge. The master and mate were on the bridge at the time and fortunately escaped injury. On looking out on the starboard side of the *Limesfield*, the master, Captain William Galbraith, observed the German submarine UB57 about one mile distant, which continued to fire more shells at the *Limesfield*.

The master then ordered the small boat to be lowered and, after destroying the confidential papers by fire, he left the steamer with the rest of the crew. After they had rowed a short distance the commander of the UB57 signalled them to stop and coming alongside the small boat questioned Captain Galbraith as to the name of his vessel and the nature of the cargo that she was carrying. The last he saw of his vessel was that she had taken fire and it was assumed that the submarine continued shelling her until she foundered. After rowing for about six hours, the crew were picked up by the Fleetwood fishing trawler *Reliance* and landed at Fleetwood at 4.00 a.m. on 8 February.

References

Lloyd's War Losses, The First World War; British Vessels Lost at Sea, 1914-1918; World Ship Society, H. Appleyard; *A History of Shipbuilding At Lytham*, Dakres; *Ramsey Courier*, Tuesday, 12.02.1918. spool MN487 MNH; UK Public Records Office Enemy Submarines in the Irish Sea, January/February 1918 ADM 137/1514.

Wreck Site

Diving

The identity of the wreck was confirmed in 1996, following the recovery of the ship's bell, inscribed 'Limesfield 1916'. The wreck of the *Limesfield* now sits upright on its keel in a general depth of 41m of water and rises to about 5.5m from the seabed. It is about 44m in length and about 8m in width. It is orientated on a north-north-east/south-south-west axis with the bow to the north-north-east.

The *Limesfield* makes an excellent wreck to dive, being largely intact and upright on its keel. There are two holds, with the bridge located amidships. The engines and boiler are found towards the stern. There is no evidence of any cargo in the holds. The hull is largely intact, but there is some damage to the starboard side. It is presumed that this damage would have been caused by the explosion of the bombs set by the crew of the German submarine. The main superstructure, originally at the rear of the vessel, has collapsed to deck level. As the wreck lies on a sandy seabed, visibility is generally good at 8m or so in summer months and sometimes excellent at 15m or more in calm weather and small tides (apart from the plankton bloom in May and early June, when it is generally more limited).

Expect the slack waters to occur more or less at the predicted low and high water times and beginning about half an hour before to three quarters of an hour after. On spring tides expect this window of slack to be of a shorter duration. The flood tide flows from the west-south-west and the ebb from the east-north-east.

Angling

I have not had a great many fish from this wreck, being mainly coalfish, pouting and whiting. In the correct conditions however, there should be quantities of pollack and, on occasions, cod, together with the chance of a ling.

Liverpool

Wreck: ★★★
Scenery: ★★★★★
Angling: ★★
Depth: 38m
Position: 54 00.361 N, 04 33.403 W
Datum: WGS84
Location: 3.9n.m. south-east of Langness
Access: Douglas (9n.m.) and Port St Mary (7.5n.m.) slipways at all stages of the tide. Castletown (5.5n.m.) slipway three hours either side of high water.

Vessel

The steel steamship *Liverpool*, of Sligo, (Official Number: 72,449), was completed in 1892 by Messrs John Jones & Sons, of Liverpool, and was built to the specifications and under the supervision of Mr Henry H. West, the naval architect for the Sligo Steam Navigation Co. She was 686 gross tons, 332 tons net, and measured 202.6ft in length, 29.1ft in the beam and had a draught of 14.4ft (61.8m x 8.9m x 4.4m). The carriage of cattle was a very important aspect of the trade that she was engaged in, so careful consideration was given to the cattle fittings. Being a larger vessel than any of her predecessors, increased accommodation was also provided for saloon and deck passengers. The saloon and cabins were fitted out in a substantial and comfortable manner. The triple-expansion steam engine, also constructed by Messrs John Jones & Sons, developed 187nhp. On her trial trip the *Liverpool* attained a speed of thirteen knots. The ship was lighted throughout by electricity.

History

The *Liverpool*, Captain Francis Devaney, master, left Liverpool on Tuesday 19 December 1916 at 5.10 p.m., bound for Sligo with a large general cargo of merchandise weighing 500 tons. The weather was a bit hazy at the time, but when she reached the Bar Lightship, it had cleared. The sea was quite smooth. Everything went well until 11.30 p.m., when a shock was felt and it was immediately ascertained that the vessel had struck a mine. The position of the vessel at this point was eleven miles south-east by south of the Chicken Rock Lighthouse. Captain Devaney ordered the engines to be stopped and the boats to be launched. He then went forward to inspect the damage, which he concluded was not enough for the vessel to be in immediate danger of sinking. After a head count of the men on board, it was quickly surmised that three men were missing. Captain Devaney then made a second journey forward in one of the boats in order to search for the three men, but received no reply. The remainder of the crew then stood off the *Liverpool* in the boats, ready to return if she did not sink.

Captain Devaney then went back to the bridge to sound the steam whistle in order to attract the attentions of a steamer coming up behind. With help from the chief mate, he also went forward to get the signal lamps and these were lit and hoisted aloft.

Soon the vessel approached the stricken *Liverpool* and identified herself as the steamship *Ruby*, of Glasgow, Captain McCawley, bound from Wales to Glasgow with a cargo of stone. The *Ruby* offered to tow the *Liverpool* to Douglas and so a hawser was passed to the *Liverpool*. The *Ruby* then commenced towing the *Liverpool* stern-first as the head was too deep in the water. After towing for some time, Captain McCawley decided to change his plan and tow the *Liverpool* to Belfast instead as the weather had quickly deteriorated, making progress to Douglas impossible. A second hawser was added and towing commenced for a second period. At about 5.30 a.m. on Wednesday 20 December, the *Liverpool* was noticed to be taking a bigger list to starboard and Captain McCawley immediately ordered the hawsers to be cut with axes. Ten minutes later, the *Liverpool* disappeared beneath the waves in a position given at the time as two and a half miles south-east by south from Langness.

The survivors of the *Liverpool* were: Captain Francis Devaney, Sligo, master; Michael McLoughlin, Raughley, first mate; John Moffatt, Sligo, second mate; T. Boyd, Manchester, chief engineer; Ivor Thomas, Rosses Point, second engineer; J. Smith, Armagh, donkeyman; J. Kilgallen, Rosses Point, sailor; James McGowan, Rosses Point, sailor; A. Petrie, Sligo, sailor; J. Moffatt, Sligo, sailor; J. McGowan, Rosses Point, steward; J. Burns, Liverpool, fireman; J. Smith, Omeath, fireman and W. Bannon, Omeath, fireman. The three men who died were Daniel Garvey, Sligo, winchman; J. Costello, Sligo and J.P. Gillen, Rosses Point, the latter being the sole passenger on board. It was the opinion of Captain Devaney that Costello was killed by the force of the explosion, while Garvey and Gillen were drowned, being unable to get through the wreckage. The survivors were landed by the *Ruby* at Clydebank.

A lifebuoy marked with the name of the 'SS *Liverpool*, of Sligo', and a quantity of general wreckage, was washed up near Port St Mary later the same day.

References

Lloyd's War Losses, The First World War; British Vessels Lost At Sea, 1914-1918; Isle of Man Times, 23.12.1916. spool N34 MNH; World Ship Society, H. Appleyard; *History of Steam Navigation*, Kennedy (1903); *Sligo Independent*, Saturday, 30.12.1916; *Sligo Champion*, 10.08.1918; *Lloyd's Register*; UK Public Records Office ADM 137/2960.

Wreck Site

Diving

The identity of the wreck of the *Liverpool* was confirmed in April 1997 following the recovery of her bridge bell inscribed 'SS *Liverpool* 1892'.

Liverpool.

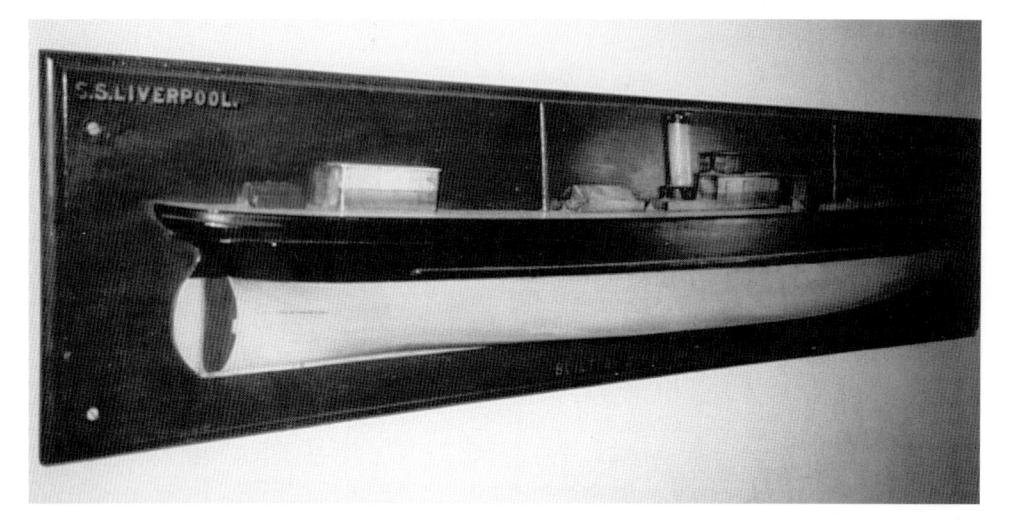

Builder's half model of the *Liverpool.*

The wreck sits upright on its keel in a general depth of 38m of water and rises to about 5m from the seabed. The wreck is about 56m in length and about 12m in width. It is orientated on a north-east/south-west axis with the bow to the north-east.

The bow has been completely destroyed by a combination of the initial mine explosion and then the impact of the vessel with the seabed. All that greets the diver today is a jumble of metal. Moving aft of the bow is the section where the cattle stalls were located and the cargo hold still full of the merchandise that she was carrying, including building materials, crockery, bottled beer and shoes. Most cargo remains in the hold, but is buried deep in the wreckage.

Continuing to swim from bow to stern, the next section to be encountered is the bridge area immediately in front of the massive boiler, which forms the highest part of the wreck along with the engine. The engine is an impressive sight, rising 5m from the seabed, and often has shoals of pollack swimming around it. Moving towards the stern from the engine is where the passenger accommodation was situated. Finally, the stern section is almost intact down from the original deck level to the keel. It is in this area that pieces of the ship's crockery etc. have been found. The graceful shape of the classic counter stern can be seen, complete with the intact single propeller standing clear of the seabed. The wreck of the *Liverpool* is one of the most memorable sites in Manx wreck diving and well worth preserving for future generations of divers.

As the wreck lies on a sand and shingle seabed, visibility is generally good at 8m or so in the summer months and sometimes excellent at 15m or even 20m in calm weather and small tides (apart from the plankton bloom in May and early June, when it is generally more limited).

Expect the slack waters to occur more or less at the predicted low and high water times and beginning about half an hour before to three quarters of an hour after. On spring tides, expect this window of slack to be of a shorter duration. The flood tide flows from the west-south-west and the ebb from the east-north-east.

Angling

This is not a particularly good wreck for angling. The wreck holds moderate numbers of pollack to 5lb during the summer and autumn months. Occasional large shoals of coalfish can be a nuisance. Some large ling to 20lb have been taken over the years together with pout, ballan wrasse and cuckoo wrasse. Whilst diving the wreck some very large conger eels have also been seen and there is potential for fish to more than 60lb from this wreck; anchoring in the correct position over the wreck would however be essential for success.

Lucy

Wreck: ★★★★★
Scenery: ★★★★
Angling: ★★★★★
Depth: 41m
Position: 53 58.107 N, 04 02.902 W
Datum: WGS84
Location: 18.2n.m. south-east of Douglas Head
Access: Douglas (18.2n.m.) slipway at all stages of the tide.

Vessel

The steel steamship *Lucy*, of Liverpool, (Official Number: 110,569), weighed 155 tons gross, 36 tons net, and was built in 1899 by Scott & Sons, of Bowling. She was 90ft in length, had a beam of 20.7ft and a draught of 9.5ft (27.4m x 6.3m x 2.9m). The *Lucy* was equipped with a compound steam engine developing 32rhp and built by Fisher & Co., of Paisley. She was owned by J. Monks & Co. Ltd, of Liverpool.

History

The *Lucy* left Weston Point, on the River Mersey, on Thursday 21 July 1910, bound for Douglas with a cargo of 179 tons of moulding sand consigned for Gelling's Foundry Co., of Douglas. At midnight, when in a reported position of fourteen miles south-south-east of Douglas Head, she sprang a leak and foundered. The crew of four men took to the small boat and were eventually picked up by the trawler *Desideratum* and landed at Fleetwood.

References

Isle of Man Examiner, Saturday, 30.07.1910. spool EX14 MNH; Board of Trade Casualty Returns, Guildhall Library; *Lloyd's List*, Saturday, 23.07.1910; *Lloyd's Register 1910*; *Monk's Navy*, Fenton.

Wreck Site

Diving

The identity of the wreck of the *Lucy* has not been confirmed. The position of the wreck, its dimensions and the type of vessel clearly point to it being the *Lucy*.

The wreck sits a general depth of 41m of water and rises to about 4m from the seabed. The wreck is about 25m in length and about 6m in width. It is orientated on a north/south axis.

It lies upright on its keel and is mostly intact. It has a single hold, without signs of any cargo. The engine and boiler are situated close to the stern. The entire wooden superstructure has rotted away.

As the wreck lies on a sandy seabed, visibility is generally good at 8m or so in the summer months and sometimes excellent at 15m or more in calm weather and small tides (apart from the plankton bloom in May and early June, when it is generally more limited).

Expect the slack waters to occur more or less at the predicted low and high water times and beginning about half an hour before to three quarters of an hour after. On spring tides expect this window of slack to be of a shorter duration. The flood tide flows from the west and the ebb from the east.

Angling

The *Lucy* produces large numbers of pollack from June to October. Most fish are in the range of 4lb to 8lb, but there is always a chance of a double-figure fish. Large shoals of similarly sized coalfish also make an appearance from time to time. July and August see cod taken, but numbers do vary from year to year. Ling are sometimes present as well as pouting.

Manchester

Wreck: ★★★★★
Scenery: ★★★★★
Angling: ★★★★★
Depth: 55m
Position: 53 52.080 N, 04 35.025 W
Datum: WGS84
Location: 11.2n.m. south of Langness
Access: Douglas (17.2n.m.) and Port St Mary (13.2n.m.) slipways at all stages of the tide. Castletown (12.4n.m.) slipway three hours either side of high water.

Vessel

The Norwegian iron screw steamer *Manchester* (ex *Glanwern*), of Christiana (modern-day Oslo), 915 tons gross, 538 tons net, was built in 1882 by W. Doxford & Sons, of Sunderland. She had a single well deck and was fitted with a compound steam engine developing 110nhp constructed by the shipbuilder. She measured 212ft in length, had a beam of 30ft and a draught of 15.5ft (64.6m x 9.1m x 4.7m). At the time of her loss she was owned by Winga & Co., of Christiana, (Acties, of Manchester, managers).

History

On Thursday 23 November 1905, the steamer *Frieda*, of West Hartlepool, docked at Maryport, Cumbria. She carried the fifteen survivors of the *Manchester*, N. Pedersen, master, after the two vessels had collided at 2.00 a.m. that morning when twelve miles south-south-west of Langness.

The weather was extremely rough at the time and the *Frieda* struck the *Manchester* amidships, sheered off and struck her twice more. The crew of the *Manchester* launched their lifeboat and all got safely into it, except Anderson, the cook, who was sleeping in the storeroom. He was supposed to have been injured in the collision and was not seen again. The *Frieda* stopped close by the lifeboat, but the men in the lifeboat had to wait until their craft was on the crest of a wave until they could spring for either the rail of the *Frieda* or for ropes flung to them by the crew of the *Frieda*. The lifeboat was severely damaged as it bumped against the hull of the *Frieda*, but all fifteen men were eventually rescued, though several of their number had very narrow escapes from death.

The *Manchester* was bound from Porsgrund in Norway to Manchester with a general cargo. The next day, the Isle of Man Steam Packet vessel from Liverpool to Douglas passed through a great quantity of floating wreckage from the wreck of the *Manchester*.

References

Isle of Man Examiner, 02.12.1905. spool EX12 MNH; *Manx Sun*, Saturday, 02.12.1905. spool N78 MNH; *Isle of Man Times*, spool N25 MNH; Lloyd's Register of Shipping; World Ship Society, H. Appleyard; Board of Trade Casualty Returns, Guildhall Library.

Wreck Site

Diving

The identity of the wreck of the *Manchester* was confirmed in 2002 following the recovery of her bell, inscribed 'Glanwern 1882', which was the *Manchester*'s original name.

The wreck sits upright on its keel in a general depth of 55m of water and rises to about 8m from the seabed. The wreck is about 70m in length and about 10m in width. It is orientated on an east-north-east/west-south-west axis.

The *Manchester* is a wreck only for very experienced divers and is at the limits of air diving, so is probably more suited to technical divers using tri-mix. The wreck has been visited by only a very few divers so she is worthy of further exploration.

As she lies on a sandy seabed, visibility is generally good at 8m or so in summer months and sometimes excellent at 15m or more in calm weather and small tides (apart from the plankton bloom in May and early June, when it is generally more limited).

Expect the slack waters to occur more or less at the predicted low and high water times and beginning about half an hour before to three quarters of an hour after. On spring tides, expect this window of slack to be of a shorter duration. The flood tide flows from the west-south-west and the ebb from the east-north-east.

Ship's bell recovered by a diver from the steamship *Manchester*.

Angling

The *Manchester* provides large numbers of pollack in the range of 5lb–10lb, with occasional larger fish. The wreck also holds large coalfish and fishes best on spring tides when the tide is at full flow. There is a good chance of ling and conger eels using the right techniques during slack water periods.

Mhari-L

Wreck: ★★★★★
Scenery: ★★★★★
Angling: ★★★
Depth: 50m
Position: 53 49.774 N, 04 16.124 W
Datum: WGS84
Location: 18.6n.m. south-east of Langness
Access: Douglas (20.4n.m.) and Port St Mary (22.1n.m.) slipways at all stages of the tide. Castletown (20n.m.) slipway three hours only either side of high water.

Vessel

The steel motor fishing vessel *Mhari-L*, of Hull (H460), 50 tons gross, 27 tons net, was built at Hepworths, of Knottingley in 1978 and was equipped with a 735hp diesel engine. The *Mhari-L* measured 56ft in length (17.1m). She was owned by Jack Robinson Ltd, of Hull and operated as a scallop dredger, based at Kirkcudbright, south-west Scotland.

History

The *Mhari-L* was dredging for scallops off the south-east coast of the Isle of Man on Friday 20 February 1985, when she suddenly and mysteriously disappeared along with her crew of five men. She was due back in Kirkcudbright by midnight and when she didn't arrive, the alarm was raised with the rescue services. Ramsey Coastguard initiated and coordinated searches using Nimrod aircraft, helicopters, naval craft, merchant shipping and fishing vessels. Despite the extensive searches, no trace could be found of her, apart from the boot of one of the men, which was recovered by a fishing vessel on Saturday 21 February. Her last known position was eighteen to twenty-five miles south-east of Douglas at 5.00 a.m. on 20 February. At 3.30 p.m. on Sunday 22 February the search was called off by Ramsey Coastguard, but shipping in the area was requested to maintain a lookout for any signs of the *Mhari-L*.

It was not until Tuesday 22 April that her wreck was located by the Navy minehunter HMS *Bildeston*. Later, on Thursday 2 May, Royal Naval Divers, operating from the Navy's marine recovery vessel *Seaforth Clansman* and under the command of Lieutenant Commander Robin Gay, found that the *Mhari-L*'s trawl had snagged an underwater object, later confirmed to be a telephone cable.

Rumours had abounded (and continue to this day) that she was sunk by a submarine catching her dredgers and dragging her under. It seems far more plausible that the *Mhari-L* foundered as the result of snagging the cable, pulling it to the gunnel of the boat and then trying to hoist it on to the derrick in order to allow the crew to free the scallop dredges from the cable. The sheer weight of the cable and any swell in the sea at the time could well have destabilised the vessel. At this point it is likely that the *Mhari-L* capsized with the loss of all hands. The skipper, Stuart Campbell, had been known to have successfully accomplished this hazardous manoeuvre several months before on another cable.

The remainder of the crew was Keith Campbell, William Maxwell, Mark Amos and George McKeand.

References

Isle of Man Times, Tuesday, 19.03.1985. spool MN27 MNH, Hydrographic Department; *Olsen's Nautical Almanac, 1981*.

Wreck Site

Diving

Divers from the Royal Navy identified the wreck as being the *Mhari-L* in 1985. The wreck sits in a general depth of 50m of water and rises to about 5m from the seabed. The wreck is about 20m in length and about 5m in width. It is orientated on a north-north-east/south-south-west axis and rests on a sloping seabed.

Due to the depth, the *Mhari-L* is only for the experienced diver. It lies upright on its keel and is mostly intact. There is little marine growth on the wreck and it has been reported that the ship's wheel still remains in the wheelhouse.

As the wreck lies on a sandy seabed, visibility is generally good at 8m or so in the summer months and sometimes excellent at 15m or more in calm weather and small tides (apart from the plankton bloom in May and early June, when it is generally more limited). The wreck can be dark on occasions however, so a good torch is a necessity.

Expect the slack waters to occur more or less at the predicted low and high water times and beginning about half an hour before to three quarters of an hour after. On spring tides, expect this window of slack to be of a shorter duration. The flood tide flows from the west-south-west and the ebb from the east-north-east.

Angling

The main species to be caught on the *Mhari-L* are pollack, coalfish and cod, possibly into double figures. There are occasional ling with conger eels a possibility.

Octavia

Wreck:	*****
Scenery:	*****
Angling:	***
Depth:	24m
Position:	54 10.216 N, 04 00.268 W
Datum:	WGS84
Location:	13.3n.m. south-east of Maughold Head
Access:	Douglas (16.4n.m.) slipway at all stages of the tide. Laxey (14.2n.m.) slipway three hours either side of high water. Ramsey (14.8n.m.) slipway two hours either side of high water and beach launch possible in front of the Lifeboat House.

Vessel

The steel steam trawler *Octavia*, of Hull (H876), (Official Number: 123,238), 174 tons gross, 68 tons net, was built in 1906 by Cook, Welton and Gemmell, of Beverley, near Hull. She was 108.5ft in length, had a beam of 21.6ft and a draught of 11.5ft (33.1m x 6.6m x 3.5m). She was powered by a triple-expansion steam engine developing 45nhp at a pressure of 200 pounds, which was built by Amos and Smith, of Hull. This gave her a speed of 9.5 knots. The *Octavia*'s owner at her date of loss was Mr R. Hudson, of Preston, a retired police officer, who operated the trawler out of Fleetwood, Lancashire.

History

On Saturday 12 February 1937, two steam trawlers, the *Octavia*, of Hull and the *George Cousins*, of Fleetwood (LO66), 122 tons gross and owned by the Mac Line Ltd, of Fleetwood, were in collision about twelve miles south-east of Maughold Head during the hours of darkness. The *Octavia* was so badly holed that she sank within a few minutes. Fortunately, no loss of life was involved in the collision and the nine members of the crew of the *Octavia* were able to scramble aboard the *George Cousins* a few minutes before the *Octavia* went down, taking the crew's belongings with her.

Two of the crew of the *Octavia* had a terrifying experience. H. Haslam, the bosun, and a deckhand, W. Durbin, were asleep in their bunks at the time of the collision. The door leading to the forecastle was jammed and seawater began to rush in through a gaping hole. A lamp was upset in the forecastle and spilt paraffin ran all over the cabin floor and was ignited by the stove. For a few minutes the rest of the crew thought the two men were lost, but luckily the men on both sides of the forecastle door were able to force it open and the two men trapped inside managed to reach the deck. By this point the *Octavia* was rapidly heeling over.

The mate, D. Anderson and a deckhand, J. Crellin, were both from Peel on the Isle of Man.

References

Ramsey Courier, Friday, 19.02.1937. MNH; *Peel City Guardian*, Saturday, 20.02.1937. MNH; Lloyd's List via Lancashire County Council Museum Service; Hull Maritime Museum; *Cook, Welton and Gemmell, Shipbuilders of Hull and Beverley 1883-1963*, Thompson, Newton, Robinson and Lofthouse.

Wreck Site

Diving

The identity of the wreck of the *Octavia* was confirmed in 1993, following the recovery of her bell inscribed 'Octavia 1906'. The wreck sits in a general depth of 24m of water and rises to about 6m from the seabed. It is about 40m in length and 10m in width. It is orientated on a north-east/south-west axis with the bow facing north-east.

The *Octavia* is an enjoyable dive and makes for an impressive sight as it is rare to encounter such an intact wreck in such relatively shallow water in the seas around the Isle of Man. The wreck lies upright on its keel, but leans slightly to starboard. The superstructure and bridge are well flattened and the wooden decking has gone allowing access to the inside of the hull. The whole of the upper structures are covered with plum-rose anemones. When seen from above the wreck appears a ghostly white colour with flecks of orange.

Swimming around the hull close to the seabed, the propeller can still be seen in its place. Unusually, as they normally corrode to nothing very quickly, the smoke stack is still present, lying on the seabed parallel to the wreck just a few metres off

Octavia. (Copyright: Hull Maritime Museum)

on the starboard side. Further along the starboard side towards the bow there can be seen the split in the hull caused by the *George Cousins*' bow. In other places, especially on the port side, it is noticeable that some of the hull plates are now falling off onto the seabed. This process has perhaps been aided by scallop dredgers, which have smashed into the side of the wreck on occasion, for some of the damage appears quite recent.

Crabs and lobsters are both numerous and large on this wreck. Indeed, some of the lobsters deep inside the wreck in sections such as the engine room are some of the largest around the Isle of Man. Large shoals of fish circle around the wreck.

As the wreck lies on a sandy seabed, visibility is generally good at 8m or so in the summer months and sometimes excellent at 15m or more in calm weather and small tides (apart from the plankton bloom in May and early June, when it is generally more limited). There are occasions after unsettled weather and spring tides, however, when the visibility can be quite limited and down to just several metres.

Expect the slack waters to occur more or less at the predicted low and high water times and beginning about an hour and a half before to one hour after. On spring tides expect this window of slack to be of a shorter duration. The flood tide flows from the south-west and the ebb from the north-east.

Angling
The most common species on the *Octavia* are pollack and coalfish. The pollack reach about 8lb, but larger specimens have been seen underwater while diving. Hordes of pouting keep close to the wreck and on occasions cod will make an appearance. Conger eels lurk in the midst of the wreckage.

Oona Hall

Wreck: *****
Scenery: ****
Angling: ***
Depth: 51m
Position: 54 16.466 N, 04 51.280 W
Datum: WGS84
Location: 6.3n.m. west-north-west of Peel
Access: Peel (6.3n.m.) slipway at all stages of the tide.

Vessel

The steel steam trawler *Oona Hall*, of Fleetwood (FD23), 158 tons gross, 57 tons net, was built in Aberdeen in 1907 by Hall, Russell & Co. Ltd, of Aberdeen. She was 105.6ft in length, had a beam of 21.2ft and a draught of 11.1ft (32.2m x 6.5m x 3.4m). At the time of her loss, the *Oona Hall* was owned by Mr R. Bettess. She was equipped with a triple-expansion steam engine.

History

On 28 May 1940, the French Armed Auxiliary Cruiser *Ville d'Alger* was leading a French Transport, escorted by four destroyers, through the Irish Sea, on passage from Namsos, Norway. She was carrying *Chausseurs Alpins*, French Mountain troops, part of the Allied Expeditionary Force sent to aid in the failed defence of Norway. As the French convoy passed the west coast of the Isle of Man, it encountered a sea mist.

Shrouded in the mist and in the path of the convoy, the steam trawler *Oona Hall* was unaware of her impending doom. The *Ville d'Alger* ran down the trawler, drowning eleven of the twelve crewmen, in a position given as eight miles north-west by north of Peel breakwater. The sole survivor of the *Oona Hall* was picked up by the *Ville d'Alger*. He could recollect little of the incident, being asleep when the crash came. Instinctively rushing for the openness of the deck, he was knocked senseless by some falling wreckage. He only regained consciousness when he was pulled from the sea.

References

Fleetwood's Fishing Industry, Horsley and Hirst; World Ship Society, K. O'Donoghue; *Manx Independent*, 12.12.1987. Page 18, spool MN86 MNH.

Wreck Site

Diving

The identity of the wreck of the *Oona Hall* was established in the year 2000 after the wreck was dived. It was deduced to be the *Oona Hall* from the type of vessel, dimensions and location.

The wreck lies in a general depth of 51m of water and rises to about 5m from the seabed. It is about 35m in length and about 7m in width. The *Oona Hall* is both upright and intact. The superstructure, incorporating the wheelhouse at the front, is situated towards the stern and is complete. There are even the remains of an electric lamp used for illuminating the work deck still on top of the wheelhouse. Between the superstructure and the transom stern can be seen the gallows used to haul the warps connected to the nets. One of the most notable features is just how far the wreck has sunk into the muddy seabed. From the mud to her gunnel, the distance is less than 2m.

As the *Oona Hall* lies on a muddy seabed, visibility can be poor for Manx standards at less than 5m in the summer months, and it is especially poor on spring tides.

Expect the slack waters to occur more or less at the predicted low and high water times and beginning about half an hour before to three quarters of an hour after. On spring tides expect this window of slack to be of a shorter duration. The flood tide flows from the south and the ebb from the north.

Angling

The wreck was exhaustively fished in the early 1980s, so does not hold the quantity of fish it used to at that time. Pollack and coalfish to 6lb are still present in fair numbers.

Opal

Wreck: ★★★★★
Scenery: ★★★★
Angling: ★★★★★
Depth: 52m
Position: 53 47.383 N, 04 25.858 W
Datum: WGS84
Location: 17.5n.m. south-south-east of Langness
Access: Douglas (21.5n.m.) and Port St Mary (20.3n.m.) slipways at all stages of the tide. Castletown (18.9n.m.) slipway three hours either side of high water.

Vessel

The steel steamship *Opal*, of Glasgow, (Official Number: 102,659), 599 tons gross, 237 tons net, was built in 1894 by Scott & Sons, of Bowling. She was 180ft in length, had a beam of 29.1ft and a draught of 10.6ft (54.9m x 8.9m x 3.2m). The *Opal* was of a well deck design, with her machinery and superstructure situated aft. She was owned by Mr W. Robertson and was equipped with a 99rhp triple-expansion steam engine built by Muir and Houston, of Glasgow.

History

The *Opal* was bound from Llandulas, North Wales, to Belfast, with a cargo of limestone on 18 December 1916, when, after hitting a mine laid by the German submarine U80, she was lost off the south-east coast of the Isle of Man with her twelve crew members, including the master.

References

Lloyd's War Losses, The First World War, British Vessels Lost At Sea, 1914-1918; *Dictionary of Disasters at Sea*, Hocking; *Steam Coasters*, Waine; *British Merchant Ships Sunk By U-Boats In The 1914-1918 War*, Tennent; World Ship Society, H. Appleyard; *Lloyd's Register*; UK Public Records Office ADM137/2960.

Wreck Site

Diving

The identity of the wreck has not been verified. Divers in 1998, however, described it as the wreck of a coaster, and then in 1999 reported that its cargo consisted of limestone. Other divers have reported that the wreck is a diesel-powered motor coaster and not a steamship, so there is still a mystery to be solved by enterprising divers.

The wreck sits upright in a general depth of 52m of water and the wreck rises to about 6m from the seabed. It is about 50m in length and about 10m in width. The wreck is orientated on a south-east/north-west axis with the bows facing south-east. The bow and midships sections are intact, but the stern area has broken off and lies a short distance away from the main wreck.

As the wreck lies in an area of sand ripples, visibility is generally good at 8m or so in summer and sometimes excellent at 15m or more in calm weather and small tides (apart from the plankton bloom in May and early June, when it is generally more limited).

Expect the slack waters to occur more or less at the predicted low and high water times and beginning about half an hour before to three quarters of an hour after. On spring tides, expect this window of slack to be of a shorter duration. The flood tide flows from the west and the ebb from the east.

Angling

This wreck produces large numbers of pollack in the range of 6lb to 10lb with the occasional fish into double figures. A few coalfish have been taken. There is the potential for ling and conger eels to large proportions.

Paddle Wheel

Wreck: ★★★★★
Scenery: ★★★
Angling: ★★
Depth: 29m
Position: 54 07.802 N, 04 21.098 W
Datum: WGS84
Location: 4.1n.m. east-south-east of Douglas Head
Access: Douglas (4.1n.m.) and slipway at all stages of the tide. Laxey (5.8n.m.) slipway three hours only either side of high water.

Vessel

No details are available.

History

The origins of the paddle wheel still remain a mystery to me. The wheel is from a ship, but it is unclear whether it was the result of an accident to a ship or part of the deck cargo of a ship, which was subsequently lost over the side during stormy weather.

Wreck Site

Diving

The identity of the wreck of the *Paddle Wheel* has been dived for at least twenty years. It sits on the horizontal plane in a general depth of 29m of water and rises to about 4m from the seabed. The wheel is about 12m in diameter.

Being close to Douglas harbour and in a reasonable depth of water, the *Paddle Wheel* serves as a good training or warm-up dive in the spring. It consists of an iron wheel structure with nine arms radiating out both top and bottom from a central hub. At the end of each two arms is the paddle structure, or at least the metal for holding a wooden paddle. Each pair of arms is strengthened with cross struts. It is an impressive structure and occasional lobsters can be observed.

As the wheel lies on a sandy seabed visibility is generally good at 8m or so in summer months and sometimes excellent at 15m or more in calm weather and small tides (apart from the plankton bloom in May and early June, when it is generally more limited).

Expect the slack waters to occur more or less at the predicted low and high water times and beginning about half an hour before to three quarters of an hour after. On spring tides expect this window of slack to be of a shorter duration. The flood tide flows from the south-west and the ebb from the north-east.

Angling

There can sometimes be a surprising number of fish on such a small structure. Usually they are shoals of coalfish to 6lb, but on occasion the shoals are composed of pollack as well and are of a similar size to the coalfish. Cod and small ling have also been taken on the wreck together with hordes of pouting and, in the height of the summer, mackerel.

Peveril

Wreck: ★★★
Scenery: ★★★★★
Angling: ★★★★
Depth: 38m
Position: 53 59.247 N, 04 10.753 W
Datum: WGS84
Location: 13.8n.m. south-east of Douglas Head
Access: Douglas (13.8n.m.) and slipway at all stages of the tide. Laxey (16.1n.m.) slipway three hours either side of high water.

Vessel

The steel steamship *Peveril*, of Douglas, (Official Number: 76,307), 595 tons gross, 243 tons net, was owned by the Isle of Man Steam Packet Co. Ltd, of Douglas. She was built in 1884 by the Barrow Shipbuilding Co., of Barrow-in-Furness, Cumbria. The same company built both triple-expansion steam engines, which were capable of producing 1,200ihp through her twin screws and giving her a maximum speed of thirteen and a half knots. The *Peveril* was 207ft in length, had a beam of 26ft and a draught of 13ft (63.1m x 7.9m x 4m).

History

On Saturday 16 September 1899 at 7.50 p.m., the *Peveril*, Captain W. Woods, master, departed from the Queen's half-tide dock, Liverpool, with a heavy and valuable cargo of various merchandise together with two passengers. It was nearly high water, the weather clear and the wind was a fresh breeze from the north-north-west. The *Peveril* proceeded down the Mersey and reached the Bar Lightship at 9.17 p.m., with the master in charge. A course of north-northwest standard compass was then steered to take the vessel to her destination at Douglas on the east coast of the Isle of Man. The master left the bridge shortly after the course was set by the first officer, Thomas Webb. He also then left the bridge and the second officer took over in charge. Thomas Webb returned to the bridge at 12.10 a.m. on 17 September, the vessel going at full speed and still on the same course. About a quarter of an hour afterwards, he observed a vessel's masthead light from three to four points on the starboard bow.

The iron twin-screw steamship *Monarch*, of Belfast, (Official Number: 90,117), 113 tons net, owned by Mr Alexander King, of Ardvara, Cultra, Co Down, was built in 1884 by Messrs M'Llwaine, Lewis & Co. Ltd, of Belfast. She measured 155ft in length, had a beam of 22ft and a draught of 11ft (47.3m x 6.7m x 3.4m) and was powered by a compound steam engine.

On Saturday 16 September 1899 at 7.30 p.m., under the command of Captain McCulloch, the *Monarch* left Workington with a cargo of 350 tons of flue dust bound for Swansea. She passed St Bee's Head at 8.35 p.m. and a south-westerly course was set to take her to the Skerries, off the north-west tip of Anglesey. Her course would take her southwards along the east coast of the Isle of Man.

On board the *Peveril*, an able seaman, Joseph Corris, was on the lookout, another able seaman at the wheel and two others on the deck. The vessel was going at between twelve and thirteen knots. Soon after seeing the other vessel's light, Thomas Webb observed the port light of the other vessel, which appeared to be moving in a south-westerly direction. The *Peveril*'s regulation lights were properly swung and burning brightly. When the other vessel was about one to two miles distant, Thomas Webb was able to make out the red light, amidships and burning brightly, and at this point he became aware that the two vessels were on a collision course. He ordered the helm to be put hard at starboard and gave two blasts on the ship's whistle.

All went well on board the *Monarch* until a little before midnight, when the green light of a steamer was observed. The *Monarch*, in accordance with the steam sailing instructions, held her course, showing her red light on the port side to the other vessel, while the green light on the other indicated that they were 'crossing vessels'.

When the vessels were in dangerous proximity to each other and Captain McCulloch of the *Monarch* found that a collision was inevitable, he ordered the engines to be reversed. With her port bow, the *Monarch* struck the *Peveril* amidships and in doing so, carried away her own hull plates for about 20ft on the port side, the stem being completely carried away down to within two streaks of the keel and her fore peak was flooded with water. The bulkhead held firm, however, and there was no leakage to be seen in the forehold or in any other part of the ship.

It was 12.40 a.m. on Sunday 17 September, with the tide on the ebb, the weather fine and the wind in the north-north-west, blowing a fresh breeze, with a lumpy sea, when the other vessel struck the *Peveril* amidships just abreast of the funnel. The *Monarch* rebounded clear of the *Peveril* and, as the *Peveril* shot ahead of the *Monarch*, Thomas Webb stopped the *Peveril*'s engines. As soon as the collision occurred the *Peveril*'s master, Captain Woods, came on deck and took charge. Water was pouring into the engine room at an alarming rate and it was soon evident that she was in a sinking state. Captain Woods ordered the crew on deck and the lifeboats were put out. Not long after, the crew of the *Peveril* abandoned ship and in the two lifeboats pulled over to the *Monarch*, which had been standing by the stricken steamer. The *Monarch* continued to stand by the *Peveril* for another forty minutes until the *Peveril* eventually sank.

The crew of the *Peveril* watched her foundering with breathless and nervous anxiety from the deck of the *Monarch*. The moon was shining brightly at the time and as the *Peveril*, which had been successfully sailed through many a terrible gale, made her final plunge into the deep, the old hands, who had spent many happy years on board her, heaved pitiful sighs and wept.

Captain McCulloch of the *Monarch* took soundings and an observation of the Douglas Head Lighthouse, north-north-west and fourteen miles distant, thus showing the clearness of the night. He took the *Peveril*'s two boats in tow and made for Douglas.

The *Peveril* had a valuable cargo on board. The crew and stewards lost all their belongings. The crew of the *Peveril* was Captain W. Woods, master; T. Webb, first mate; J. Collister, second mate; T. Cowell, carpenter; I.M. White, purser; W. Creggs, seaman; R. Connell, seaman; J. Corris, seaman; J. Clague, seaman; A. Quayle, seaman; J. Cowley, seaman; J. Teare, seaman; J. Casement, first engineer; F. Duff, second engineer; R. Cubbon, donkeyman; W. Craine, greaser; T. Poole, fireman; T. Clague, fireman; J. Stewart, fireman; J. Crellin, fireman; J. Crowe, fireman; J. Bird, chief steward; McCann, second steward; Mrs Shaw, stewardess; Thomson, pantry man; McLaverty, saloon steward; J. McGuire, cook; Williams, barman; Nelson, steerage steward; Gross, cook's boy; J. Temple, cargo clerk; and J. Kelly, stores department. The passengers were M. Ruthven and R.H. Pitt.

References

Isle of Man Times, spool N21 MNH; *Island Lifeline*, Chappell; *Mona's Herald*, spool N115; *Manx Sun*, spool N74 MNH; Board of Trade Casualty Returns, Guildhall Library; UK Public Records Office CUST104/297.

Shipwrecks of the Isle of Man

Peveril.

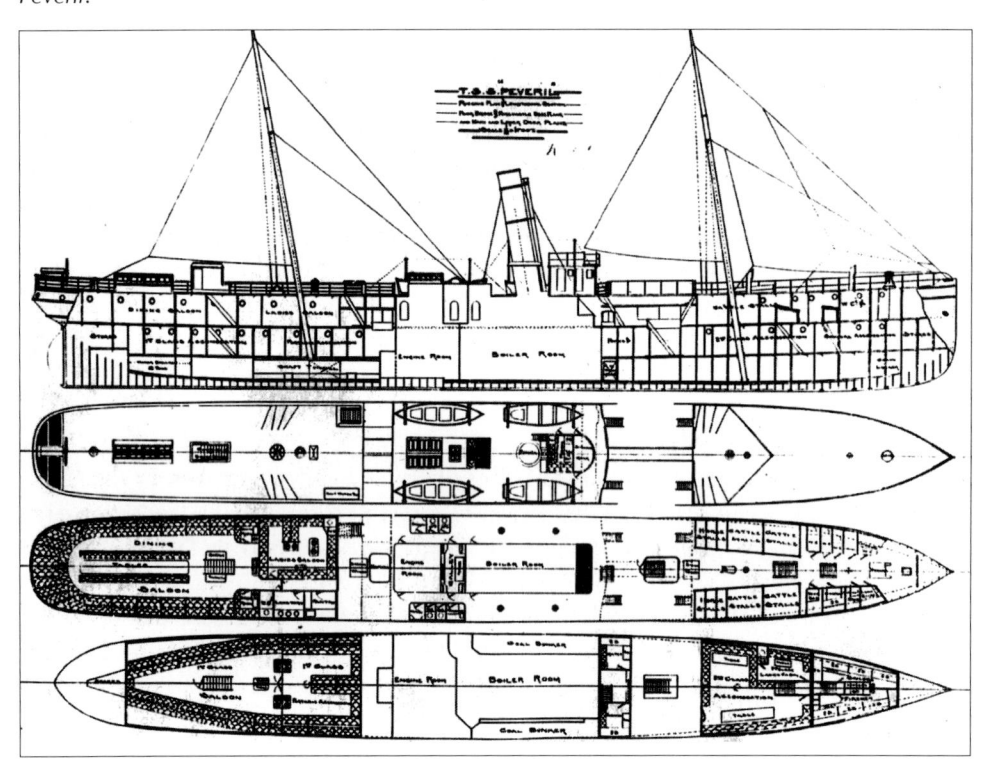

Plans of the steamship *Peveril*. (Steve Taggart)

Wreck Site

Diving

The wreck of the *Peveril* was confirmed in 1984 by the recovery of a number of artefacts, including the ship's wheel hub bearing her name. It sits a general depth of

38m of water and rises to about 4m from the seabed. The wreck is about 50m in length and about 10m in width. She is orientated on a north-north-east/south-south-west axis.

The *Peveril* lies upright on its keel and is very flattened. The boiler and engine form a large part of what stands clear of the seabed. Appearances can be deceiving, however, and the *Peveril* makes a fascinating wreck to dive. The holds still contain the general cargo, which she was carrying on her last fateful voyage across the Irish Sea, including children's toilets destined for a primary school in Douglas! Crockery with the Isle of Man Steam Packet Co. Ltd logo and silver cutlery can still be found in the sediment where once the galley was located just behind the boiler towards the stern. One of the most remarkable items recovered was an intact Edison light bulb, obviously dating from 1899 or a year or two earlier! All manner of items still remain in her holds and being designed for the carriage of passengers in the summer months, there is a large and varied amount of fittings etc. hidden amongst other parts of the wreckage.

As the wreck lies on a sandy seabed, visibility is generally good at 8m or so in the summer months and sometimes excellent at 15m or more in calm weather and small tides (apart from the plankton bloom in May and early June, when it is generally more limited). On occasions the wreck can be very dark, however, so a good torch is recommended.

Expect the slack waters to occur more or less at the predicted low and high water times and beginning about half an hour before to three quarters of an hour after. On spring tides, expect this window of slack to be of a shorter duration. The flood tide flows from the west-south-west and the ebb from the east-north-east.

Angling
Unusually for Manx wrecks, the main species on the *Peveril* in years gone by used to be cod with some larger specimens to 12lb present and the average fish in the range of 5lb to 8lb. The last few years have seen a dramatic decline in cod numbers and now the predominant species is the pollack. Pollack are generally in the range of 3lb to 6lb. At times, large shoals of small coalfish can be a nuisance.

On the positive side, the *Peveril* still produces some good ling fishing and each year fish in the range of 8lb to 15lb are caught. The one or two specimens to 20lb are taken each season. The broken wreckage harbours a large conger eel population and anchoring for them could prove productive.

Polarlight

Wreck: ★★★★★
Scenery: ★★★★★
Angling: ★★★
Depth: 30m
Position: 54 26.792 N, 04 20.400 W
Datum: WGS84

Location: 1.9n.m. north-east of the Point of Ayre

Access: Ramsey (7.6n.m.) slipway two hours either side of high water or beach launch possible in front of the Lifeboat House. Peel (18.9n.m.) slipway at all stages of the tide.

Vessel

The steel motor vessel *Polarlight*, of London, (Official Number: 339,094), 199 tons gross, 149 tons net, was completed in April 1970 by J.R. Hepworth & Co. (Hull) Ltd at Paull, near Hull. She measured 137.3ft in length, had a beam of 25.3ft and a draught of 8.8ft (41.9m x 7.7m x 2.7m). The *Polarlight* was equipped with an eight-cylinder oil engine built by Rolls Royce and developing 345bhp that gave her a speed of nine knots. At the time of her loss, the *Polarlight* was owned by the Clyde Shipping Co. Ltd, of Glasgow and managed by the Glenlight Shipping Co. Ltd, of Ardrossan.

History

At 12.29 p.m. on Tuesday 28 February 1989, whilst the *Polarlight* was in a position one mile north of the Point of Ayre, on a journey from Magheramorne, Larne, to Ramsey with a cargo of 300 tons of cement consigned for Mannin Fuels Ltd of Ramsey, she developed a serious list to starboard after the cargo shifted in a force nine gale. The master, John Moffat, decided the degree of list posed a threat to his ship and issued a mayday call on the ship's radio before ordering his three crewmen to abandon ship. The *Polarlight* capsized less than four minutes after the crew abandoned her and then quickly foundered.

Ramsey Lifeboat was launched, as was a helicopter from RAF Valley in Anglesey scrambled by Coastguards at Liverpool. The first vessel on the scene was the ro-ro ferry *Spheroid*, which positioned herself upwind of the life raft to provide shelter, but it was the Manx Government's fishery protection vessel *Enbarr*, which had been about three miles from the scene, that was able to effect a rescue. Despite rough conditions, the *Enbarr* manoeuvred into position alongside the life raft containing the four men from the stricken ship and took them on board. Two of the men, including John Moffat, had spent some time in the icy sea before enduring forty minutes in their open dinghy.

The *Polarlight*'s crew consisted of John Moffat, master; Ronald Bell, mate; David Hodgkinson and Michael Murray, none of whom were injured.

References

Isle of Man Examiner; *Isle of Man Courier*; World Ship Society, N. Davidson; Clyde Shipping Co., Harvey & Telford.

Wrecks in Open Water

Polarlight. (Copyright: Andrew Denholm)

The propeller on the wreck of the *Polarlight*. (Copyright: Phil Hutchinson)

Wreck Site

Diving

The position of the wreck of the *Polarlight* has been known to local divers for more than ten years. The *Polarlight* sits in a general depth of 30m of water and rises to about 6m from the seabed. The wreck is about 42m in length and about 10m in width. It is orientated on an east/west axis with the bow facing to the east.

The *Polarlight* is intact and lies on its starboard side with the cargo hold covers and cargo lying on the seabed next to the wreck. At the rear of the ship is the wheelhouse, still intact, but with entry to it now barred by collapsing wreckage. Behind the wheelhouse on the starboard side is an open hatch with a stairway down to the engine room. The hull at the stern is completely encrusted with plumrose anemones, which very nearly obscures the row of intact portholes right around the stern. The non-ferrous propeller and rudder are also intact.

Moving forward past the wheelhouse the cargo hold is encountered. Little cargo remains as it mostly spilled onto the seabed as the ship foundered; divers are therefore free to explore its cavernous interior. Forward of the hold lies the intact bow section with steel mast protruding horizontally.

All in all, the *Polarlight* is suitable for moderately experienced wreck divers. Most divers who visit the wreck enjoy the *Polarlight* due to its recognisable form, the good visibility, the profuse marine life and clean nature of the wreck.

As the wreck lies on a sandy/shell grit seabed, visibility is generally good at 8m or so in the summer months and sometimes excellent at 15m or more in calm weather and small tides (apart from the plankton bloom in May and early June, when it is generally more limited).

Expect the low water slack period to occur more or less at the predicted time and beginning about half an hour before to an hour after. Slack water periods over the high water begin about one and a half hours before the predicted time and last for less than an hour. On spring tides expect both windows of slack to be of a shorter duration. The flood tide flows from the north-west and the ebb from the south-east.

Angling

There are plenty of good size pollack on the *Polarlight*, together with coalfish. Many conger eels lie in the wreckage and ling are a possibility in the height of summer. Cod should frequent the wreck on occasion.

PT1

Wreck: ★★★★★
Scenery: ★★★★★
Angling: ★★★★
Depth: 60m
Position: 53 52.563 N, 04 43.717 W
Datum: WGS84
Location: 10.6n.m. south-south-east of the Calf of Man
Access: Port St Mary (11.7n.m.) and Douglas (18.6n.m.) slipways at all stages of the tide. Castletown (12.1n.m.) slipway three hours only either side of high water.

Vessel

The steel paddle tug *PT1*, 103 tons gross, was built for the war in Mesopotamia by George Brown, of Greenock in 1917. She was powered by a pair of compound diagonal steam engines developing 240ihp, built by McKie and Baxter, which gave her a speed of nine knots. She was 110ft in length, had a beam of 20ft and a draught of 8ft (33.5m x 6.1m x 2.4m).

She was originally ordered by Royal Indian Marine with the name *T44*, along with a series of tunnel screw tugs, but during construction it was decided to give the paddle tugs their own serial numbers, all of them commencing 'PT'. When completed, the *PT1* was under the jurisdiction of the Inland Transport of the Royal Engineers.

History

The *PT1*, Captain McLeod, master, left Greenock at 10.00 a.m. on 9 May 1917 and carried a crew of nineteen men: the captain, one lieutenant, four second lieutenants, one sergeant, two corporals and ten sappers.

When nine miles south of the Calf of Man, she commenced to take water in rapidly, presumably as the result of a mechanical failure, and the crew were ordered to take to the lifeboats. The starboard boat got clear with eight of the crew, but the port boat became jammed under the port paddle box and capsized, the occupants being thrown into the water. Five were picked up, but six men were drowned. The survivors were in the open lifeboat for about one and a half hours before they were picked up by a trawler and taken into Peel. Later, Sapper Chateris died from exposure as a result of having been immersed in the sea.

The crew list for the *PT1* was Captain McLeod; Lieutenant M.D. Kerr; Second Lieutenant C. Casper; Second Lieutenant J. Brown; Second Lieutenant E. Evans; Second Lieutenant A.H. Seddon; Sergeant Steel; Corporal Atkins; Corporal Fife; Sapper Young; Sapper Swanger; Sapper Green; Sapper J. McDonald; Sapper J. Lucas; Sapper O'Donnell; Sapper G. Woods; Sapper J. Teasdale; Sapper Hockridge; Sapper Chateris. Of these men Captain McLeod, Sergeant Steel, Corporal Atkins, Sapper Young, Sapper Swanger and Sapper Green were drowned.

References

The Isle of Man and the Great War, Sargeaunt; P.N. Thomas; World Ship Society, D. Asprey, World Ship Society; Isle of Man Governor's Papers 9485 MNH.

Wreck Site

Diving

The wreck is assumed to be that of the *PT1* due to the wreck's location and dimensions. The *PT1* sits in a general depth of 60m of water and rises to about 5m from the seabed. The wreck is about 40m in length and about 6m in width. It is orientated on an east-north-east/west-south-west axis. The wreck is intact and upright, and too deep for divers using air, though it is accessible to those using tri-mix.

As the wreck lies on a sandy seabed, visibility is generally good at 8m or so in the summer months and sometimes excellent at 15m or more in calm weather and small tides (apart from the plankton bloom in May and early June, when it is generally more limited).

Expect the slack water period to occur more or less at the predicted low and high water time and beginning about half an hour before to three quarters of an hour after. On spring tides, expect both windows of slack to be a shorter duration. The flood tide flows from the south-west and the ebb from the north-east.

Angling

The wreck mainly produces pollack in the range of 5lb to 10lb. Other species, such as coalfish and ling, should be taken.

Queen of the Isles

Wreck: ★★
Scenery: ★★
Angling: ★
Depth: 19m
Position: 54 16.080 N, 04 08.600 W
Datum: WGS84
Location: 6.2n.m. east-south-east of Maughold Head
Access: Douglas (13.7n.m.) slipway at all stages of the tide. Laxey (9.3n.m.) slipway three hours either side of high water. Ramsey (9.1n.m.) slipway two hours either side of high water and beach launch possible in front of the Lifeboat House.

Vessel

The iron steamship *Queen of the Isles*, of Beaumaris, (Official Number: 14,820), 146 tons gross, 84 tons net, was built in 1853 by Thomas Toward, of Newcastle. She was 126.5ft in length, had a beam of 18.2ft and a draught of 9ft (38.6m x 5.5m x 2.7m). The *Queen of the Isles* was originally built as a paddle steamer, but was converted to a schooner-rigged, twin-screw steamship in 1885. She was equipped with twin steam engines developing 60hp. At the time of her loss, she was owned by Mr Thomas Roberts, of 3 Berry Street, Conway, North Wales.

History

The *Queen of the Isles*, William Hughes, master, was bound from Belfast for Garston, with a light general cargo. At 1.00 a.m. on Sunday 15 September 1889, the master,

The loss of the *Queen of the Isles* as reported in the *Ramsey Courier*. (Copyright: Manx National Heritage)

who was on deck at the aft of the steamer, heard a sudden and tremendous noise coming from the engines below. The steamship, which had been proceeding at full speed in a southerly direction, was shaken violently. William Hughes immediately ran down to the engine room to see what had caused the problem.

William Williams, the engineer, had been standing near to the engines when he heard a crash on the port side and saw the port engine suddenly revolve at high speed. He shut down the steam to the engine, threw it out of gear and then went round the back of the engines by the starboard side to see what had caused the crashing sound. All that faced him was a fountain of seawater gushing from a hole in the hull plating in the bottom of the ship.

At this moment, the master arrived in the engine room and quickly saw that his vessel was doomed as she was filling very rapidly. William Williams stopped the starboard engine and eased on the safety valves and went with William Hughes on to the deck. William Hughes then gave the order to abandon ship and to launch the small boat. Within ten minutes, the master and six crewmen had secured a portion of their clothing and launched the small boat. They stood by in the small boat at a safe distance away from the *Queen of the Isles*, which foundered about twenty-five minutes later, just after 2.00 a.m., in a position six miles south by east of the Bahama Lightship (about six miles east-south-east of Maughold Head). The night was fine though a little hazy, and the sea calm with a light southerly wind, as they rowed to the Bahama Lightship.

Captain D. Kneale, master of the Bahama Lightship stated that at 3.00 a.m. on 15 September, a small boat with seven men came alongside the Lightship. The morning was fine, with a very light south-east wind and the sea as smooth as glass. The men were taken on board and reported to Captain Kneale that they were the crew of the steamer *Queen of the Isles*. Some time afterwards, when it was daylight, a steamer belonging to the Strath Line hove in sight and Captain Kneale, thinking it would be a good opportunity for the unfortunate crew to get to their homes, signalled to the steamer to come alongside. Although the steamer passed so close to the Lightship that the name *Topaz* could clearly be made out, the only reply to the signals was that the man at the wheel of the steamer held up his hand. The steamer proceeded on her way without altering course.

In a short time, another steamer was noticed coming along, but notwithstanding the signals were still flying and that she passed close by the Lightship, not the slightest notice was taken of the signal. Shortly afterwards, a third steamer hove in sight and she was signalled to also, but with no greater success. The crew of the trawler *Anna Maria*, of Douglas, Whiteway, master, which was about two miles off the Lightship, upon hearing the gun, bore down on the Lightship and took in tow the small boat, complete with the crew of the *Queen of the Isles* and towed them into Ramsey Bay, after which the crew of the steamer rowed their small boat to the Queen's Pier and landed safely.

The engineer, William Williams, later confirmed on oath that, in his opinion, the *Queen of the Isles* had foundered following her port propeller shaft breaking between the main bearings and the stuffing box, and the flailing shaft then puncturing the hull plate below it.

The trawler *James and Frances*, of Ramsey, arrived in Ramsey harbour on Friday night 18 October 1889 and reported the loss of a trawl net. It is supposed that the trawler fouled the wreck of the steamer *Queen of the Isles*, which had sunk a few weeks earlier, six miles south by east of the Bahama Lightship.

References

Isle of Man Times, spool N12 MNH; *Mona's Herald*, spool N109 MNH; *Manx Sun*, spool N68 MNH; *Ramsey Courier*, Saturday, 21.09.1889. spool MN102 MNH; Roy S. Fenton, author of *Cambrian Coasters*; *Mona's Herald*, Wednesday, 23.10.1889. spool N109 MNH; Board of Trade Casualty Returns, Guildhall Library; UK Public Records Office CUST104/232.

Wreck Site

Diving

The identity of the wreck has not been definitely confirmed, but the size of the wreck and its location strongly suggest it is that of the *Queen of the Isles*. It sits in a general depth of 19m of water and rises to about 3m from the seabed with the highest point being the boiler. The wreck is about 35m in length and about 10m in width. It is orientated on a south-south-east/north-north-west axis.

The wreck of the *Queen of the Isles* has been extensively salvaged at some point in the past and the remains are very sparse. Even the brass and copper components of the boiler have been removed and the engines are gone. Wreckage is scattered about over quite a large area; despite the salvage operations, however, the general outline of the vessel can just be made out. The wreck is worth a look, and items of crockery have been observed. It is a suitable dive for the inexperienced diver and a 'gentle' wreck to dive with slack tides, good visibility and easily navigated.

As the wreck lies on a sandy seabed, visibility is generally good at 8m or so in the summer months and sometimes excellent at 15m or more in calm weather and small tides (apart from the plankton bloom in May and early June, when it is generally more limited). There are plenty of lobsters and crabs on the wreck.

Expect the slack waters to occur more or less at the predicted low and high water times and beginning about an hour before to at least an hour after. On spring tides expect this window of slack to be of a shorter duration. The flood tide flows from the south-west and the ebb from the north-east.

Angling

The *Queen of the Isles* is not really an angling wreck as it affords little protection to fish. On the sonar she appears more of a mound that a real wreck. Mostly there are shoals of pouting, but there is potential for other species on occasion.

Rian

Wreck: *
Scenery: *
Angling: *
Depth: 12m
Position: 54 20.720 N, 04 19.600 W
Datum: OGB
Location: 2.3n.m. north-east of Ramsey
Access: Laxey (9.3n.m.) slipway three hours either side of high water. Ramsey (2.3n.m.) slipway two hours either side of high water and beach launch possible in front of the Lifeboat House.

Vessel

The steel motor vessel *Rian*, of Groningen, 232 tons gross, 131 tons net, was built in 1934 by Gebr Van Diepen, of Waterhuizen. She was equipped with a three-cylinder four-stroke CSA oil engine by Humboldt-Deutzmotoren, A.G. Koln-Deutz. Her owner was D. Buining, of Groningen, the Netherlands. She was 113.4ft in length, had a beam of 22.1ft and a draught of 8.3ft (34.6m x 6.7m x 2.5m).

History

Early on Sunday morning 3 February 1946, Ramsey Lifeboat was launched in answer to distress flares at sea. When the lifeboat reached the vessel from which the flares had emanated, it was found that the Dutch coaster *Rian* had sunk following a collision with the Dutch submarine escort vessel Jan Van Gelder, about two and a half miles off Ramsey. The crew of the *Rian*, after putting off in the ship's lifeboat, were picked by the escort vessel, which anchored later in Ramsey Bay, having suffered some damage. The crew were transferred to the lifeboat and they were later provided with accommodation at the Prince of Wales Hotel. The *Rian*, Captain Henrikus Meertens, master, was carrying 247 tons of coal from Maryport to Parr, Cornwall.

Captain Meertens later recalled:

Most of the crew were asleep at the time when there was a crash and water began rushing in to flood the engine room. We had to get the ship's boat over the side and jump in with all speed, as our vessel began to sink rapidly. We had to leave all our belongings behind. I had a motorcycle on board which I had just bought, and she went down too, but we managed to save our dog which was the crew's mascot.

References

Isle of Man Examiner, 08.02.1946. MNH; World Ship Society, K. O'Donoghue; *Ramsey Courier*, Friday, 08.02.1946. spool MN536 MNH.

Wreck Site

Diving

The identity of the wreck has not been definitely confirmed, but the size of the wreck and its location strongly suggest it is that of the *Rian*.

The wreck lies in a general depth of 12m of water and rises to about 1.5m from the seabed in a scour.

The wreck of the *Rian* was struck on 11 February 1952 and presumably at that time was dispersed with explosives in order to prevent it posing any further danger to ships navigating the area. Only very scattered wreckage now exists.

As the wreck lies on a sandy seabed, visibility is generally good at 8m or so in the summer months and sometimes excellent at 15m or more in calm weather and small tides (apart from the plankton bloom in May and early June, when it is generally more limited).

Expect the slack waters to occur more or less at the predicted low and high water times and beginning about an hour before to at least an hour after. On spring tides expect this window of slack to be of a shorter duration. The flood tide flows from the south and the ebb from the north.

Angling

It is not a wreck for angling.

Ringwall

Wreck: *****
Scenery: *****
Angling: **
Depth: 38m
Position: 54 07.018 N, 04 53.580 W

Datum: WGS84
Location: 4.2n.m. west-north-west of Bradda Head
Access: Port St Mary (7.6n.m.) and Peel (9.7n.m.) slipways at all stages of the tide. Port Erin (4.9n.m.) beach launch possible by the harbour.

Vessel

The steel steamship *Ringwall*, of Liverpool, (Official Number: 143,711), (ex *Mary Summerfield*), 407 tons gross, was built in 1921 by Day, Summers & Co. Ltd, of Southampton for the Summerfield Steamship Co. Ltd. She was 143ft in length, had a beam of 25.1ft and a draught of 11.6ft (43.6m x 7.7m x 3.5m). The *Ringwall* had a single well deck constructed of steel with her machinery and superstructure placed at the aft end of the vessel. The engines developed 60hp and were also built by Day, Summers & Co. Ltd, of Southampton. Her owner, at the time of her loss, was Wallace Brothers Ltd, of Dublin, who had renamed her *Ringwall* in 1928.

History

On 27 January 1941, the *Ringwall*, Captain John Hughes, master, left Dublin, in ballast, bound for Silloth. Later that day, she hit a mine off the south coast of the Isle of Man and foundered with the loss of her crew of eight men. The crew

Ringwall. (Copyright: John Clarkson)

was: J. Hughes, E. Hunt, D. McKay, J. O'Reilly, R. Prendergast, J. Reilly, M. Smyth and J. Tallon.

References

British Vessels Lost At Sea, 1939-1945; Lloyd's Register of Shipping; *Britain's Sea War*, Young; *Ramsey Courier*, 07.02.1941. MNH; Lloyd's Register Wreck Returns 1940-49, Guildhall Library; Gerald Hughes; Interview with Nancy Hughes, daughter of Captain John Hughes.

Wreck Site

Diving

The identity of the wreck must have been confirmed many years ago. For a long time it was known locally as the *Mary Summerfield*. As this was the *Ringwall's* name when launched, it strongly suggests that a diver had recovered the bell.

The *Ringwall* lies in a general depth of 38m of water and rises to about 5m from the seabed. The wreck is about 40m in length and about 8m in width. It is orientated on a south-east/north-west axis.

The wreck of the *Ringwall* sits upright on her keel and is largely intact. Evidence of the damage caused by the mine can be seen on the hull.

As the wreck lies on a sandy seabed so that visibility is generally good at 8m or so in the summer months and sometimes excellent at 15m or more in calm weather and small tides (apart from the plankton bloom in May and early June, when it is generally more limited).

Expect the slack waters to occur more or less at the predicted low and high water times and beginning about half an hour before to at three quarters of an hour after. On spring tides expect this window of slack to be of a shorter duration. The flood tide flows from the north-west and the ebb from the south-east.

Angling

The *Ringwall* has been fished extensively for many years, so large fish can't be expected. It produces large numbers of pollack, however, and coalfish up to 8lb. Ling are taken occasionally and pouting are always present.

Robert Dee

Wreck: ★
Scenery: ★
Angling: ★
Depth: 25m
Position: 54 15.480 N, 04 18.880 W
Datum: OGB
Location: 1n.m. south-east of Port Cornaa, south of Maughold Head

Access: Douglas (8.5n.m.) slipway at all stages of the tide. Laxey (3.3n.m.) slipway three hours either side of high water. Ramsey (5.6n.m.) slipway two hours either side of high water and beach launch possible in front of the Lifeboat House.

Vessel

The wooden motor fishing vessel *Robert Dee*, of Ramsey (RY11), 20 tons gross, was built in France in 1959. She measured 41ft in length (12.5m).

History

A collision between two fishing boats occurred in the fog of the early morning on Thursday 17 May 1978 at a point two and a half miles south of Maughold Head. The *Robert Dee* was fishing when hit by the *Jacob Johannes*, Castletown, 47 tons, and owned by Henry Goldsmith of Port St Mary, which was on passage from Douglas to Ramsey.

Robert Dee. (Copyright: Michael Craine)

On board the *Robert Dee* were the owner and skipper John Barry Williams, of Main Road, Kirk Michael, crewman Jackie Eves, 3 Albert Square, Ramsey and the owner's dog. The steel hull of the *Jacob Johannes* cut straight into the wooden hull of the *Robert Dee* and the latter sank immediately. The two crewmen of the *Robert Dee*, together with their dog, clambered on board the *Jacob Johannes*, all managing to escape injury. They were later taken back to their homeport of Ramsey. It was later reported that the skipper of the *Jacob Johannes* never even realised he had run down a vessel, until the two crewmen of the *Robert Dee* had suddenly clambered on board his own.

References

Isle of Man Examiner, spool MN64 MNH; *Olsen's Fishermen's Nautical Almanac*, 1981; B. Kelly, Port St Mary; *Ramsey Courier*, Friday, 18.05.1978. spool MN578 MNH.

Wreck Site

Diving

The wreck of the *Robert Dee* was dived in the years following her loss. The wreck, which was intact in those days, has deteriorated considerably over the years. It lies in a general depth of 25m of water and rises to barely 1m from the seabed. The remains are about 15m in length and about 8m in width.

The wreck will now compose of the more resilient parts of the vessel such as the engine, fuel tank, propeller and propeller shaft. There may be some interesting metallic finds amongst the clutter.

The sandy seabed usually ensures that visibility is good at around 8m or so in summer and sometimes excellent at 15m or more in calm weather and small tides (apart from the plankton bloom in May and early June, when it is generally more limited).

Expect the slack waters to occur more or less at the predicted low and high water times and beginning about half an hour before to three quarters of an hour after. On spring tides, expect this window of slack to be of a shorter duration. The flood tide flows from the south-west and the ebb tide from the north-east.

Angling

The *Robert Dee* now only produces pouting, small pollack and shoals of mackerel.

Romeo

Wreck: ****
Scenery: *****
Angling: ****
Depth: 46m
Position: 54 22.357 N, 04 52.069 W

Datum: WGS84
Location: 10.9n.m. north-west of Peel
Access: Peel (10.9n.m.) slipway at all stages of the tide.

Vessel

The steel steamship *Romeo*, of Hull, (Official Number: 82,494), 1,730 tons gross, 982 tons net, was built in 1881 by Earle's Co. Ltd, of Hull. She was 275ft in length, had a beam of 34.6ft and a draught of 19.9ft (83.8m x 10.5m x 6.1m). The *Romeo* was equipped with a compound steam engine developing 333nhp, which gave her a top speed of ten knots. She was owned by Ellerman's Wilson Line Ltd, of Hull.

History

The *Romeo*, J. Neile, master, left Scapa on 23 February 1918, bound for Liverpool. She was on Admiralty charter for carrying meat and provisions to the Fleet, but was returning to Liverpool in ballast after having called in at Stornoway, remaining there for six days. She was equipped with a twelve-pound gun for defence against enemy submarines.

On 3 March 1918 at 2.40 a.m., she was about ten miles south of the Mull of Galloway, steaming at ten knots and zigzagging. The weather was fine with occasional snow showers, the wind light and the sea smooth. The first officer was in charge on the bridge. There was a lookout on the forecastle head, another on the

Romeo. (Copyright: Hull Maritime Museum)

bridge and one on the gunner's aft platform. All lights on the ship were carefully screened and no navigation lights were burning.

A green and red light suddenly appeared off her port bow. Fearful of a collision with another ship, the order was given to show the *Romeo's* navigation lights at her bow. This was a fateful mistake as she had been tricked by German submarine U102 into giving away her exact position. Within a couple of minutes a torpedo slammed into the *Romeo's* port side between the stoke-hole and engine room. The explosion was terrific and split the ship in half. At first she took a list to port, and then righted herself before sinking like a stone in less than two minutes of the explosion. There was no time for the crew to launch any of the lifeboats and the crew of thirty-seven men was thrown into the water.

The two gun crew, John Compagnon and William Camomile, managed to cling to a swamped boat and eventually bailed it out. Shortly afterwards, they spotted a sailor in the water and hauled him out in to the lifeboat, but he later died at about 10.00 a.m. At daylight the two gunners managed to get the mast and sail up before being picked up by the steamship *Ardgarvel* at 11.00 a.m., and later landed at Greenock.

The only other survivor from the *Romeo* was the wireless operator, Arthur Seddon. He was picked up by a trawler and landed at Holyhead by the patrol boat *Kilgobnet* at 11.00 a.m. on 4 March.

References

British Vessels Lost At Sea, 1914-1918; *Dictionary of Disasters At Sea*, Hocking; *British Merchant Ships sunk by U-Boats in the 1914-1918 War*, Tennent; UK Public Records Office, Irish Sea German Submarines, March 1918, ADM 137/1515.

Wreck Site

Diving

The wreck of the *Romeo* was confirmed in the late 1990s by the recovery of the ship's bell bearing her name. For many years, the wreck was known to local people as simply the 'liner'. She was often confused with the steamship *Champagne*, owned by the Pacific Steam Navigation Co. and an ocean-going passenger/cargo vessel. The description of a 'liner' was partly correct, however as before being requisitioned by the Admiralty, the *Romeo* was engaged by Ellerman's Wilson Line in carrying both passengers and cargo between Sweden and Hull. Many of the passengers were emigrants crossing to England for further passage to North America.

The wreck of the *Romeo* lies in a general depth of 46m of water and rises to about 8m from the seabed. It is about 150m in length and about 20m in width. The wreck lies in two sections with about 50m separating them. The split is aft of the centrally located boilers. It is a large wreck, with the bow section lying on its side and quite broken up. Separate dives are required for each section. The *Romeo* makes for an excellent dive, but, owing to the depth, is only for the experienced diver.

As the wreck lies on a muddy seabed, visibility can be reduced on large tides but is generally in the region of 6m or so in the summer months and sometimes more at 10m or more in calm weather and small tides (apart from the plankton bloom in May and early June, when it is generally more limited). On occasions, the wreck can be very dark so a good torch is recommended.

Expect the slack waters to occur more or less at the predicted low and high water times and beginning about half an hour before to three quarters of an hour after. On spring tides expect this window of slack to be of a shorter duration. The flood tide flows from the north-west and the ebb from the south-east.

Angling

The wreck produces good pollack fishing with fish in the range of 5lb to 10lb, together with shoals of coalfish. There is the potential for cod and ling at the right time of year.

Rostrevor

Wreck: ★★★★
Scenery: ★★★★★
Angling: ★★★★★
Depth: 57m
Position: 53 52.257 N, 04 26.138 W
Datum: WGS84
Location: 12.6n.m. south-east of Langness
Access: Douglas (16.4n.m.) and Port St Mary (15.6n.m.) slipways at all stages of the tide. Castletown (14.1n.m.) slipway three hours either side of high water.

Vessel

The steel screw steamship *Rostrevor*, of Newry, (Official Number: 108,644), 298 tons gross, 82 tons net, was built in 1899 by J. Fullerton & Co., of Paisley. She was 142.5ft in length, had a beam of 21.3ft and a draught of 10.4ft (43.4m x 6.5m x 3.2m). The *Rostrevor* was equipped with a compound steam engine developing 61nhp and built by Hall-Brown, Buttery & Co., of Glasgow. She was owned by the Newry and Kilkeel Steam Ship Co. Ltd and was managed by J. Fisher & Sons, of Newry.

History

The *Rostrevor* left Newry on Wednesday evening 18 April 1917, with a cargo of granite setts, bound for Manchester. Early the next day, Thursday 19 April, she encountered a north-east gale, capsized and foundered in a position reported to be 25m north-west of the Skerries Rock after her cargo had shifted. The crew managed to get in the boats safely and were picked up by a passing passenger steamer.

References

Ramsey Courier, Friday, 20.04.1917 MNH; Lloyd's Register of Shipping; UK Parliament Sessional Papers, 1920; *British Shipping Fleets, Joseph Fisher & Sons*, Fenton and Patterson.

Wreck Site

Diving

The identity of the wreck is assumed to be that of the steamship *Rostrevor*, but as yet no positive identity has been achieved. Interestingly, a diver in 2000 recovered a brass steering stand marked with 'Paisley 1899', which would certainly match with the place and date of manufacture of the *Rostrevor*.

The *Rostrevor* sits upright in a general depth of 57m of water and rises to about 8m from the seabed. The wreck is about 45m in length and about 7m in width. It is orientated on a south-east/north-west axis. The midships and stern sections of the wreck are reasonably intact, but the bow is greatly damaged.

As the wreck lies in an area of sand ripples, visibility is generally good at 8m or so in summer and sometimes excellent at 15m or more in calm weather and small tides (apart from the plankton bloom in May and early June, when it is generally more limited).

Expect the slack waters to occur more or less at the predicted low and high water times and beginning about half an hour before to three quarters of an hour after. On spring tides, expect this window of slack to be of a shorter duration. The flood tide flows from the west and the ebb from the east.

Angling

The *Rostrevor* produces large numbers of decent sized pollack in the 5lb to 12lb range, with the occasional coalfish. The wreck is noted for its ling, with fish over 25lb having been caught in the height of the summer. Large conger eels are a distinct possibility.

Skerries

Wreck: *****
Scenery: *****
Angling: *****
Depth: 53m
Position: 53 51.185 N, 04 21.730 W
Datum: WGS84
Location: 15.4n.m. south-east of Langness
Access: Douglas (18.2n.m.) and Port St Mary (18.6n.m.) slipways at all stages of the tide. Castletown (16.6n.m.) slipway three hours either side of high water.

Vessel

The steel steamship *Skerries*, of Glasgow, (Official Number: 124,137), 4,278 tons gross, 2,702 tons net, was built in 1906 by Russell & Co., of Glasgow. She was 370.4ft in length, had a beam of 49.8ft and a draught of 19.1ft (112.9m x 15.2m x 5.8m). The *Skerries* was fitted with a triple-expansion steam engine, developing 410nhp and built by Rankin and Blakemore, of Greenock. She was owned by the Clyde Shipping Co. Ltd, of Glasgow.

History

At 3.00 p.m. on 4 November 1916, the *Skerries*, bound from Barrow-in-Furness, Cumbria, for Barry Roads, South Wales, in ballast, was proceeding at six knots in a strong south-westerly gale when an explosion took place in the after part of the ship. She had struck a mine laid by U80, some distance south of the Isle of Man. The ship sank in about three minutes, but, fortunately, the crew of forty-six men managed to launch the boats successfully and so abandon ship.

As the master's boat was trying to get clear of the sinking steamship, the master inexplicably seized a rope which was hanging from the ship and was dragged overboard and drowned. After searching the vicinity, the boats made for the Isle of Man. On arriving in the Isle of Man, it was found that one of the crew, a Chinaman, was missing. He and the master were the only two casualties from the loss of the *Skerries*.

Various positions of loss have been given for the *Skerries* and in the official war loss records it is given as fifteen miles north-north-west of the Skerries, Anglesey. A note was made on the official loss ledger in 1919, stating that if this position were correct, then the *Skerries* must have hit a floating mine as the minefield had been laid twenty minutes north-east of the position. In reality, it has been proved that the wreck lies in the position where the minefield was actually located, some eighteen miles south of Douglas Head.

References

Dictionary of Disasters at Sea During the Age of Steam, Hocking; *Lloyd's War Losses, The First World War*; *British Merchant Ships Sunk by U-Boats in the 1914-1918 War*, Tennent; World Ship Society, H. Appleyard; *Lloyd's Register*; UK Public Records Office ADM 137/2960; *Clyde Shipping Co.*, Harvey and Telford.

Wreck Site

Diving
The identity of the wreck is assumed to be that of the steamship *Skerries* due to the size and location of the wreck.

The wreck of the *Skerries* lies in a general depth of 53m of water and rises to about 10m from the seabed. The wreck is about 120m in length and about 15m in width. It is orientated on a north-north-east/south-south-west axis.

The *Skerries* lies on her keel with a forty-five degrees list to starboard and the starboard gunnel is the highest point of the wreck. The hull is very broken with the keel facing to the east-south-east. There is a large spare propeller on the deck. It is a large wreck and, compared to others around the Isle of Man, is largely unexplored.

As the wreck lies in an area of sand/shingle, visibility is generally good at 8m or so in the summer months and sometimes excellent at 15m or more in calm weather and small tides (apart from the plankton bloom in May and early June, when it is generally more limited).

Expect the slack waters to occur more or less at the predicted low and high water times and beginning about half an hour before to three quarters of an hour after. On spring tides, expect this window of slack to be of a shorter duration. The flood tide flows from the west and the ebb from the east.

Angling

The *Skerries* used to be the best angling wreck around the Isle of Man in the 1980s and early 1990s, but has been heavily fished by charter boats operating from ports in North Wales in recent years. Pollack to 18lb have been taken plus many double figured coalfish. The best time to catch the big pollack and coalfish is when the tide is running at its strongest on a spring tide in the July to November period. Large ling are also present and the largest cod to come off her has been 23lb. Many extremely large conger eels lurk in the wreckage.

Sustain

Wreck: ★★★★
Scenery: ★★★
Angling: ★★
Depth: 46m
Position: 54 31.597 N, 04 20.258 W
Datum: WGS84
Location: 6.9n.m. north-north-east of the Point of Ayre
Access: Peel (22.7n.m.) slipway at all stages of the tide. Ramsey (12.6n.m.) slipway two hours either side of high water and beach launch possible in front of the Lifeboat House.

Vessel

The wooden motor fishing vessel *Sustain*, of Peel (PL25), 20 tons gross, was built in 1950 by Martin at Granton near Edinburgh. She was 45ft in length (13.7m).

Sustain. (Copyright: Michael Craine)

History

The *Sustain*, Tony Kneale, skipper, sank seven miles off the Point of Ayre, on Wednesday 16 November 1983, after her bilge pumps failed and she became waterlogged. Her trouble had started when she fouled her propeller while hauling the queenie gear, which caused her to take in water through a damaged stern gland.

Ramsey Lifeboat was launched at 11.33 a.m., after the *Sustain* had radioed coastguards a few minutes earlier at 11.26 a.m. The lifeboat's services were not required as the crew of the *Sustain* were transferred to another fishing boat, the *Still Waters*, and subsequently were landed at Peel. They were none the worse for their experience, despite having been in the sea before being picked up by the *Still Waters*. The *Sustain* sank shortly afterwards.

The sinking vessel was identified by a fishery protection Islander aircraft that was patrolling around the Isle of Man. The crew of the *Sustain* was Tony Kneale, Alistair Caley and Sean Barlow.

References

Isle of Man Examiner, spool MN9 MNH; *The Ramsey Lifeboats*, Seybold; Michael Craine 14.02.1996. & 10.10.2002; *Manx Star*, Friday, 18.11.1983. spool MN11 MNH.

Wreck Site

Diving

The identity of the wreck is assumed to be that of the *Sustain* due to the size and close proximity to where she sank. The wreck lies in a general depth of 46m of water and rises to about 2m from the seabed. It is about 14m in length and about 7m in width. The wreck is orientated on an east/west axis and has broken up.

As it lies in an area of sand/shingle, visibility is generally good at 8m or so in the summer months and sometimes excellent at 15m or more in calm weather and small tides (apart from the plankton bloom in May and early June, when it is generally more limited).

Expect the slack waters to occur more or less at the predicted low and high water times and beginning about three quarters of an hour before to half an hour after. On spring tides, expect this window of slack to be of a shorter duration. The flood tide flows from the west-south-west and the ebb tide from the east-north-east.

Angling

The author has no information on fishing this wreck, but would expect her to produce a few pollack, coalfish and cod on occasion.

Teasel

Wreck: ★★★★★
Scenery: ★★★★★
Angling: ★★★★
Depth: 50m
Position: 54 28.347 N, 04 11.288 W
Datum: WGS84
Location: 7n.m. east-north-east of the Point of Ayre
Access: Douglas (22.5n.m.) slipway at all stages of the tide. Laxey (17n.m.) slipway three hours either side of high water. Ramsey (11.3n.m.) slipway two hours either side of high water and beach launch possible in front of the Lifeboat House.

Vessel

The steel motor vessel *Teasel*, of Cardiff, 290 tons gross, 115 tons net, was built in 1937 by E.J. Smit & Zoon, of Westerbroek, Holland, for the Cardiff firm of

Lovering & Sons, who were owners of a small fleet of motor coasters between 1936 and 1959 on the Irish Sea coal trade. The *Teasel* was their second ship and was equipped with a seven-cylinder four-stroke C.S.A. oil engine by Humboldt-Deuzmotoren A.6. Koln-Deutz. She was 123.7ft in length, had a beam of 23.6ft and a draught of 8.7ft (37.7m x 7.2m x 2.7m).

History

On 6 January 1948, the *Teasel*, Captain W. Jones, master, who was only twenty-eight years old, carrying a crew of eight men, was bound from Belfast to Manchester, laden with a cargo of steel bars. It is thought that, when she was six miles east of the Point of Ayre with a storm-force, south-easterly wind blowing, her engines broke down, allowing the cargo to shift and so causing the *Teasel* to list heavily. Shortly after sending out a radio distress message she must have foundered.

On receiving the distress message, the Coastguards instructed the Ramsey Lifeboat, the *Lady Harrison*, to be launched and she headed for the Point of Ayre in badly deteriorating weather. The wind was soon south-east force eight to ten with visibility down to half a mile. The salvage tug *Salveda* was dispatched from Campbletown to assist in the rescue attempt. At about 8.00 p.m. word was received that the *Lady Harrison* had been blown ashore 500 yards west of the Point of Ayre Lighthouse in a wind that was now force nine to ten.

The ship's wheel on the wreck of the *Teasel*. (Copyright: Phil Hutchinson)

Coxswain Starkey of the *Lady Harrison* later stated that he had seen a light, which he took to be a Morse signal from the *Teasel*, and this being from the direction of Maughold Head, he turned the lifeboat to head towards it, but immediately ran his vessel aground on the shingle beach. The Douglas and Peel Lifeboats searched for the *Teasel* along with ten RAF aircraft from Aldergrove and several other vessels. The Douglas Lifeboat searched an area stretching from the Point of Ayre to ten miles east of Maughold Head, but found no trace of the *Teasel*. The coxswain described the sea conditions as being very bad.

On Thursday 7 January, at 12.10 p.m., the coasting steamer *Dromaine*, on a voyage from Whitehaven to Dundrum, reported finding the bodies of two members of the crew of the *Teasel* on a raft some seven miles north-east of the Point of Ayre. Also on the same day, Coastguards found wreckage, including a ship's boat from the *Teasel*, 16ft in length and complete with burnt out flares, washed ashore at Rue Point. Later still, the body of the steward, W.J. Harris, of Swansea, was washed up at Girvan in Ayrshire.

Most of the earlier historical records give the position of loss for the *Teasel* as several miles off Maughold Head, but this assumption was based on the light spotted off Maughold Head by the Ramsey Lifeboat. As her true resting place is now known, the position of loss is confirmed as seven miles north-east of the Point of Ayre.

References

Isle of Man Examiner, 1948 MNH; *The Ramsey Lifeboats*, Seybold; *Ramsey Courier*, Friday, 13.02.1948 MNH; *Isle of Man Weekly Times*, Saturday, 10.01.1948. spool MN354 MNH; *Sea Breezes*, Page 586 1982.

Wreck Site

Diving

The identity of the wreck was confirmed as the *Teasel* in 1999 by the recovery of the ship's bell bearing her name. The *Teasel* sits a general depth of 50m of water and rises to about 4m from the seabed. The wreck is about 40m in length and about 10m in width. It is orientated on a south-east/north-west axis, with the bow to the north-west. The wreck is surrounded on both sides by a scour of a depth of up to 4m and is at its deepest around the propeller.

The wreck of the *Teasel* is upright and intact. The stern is the highest point of the wreck and there is a covered walkway all around the stern section. On the top of the steel superstructure sits the ship's wheel, the wooden wheelhouse having completely rotted away. The only parts standing higher than the helm are the lifeboats davits, which on the starboard side are snagged with netting trailing down to and around the propeller. Near to the stern, an open hatch and stairway leads down to the engine room.

Forward of her superstructure lies the single hold, minus the hatch covers, but still containing her cargo of iron bars. Here on the deck, the depth is 50m. Further forward on the forecastle are the remains of a winch.

As the wreck lies in an area of sand/gravel, visibility is generally good at 8m or so in the summer months and sometimes excellent at 15m or more in calm weather and small tides (apart from the plankton bloom in May and early June, when it is generally more limited). On occasions the wreck can be very dark, so a good torch is recommended. Crabs and lobsters are large and numerous.

Expect the slack waters to occur more or less at the predicted low and high water times and beginning about half an hour before to three quarters of an hour after. On spring tides, expect this window of slack to be of a shorter duration. The flood tide flows from the south-east and the ebb from the north-west.

Angling

The author has no information on fishing this wreck, but would expect her to produce a good numbers of pollack, coalfish and cod on occasion.

Thracian

Wreck: ★★★★
Scenery: ★★★
Angling: ★
Depth: 32m
Position: 54 07.660 N, 04 47.150 W
Datum: WGS84
Location: 1n.m. north-north-west of Bradda Head
Access: Port St Mary (6.8n.m.) and Peel (6.8n.m.) slipways at all stages of the tide. Port Erin (2.5n.m.) beach launch possible.

Vessel

The steel four-masted barque *Thracian*, of Liverpool, 2,154 tons gross, 2,008 tons net, was built at Port Glasgow in 1892 to the order of Messrs W. Thomson & Co., of St Johns, New Brunswick, Canada, whose Liverpool agents were Messrs G.T. Soley & Co. (Robert & John Henderson, New Brunswick, managers). She was 282ft in length, had a beam of 42.1ft and a draught of 24.6ft (86m x 12.8m x 7.5m).

History

The wet and stormy weather that prevailed in the Isle of Man during the latter half of the week ending Sunday 14 August 1892, culminated on that Sunday evening in an awful gale from the south-south-west, accompanied by heavy rain. The wind began to rise at about 8.00 p.m. and by midnight a perfect hurricane was blowing. The gale was not of long duration and by 4.00 a.m. on Monday morning on 15 August it had moderated to a strong breeze.

Shortly after 9.00 a.m., a steam tugboat was observed to sail around Douglas Head and make for Douglas harbour. The tug turned out to be the *Sarah Joliffe*, of

Liverpool, which was described in contemporary reports as an exceptionally powerful boat. She came to anchor inside the breakwater and her master, Captain Owen Jones, at once came ashore with a sad and terrible tale to tell.

It seems that on Thursday 11 August, the *Sarah Joliffe*, one of Messrs Joliffe's fleet of Liverpool steam tugs, left Liverpool for Greenock, in order to tow to the Mersey a new large four-masted barque, the *Thracian*, of Liverpool. The barque was under the command of Captain Herbert H. Brown, of Helensborough and he was accompanied on the voyage by his wife. The *Sarah Joliffe* took ten men to Greenock to act as a temporary crew for the *Thracian* and at the Scottish port they were joined by five others, so that when the *Thracian* started in tow of the tug she had seventeen persons on board.

A start was made from Port Glasgow on Saturday evening on 13 August, and good progress seemed to have been made until Sunday afternoon of 14 August, when the vessels were between the Point of Ayre and Belfast Lough. A gale suddenly sprang up and, as the *Thracian* was in light ballast of 600 tons of rubble, the tug could not tow her along in the teeth of the gale and mountainous sea. All the *Sarah Joliffe* could do was to stand by the barque, keeping her head to the sea as much as possible. A lull in the weather followed, but at about 11.30 p.m., when the vessels were about three miles north of Port Erin on the south-western coast of the Isle of Man, there was a terrific squall. To the consternation of those on board the tug, the *Thracian* turned over.

The crew on the tug cast adrift the towing hawser to save the *Sarah Joliffe* from being dragged under and Captain Jones then bore close to the *Thracian*, which was floating keel upwards. The thick rain obscured the barque and when the *Thracian* was next seen she was about one thousand yards from the tug. She floated for a couple of minutes, but then disappeared beneath the waves.

There was no trace to be found of anyone in the water, so the *Sarah Joliffe* cruised about for several hours, but nothing further was seen of the ill-fated crew. Towards 6.00 a.m. Captain Jones, finding that nothing more could be done, steamed to Douglas, reaching there about 9.00 a.m.

The *Thracian* was on her way from the Clyde to Birkenhead, where her fitting out was to be completed and cargo was to be loaded for her first commercial voyage to San Francisco. The crew was principally composed of riggers belonging to Liverpool, eleven in total, with the remainder from Glasgow. The following is a list of the identities of some of the crew: Captain Herbert H. Brown (master), of Helensborough; Mrs Brown; Patrick Coyne (boatswain, acting mate), of Chesterfield Street, Liverpool; James Fitzgerald ('boss' rigger), (41), of Raffles Street, Liverpool; Joseph Souter (39), of Olive Street, Liverpool; Michael Naylor (43), of Hornby Street, Liverpool; Edward Dalton (32), of Twiss Street, Liverpool; Moses Harper (28), of Raffles Street, Liverpool; Edward St Clare (50), of Pitt Street, Liverpool; James Bird, of Liverpool; Michael Neary, of Liverpool; and Jerimiah Silch, of Liverpool.

Wreckage from the *Thracian* was seen floating down from Peel to Port Erin. A bucket was picked up by fisherman off Peel and a small boat was washed ashore at Niarbyl, Dalby. On Thursday 25 August 1897, the nets of a Peel fishing boat, which was fishing three miles off the Calf of Man, became entangled with an obstruction on the seabed.

At first the crew thought it was a rock, but later they realised it was the wreck of the *Thracian*.

References

Dictionary of Disasters at Sea During the Age of Steam, Hocking; *Isle of Man Examiner*, spool MN41 MNH; *Mona's Herald*, spool N110 MNH; *Ramsey Courier*, Saturday, 27.08.1892. spool MN104 MNH; World Ship Society, G.H. Somner; Board of Trade Casualty Returns, Guildhall Library.

Wreck Site

Diving

As far as it is known, the wreck of the *Thracian* has never been positively identified, but there is no doubt as to her identity as only one steel barque has been lost in this area.

The wreck of the *Thracian* sits a general depth of 32m of water and rises to about 4m from the seabed. The wreck is about 80m in length and about 10m in width. It is orientated on a south-west/north-east axis with the bow to the south-west.

The wreck of the *Thracian* is upside down, which means she is not as good a wreck to dive as might be expected. The stronger bow and stern areas are intact with the centre section quite collapsed with large holes in the hull plating visible. The four steel masts lie flat on the seabed and stretch out to the south-east on what is the vessel's starboard side. The massive anchors and chains can be seen at the bow and the rudder is still in place at the stern.

As the wreck lies in an area of sand, visibility is generally good at 8m or so in the summer months and sometimes excellent at 15m or more in calm weather and small tides (apart from the plankton bloom in May and early June, when it is generally more limited). There is quite a lot of silt on the wreckage, however, and visibility can be reduced if this is disturbed.

Expect the slack waters to occur more or less at the predicted low and high water times and beginning about an hour before to an hour after. On spring tides expect this window of slack to be of a shorter duration. The flood tide flows from the south-west and the ebb from the north-east.

Angling

Small pollack and coalfish are present at times. Ling to 10lb can be taken and large conger eels lurk amongst the wreckage.

Tuskar

Wreck: *****
Scenery: *****
Angling: ****
Depth: 50m

Tuskar. (Copyright: The World Ship Society)

Position: 54 00.224 N, 04 57.135 W
Datum: WGS84
Location: 5.1n.m. west-south-west of the Calf of Man
Access: Port St Mary (9.1n.m.) and Peel (16.4n.m.) slipways at all stages of the tide. Port Erin (8.4n.m.) beach launch possible near to breakwater.

Vessel

The steel motor vessel *Tuskar* (ex *Friso*), of Groningen, 250 tons gross, 114 tons net, was built in 1939 by Sch-Deltzijl V/H Sander. She measured 127.4ft in length, had a beam of 23.1ft and a draught of 8.3ft (38.8m x 7m x 2.5m). The *Tuskar* was equipped with a four-cylinder oil engine built by Appingedammer Bros. At the time of her loss she was owned by Mr J. Pinkster.

History

On 19 April 1961, the *Tuskar*, Captain Bos, master, was bound from Runcorn to Belfast with a cargo of salt, when at 1.15 a.m., in dense fog, she struck a rock near the Calf of Man, which in all probability was the Chicken Rock. She immediately began taking in water. Captain Bos later commented, 'We had a big hole in our port side.'

She drifted out from the Calf of Man, but, owing to water rising in the ship, Captain Bos decided to send a mayday message and abandon ship. At 5.00 a.m. the *Tuskar* sank, about four miles south-west of the Calf of Man. The crew consisted of four men and the captain's wife and all spent about an hour in the life raft before being rescued by the cable ship *Ariel*.

At 5.30 a.m. the Coastguard requested that the Port Erin Lifeboat be launched and at 6.00 a.m. the lifeboat was on her way to assist the *Tuskar*. The lifeboat met up with the *Ariel* at Bay Fine not far from Port Erin and transferred the crew of the *Tuskar* ashore at 8.40 a.m. The *Tuskar*'s crew were taken to the Bay Hotel on Port Erin promenade, where they were fed and kitted out with fresh clothes by the Shipwrecked Mariner's Society (agent Mr Woodworth).

References

Isle of Man Examiner, 20.04.1961. MNH; World Ship Society, B. Lawley; *The History of the Port Erin Lifeboats*, Morris; *Isle of Man Weekly Times*, Friday, 21.04.1961. spool MN372 MNH.

Wreck Site

Diving

As far as it is known, the wreck of the *Tuskar* has never been positively identified, but there is no doubt as to her identity. Two ship's bells were recovered in 2000, but bore no inscription of her name.

The wreck of the *Tuskar* sits a general depth of 50m of water and rises to about 8m from the seabed. The wreck is about 40m in length and about 8m in width. It is orientated on an east/west axis.

The wreck of the *Tuskar* is upright and intact. The highest part of the wreck is at the stern, where the steel superstructure rises about 3m above the deck level. On top of the superstructure is the wheelhouse, but as the upper parts of it were wooden, they have rotted away. The single hold stretches in front of the superstructure out towards the bow. The hatches are gone and, as would be expected, the hold is empty.

As the wreck lies in an area of sand, visibility is generally good at 8m or so in the summer months and sometimes excellent at 15m or more in calm weather and small tides (apart from the plankton bloom in May and early June, when it is generally more limited). Due to her depth, the wreck can be quite dark, so a good torch is recommended.

Expect the slack waters to occur more or less at the predicted low and high water times and beginning about half an hour before to three quarters of an hour after. On spring tides, expect this window of slack to be of a shorter duration. The flood tide flows from the north-west and the ebb from the south-east.

Angling

The *Tuskar* produces good quantities of pollack and coalfish to 8lb with one or two larger fish. Ling to 15lb are present together with occasional shoals of codling.

Jumbo mackerel frequent the wreck in July to September. Pouting can be troublesome at times.

U246

Wreck:	****
Scenery:	*****
Angling:	****
Depth:	45m
Position:	53 39.979 N, 04 54.292 W
Datum:	WGS84
Location:	23n.m. south-south-west of the Calf of Man
Access:	Douglas (33.1n.m.) and Port St Mary (25.5n.m.) slipways at all stages of the tide. Castletown (26.2n.m.) slipway three hours either side of high water.

Vessel

The German Type VIIC submarine, U246, 761 tons, was constructed by Germaniawerft, of Kiel and was launched on 7 December 1943 and commissioned on 11 January 1944. She was commanded by KL. E. Raabe and her crew numbered forty-eight men. She was 251ft in length, had a beam of 20.5ft and a draught of 15.8ft (76.5m x 6.3m x 4.8m).

History

From 11 January 1944 to 31 July 1944, U246 and her crew undertook training with 5 Flotille. Her first patrol as a front boat was with 3 Flotille between 1 August 1944 and 30 September 1944. Her second and fateful patrol began on 1 October 1944. On 25 October, an escort attacked her with depth charges and damaged her so seriously that she had to return to base for repairs. After recommencing her patrol, U246 radioed base for the last time on 7 March 1945 from position 56° 20' 00" N, 12° 50' 00" W, while en route for her operational area in the Irish Sea.

Wreckage brought up from a contact attacked by HM Ships *Hesperus* and *Havelock*, assisted by Sunderland 'H' of No. 201 Squadron, on 30 April was conclusively identified as coming from U246. Since U246 was to leave patrol and return home in early April, she must have been dead on the bottom when found and attacked by the two destroyers and the Sunderland aircraft. In the absence of any other attack to account for U246, her loss must be attributed to an accident, most likely a snorkel failure or battery explosion resulting from inadequate ventilation while charging. Whether the loss of U246 can be attributed to an attack by HMS *Duckworth* on 29 March has yet to be determined.

References

The U-Boat Offensive 1914-1945, Tarrant; *Register of Type VII U-Boats*, Adams and Lees; *Search, Find and Kill*, Franks; *U-Boats Destroyed*, Kemp; *German U-Boat Losses During World War II*, Niestle.

Wreck Site

Diving

U246 seems the most likely candidate for the wreck, but U1024 cannot be ruled out and, indeed, after the war, the wreck was thought to be the U242, but she has possibly been located elsewhere. U1024 surrendered to the Royal Navy and later sank under tow about twenty-three miles north-west of Anglesey on 13 April 1945. Varying reports suggest the U1024 sank off Fleetwood while under tow. In addition, there are several U-boats that simply disappeared around the coast of the British Isles during the Second World War.

The wreck lies on its starboard side in a general depth of 45m of water and rises to about 4m from the seabed. The wreck is about 70m in length and about 6m in width. It is orientated on an east/west axis.

The wreck of U246 makes for an excellent dive. It is quite broken up at both the stern and the bow. At the stern, the propellers, torpedo tubes and torpedoes can be observed and likewise the bow torpedo tubes and torpedoes are also visible. The midships section is fairly intact and the conning tower is clearly visible with its distinctive D/F aerial, periscope and snorkel. Sand is piling up on the port side.

As the wreck lies in an area of sand, visibility is generally good at 8m or so in the summer months and sometimes excellent at 15m or more in calm weather and small tides (apart from the plankton bloom in May and early June, when it is generally more limited). Due to her depth the wreck can be quite dark, so a good torch is recommended.

Expect the slack waters to occur more or less at the predicted low and high water times and beginning about an hour before to low water. On spring tides, expect this window of slack to be of a shorter duration. The flood tide flows from the west and the ebb from the east.

Angling

The wreck should produce pollack, coalfish and ling.

Vivid

Wreck: ★★★★★
Scenery: ★★★★★
Angling: ★★★
Depth: 51m

Position: 53 56.886 N, 04 44.652 W
Datum: WGS84
Location: 7.6n.m. south-south-west of Port St Mary
Access: Port St Mary (7.6n.m.) and Douglas (15.5n.m.) slipways at all stages of the tide. Castletown (8.3n.m.) slipway three hours either side of high water.

Vessel

The iron steam paddle tug *Vivid*, of Irvine, 89 tons gross, was built in 1863 by Low Walker, of Newcastle. She was 89ft in length, she had a beam of 17.8ft and a draught of 9.2ft (27.1m x 5.4m x 2.8m). Her steam engines were rated at 50nhp. The *Vivid* was owned by James Douglas, senior, of 24 Dock Street, Belfast.

History

The *Vivid*, James McCoult, master, undertook repairs in Dundalk ready for her new charters, the Manchester Ship Canal Co. She left Dundalk at 4.30 p.m. on Monday 21 March 1892 on the ebb tide and set a course for Liverpool. Everything went well until 2.00 a.m. on Tuesday 22 March; the *Vivid* was steering east by south in clear weather and a moderate northerly wind when the engineer, James Douglas, son of the owner, went below and heard an unusual noise coming from the port paddle wheel, but could not work out what was causing it. He then went back on deck and climbed onto the port paddle box, but couldn't hear the noise from there. He then immediately reported the noise to the master. James McCoult ordered the *Vivid* to proceed at half speed.

At 3.40 a.m. James Douglas went back below to the stoke-hole for the purpose of firing up when he heard a loud snatching sound. He immediately stopped the engines and saw water rushing into the stoke-holes from the bunker. He then climbed on deck and disconnected the engines, put the starboard engine ahead and rushed for the small boat. At the same time he called to the other three men that the *Vivid* was sinking.

James McCoult ordered the crew to launch the small boat and all four men got into it. For twenty minutes they watched as the *Vivid* gradually foundered in a position given by the master as five miles south-east of the Chicken Rock. Her lights suddenly disappeared and they assumed she had sunk. They then set off for Port St Mary where they arrived at 7.00 a.m.

The engineer, James Douglas, gave the cause of loss as the breaking of the port paddle shaft, and the feathering irons tearing a hole in her below the waterline. The *Vivid* was estimated to be worth about £2,000.

The crew of the *Vivid* was: James McCoult, master; James Douglas, engineer; Jas Kewley, seaman; and Jas Gorman, seaman.

References

Isle of Man Times, spool N15 MNH; *Isle of Man Examiner*, Saturday, 26.03.1892. spool MN41 MNH; *Mona's Herald*, spool N110 MNH; World Ship Society, PN Thomas; UK Public Records Office CUST 104/277.

Wreck Site

Diving

A recent dive on the wreck in 2002 has all but confirmed the identity of this wreck as that of the *Vivid*.

The wreck of the *Vivid* sits upright in a general depth of 51m of water and the wreck rises to about 7m from the seabed. The wreck is about 45m in length and about 7m in width. It is orientated on a south-west/north-east axis.

The wreck makes a wonderful dive for the experienced diver and is a fairly unique opportunity to observe up close an iron paddle tug dating from the 1860s. It is intact and lying with a forty-five degree list to port, so making the starboard gunnel the highest point of the wreck. Any wooden decking and superstructure has long rotted away. Her boiler and engines are located amidships. At first sight, it does not appear to be a paddle steamer. On closer examination, however, it can be seen that the wreck possesses no propeller and evidence for the starboard paddle box and wheel lies about 10m off to the starboard creating a second piece of main wreckage. Early sonar reports of this wreck suggested that it was in two pieces, but in reality it is complete. The ship's wheel, on top of a column, nobly stands by itself right at the stern of the vessel.

It is a deep dive and only for the experienced wreck diver. As the wreck lies on a sandy seabed, visibility is generally good at 8m or so in the summer months and sometimes excellent at 15m or more in calm weather and small tides (apart from the plankton bloom in May and early June, when it is generally more limited). She can be a dark wreck however, so a good torch is imperative. When I dived to the wreck in September 2002, the visibility exceeded 20m and light was at a good level. When off the starboard side close to the seabed, I could see the entire wreck. It proved a truly memorable diving experience.

Expect the slack waters to occur more or less at the predicted low and high water times and beginning about half an hour before to three quarters of an hour after. On spring tides, expect this window of slack to be of a shorter duration. The flood tide flows from the west-south-west and the ebb from the east-north-east.

Angling

The wreck in the late 1980s was very productive for pollack and numerous ling. Heavy fishing in recent years, however, has meant a fall in both quantity and quality of fish. Having said that, there is still plenty of pollack to 8lb or more, and the chance of ling to 20lb in the height of the summer. The wreck also produces coalfish and the occasional cod.

Westburn

Wreck: ★★
Scenery: ★★★
Angling: ★
Depth: 32m
Position: 54 17.402 N, 03 54.053 W
Datum: WGS84
Location: 14.5n.m. east of Maughold Head
Access: Douglas (22.1n.m.) slipway at all stages of the tide. Laxey (18.0n.m.) slipway three hours either side of high water. Ramsey (17.0n.m.) slipway two hours either side of high water and beach launch possible in front of the Lifeboat House.

Vessel

The motor fishing vessel *Westburn*, of Kilkeel (N171), 38 tons gross, was owned by William J. Campbell, of Kilkeel, and was built in 1947 at Fraserborough.

History

The *Westburn* sank on 17 December 1975, after catching a wire rope in the propeller, which opened up the stern gland. The crew abandoned the *Westburn* sixteen miles south-west of St Bee's Head.

References

Olsen's Fisherman's Nautical Almanac, 1981; Michael Craine 14.02.1996.

Wreck Site

Diving

As far as it is known, the wreck of the *Westburn* has never been positively identified and so doubt still exists as to the exact identity of this wreck.

The wreck of the *Westburn* lies in a general depth of 32m of water and rises to about 2m from the seabed. The wreck is about 40m in length and about 8m in width. It is orientated on a north/south axis. It is an area of broken wreckage with one main part. No other information is available.

As the seabed is composed of fine silt and mud, it is easily kicked up by careless fining and visibility is quickly reduced to zero. Visibility is generally poor at less than 5m or so in the summer months. The plankton bloom in May and early June will make the wreck very dark.

Expect the slack waters to occur more or less at the predicted low and high water times and beginning about half an hour before to an hour after. On spring tides, expect this window of slack to be of a shorter duration. The flood tide flows from the west-south-west and the ebb from the east-north-east.

Angling
No information is available.

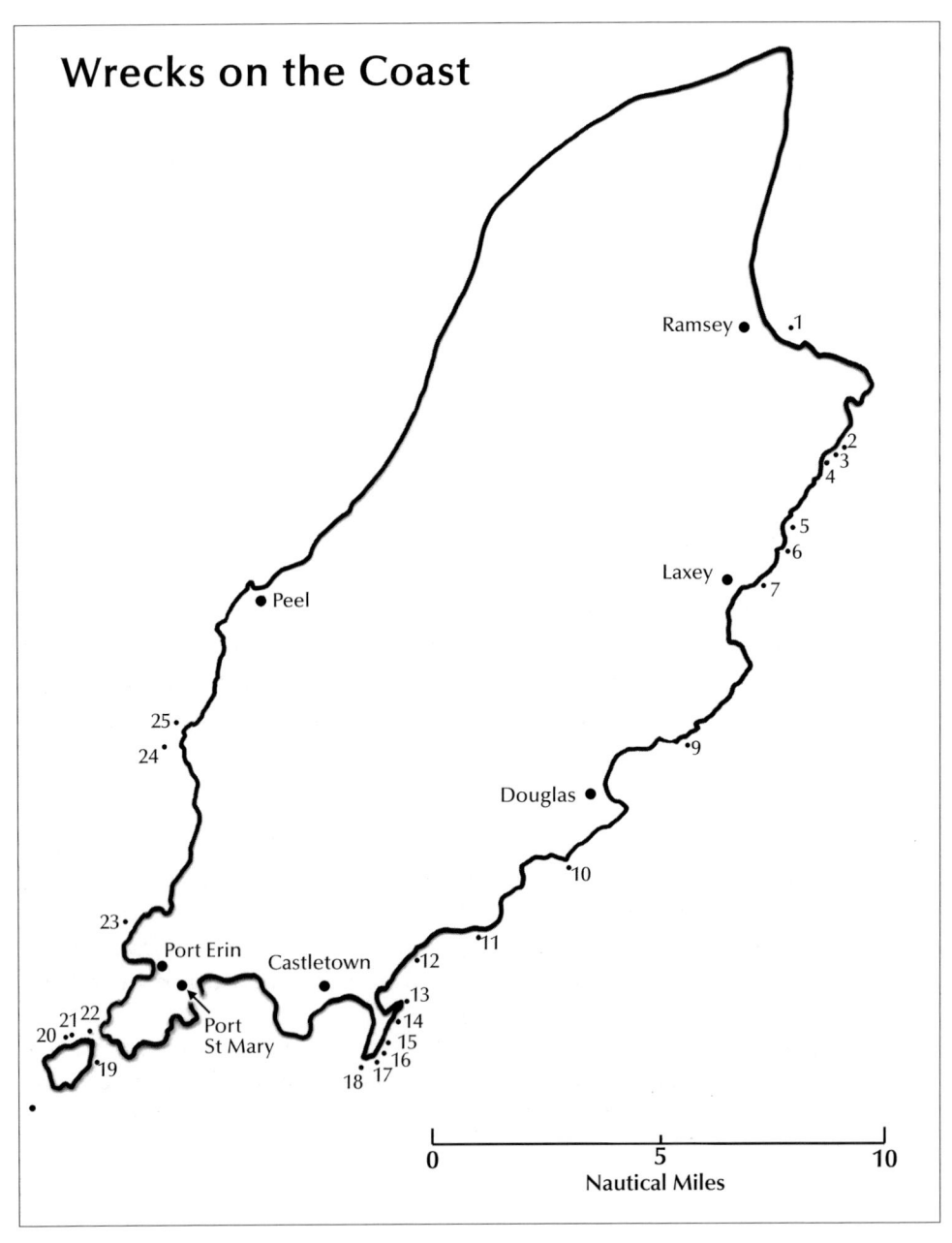

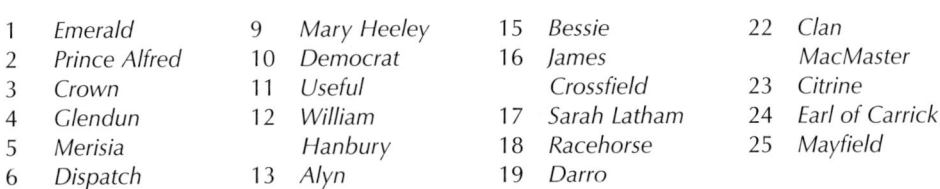

Wrecks on the Coast

1	Emerald	9	Mary Heeley	15	Bessie	22	Clan MacMaster
2	Prince Alfred	10	Democrat	16	James Crossfield	23	Citrine
3	Crown	11	Useful	17	Sarah Latham	24	Earl of Carrick
4	Glendun	12	William Hanbury	18	Racehorse	25	Mayfield
5	Merisia	13	Alyn	19	Darro		
6	Dispatch	14	Madge Wildfire	20	Mary Barrow		
7	Dunrobin			21	Incentive		
8	North British						

Wrecks on the Coast

Alyn

Depth: 5m
Position: 54 04.470 N, 04 36.180 W
Datum: WGS84
Location: Chapel Gullet, Fort Island
Access: Port St Mary (5.2n.m.) and Douglas (6.4n.m.) slipways at all stages of the tide. Castletown (3.3n.m.) slipway three hours either side of high water.

Vessel

The steel steamship *Alyn*, of Liverpool, 350 gross tons, 133 tons net, was built in 1909 by G. Brown & Co. at the Garvel Shipyard, in Greenock, (Yard Number 53) and completed for Hamilton Shipping Co. Ltd (S. Snoddy, managers). During 1911, the *Alyn* was purchased by the Zillah Shipping and Carrying Co. Ltd (W.S. Savage Ltd, managers), of Liverpool. The *Alyn* was 142.1ft in length, had a beam of 23.6ft and a draught of 9.8ft (43.3m x 7.2m x 3m).

She was powered by a single-ended manually stoked boiler raising a steam pressure of 130psi feeding a compound steam engine developing 74rhp and built by Gauldie, Gillespie & Co., of Glasgow. She had no electrical system and relied upon oil lamp illumination.

History

On 16 March 1940, the *Alyn* left Preston for an overnight voyage to Belfast with a cargo of coal. It was pitch black and drizzle fell. At 1.25 a.m. on 17 March, she ran onto the rocks at Fort Island, off Langness, a few hundred yards south-east of the Fort. The vessel's stern veered to port, her propeller still turning and fouling the rocks, shearing off the blades. By this point in the Second World War, all navigation lights, including Langness Light, had been turned off. This made journeys such as this extremely perilous for ships and their crews.

Alyn leaving Preston Docks. (Copyright: William H. Sleigh)

Her master, Captain Harry Ashcroft, immediately gave the order to send distress signals and after a while received an answer back from the shore, 'Hold on, assistance is coming'. Crewmen George William Jennings, William Henry Crebbin, James Marsh and William Marsh were on a raft on the 'house top' (the top of the superstructure), when a wave washed them and the raft overboard. They all managed to cling to the raft, which floated between the ship and the rocks for about twenty minutes.

Mr Scott, of Derbyhaven, had been awoken by the blowing of the ship's whistle and made his way to the scene, leaving his house at 1.45 a.m. No assistance was possible until the arrival of the Castletown Rocket Corps. Mr Scott called to the master to ask if he could get a line across, but the master said that was not possible.

At 3.00 a.m. when the Rocket Corps arrived, Mr Scott noticed the raft. He called to the other helpers to bring him a rope, but, owing to the high wind, he could not be understood. He made his way back to the Rocket Corp's lorry and was handed a rope. He went back to the rocks, accompanied by Mr Thomas Cubbon, but when they arrived the raft was aground on the rocks, separated from the rescuers by a gulley. One of the occupants of the raft was standing on the rocks and was assisted out of danger by Mr Scott. There were still two men on the raft and Mr Scott tried to get them off by tying the rope around his waist and handing one end to Thomas Cubbon. Having got as near as possible to the raft, he threw the other end to the two men, telling them to hold on to it and move towards him. They were either too exhausted to do this or they couldn't understand him and they instead tied the rope to the raft. The next wave washed both the men and the raft into the sea and that was the last Mr Scott saw of them. The two men who lost their lives were James Marsh and his son William Marsh, both of Liverpool.

The wreck of *Alyn* submerged at high water. (Copyright: William H. Sleigh)

The wreck of *Alyn* at low water. (Copyright: William H. Sleigh)

Meanwhile, the Rocket Corps, in charge of Coastguard Officer Owen, were preparing to establish contact with the stranded vessel, which was being swept by heavy seas. The first rocket went across the steamer forward of the bridge and the line could not be reached by the shipwrecked crew on account of the waves. A similar reason prevented the second line, which went over the stern, being secured, but the third rocket carried the line across the bridge and the crew quickly made it fast to the aft mast.

In the darkness and under the prevailing weather conditions of wind and rain, the rescue operations were particularly hazardous, and it was about 6.00 a.m. when Captain Ashcroft, of Liverpool, was finally brought ashore. True to the tradition of the sea, he was the last man to leave his ship.

The other four crewmen rescued by breeches buoy were Mark Woodward, able seaman, of Widnes; Arthur Bold, chief engineer, of Widnes; William Fisher, able seaman, of Liverpool; and George Brown, fireman, of Liverpool.

The two crewmen who reached the rocks safely on the raft were William Crebbin, mate, of Liverpool (formerly of Port St Mary) and George Jennings, second engineer, of Cheshire.

The lifeboats at Douglas and Port St Mary were launched and stood by when the rescue operations were in progress. When the rescued men reached the rocks, they had to be helped about 100m to the safety of the grassy part of Fort Island.

The next morning the *Alyn* lay parallel to the coast, about 6m out from the rocks. She was complete except for the sheared propeller and missing boats, the davits swinging out over the water.

In less than a week, the bow section had broken off and fallen to one side. The ship rapidly disintegrated and by late April 1940 only the shells of bow and stern remained, with the main mast and ship's wheel on her former open bridge.

References

Isle of Man Examiner, spool EX35 MNH; *Sea Breezes*, 1986; World Ship Society, K. O'Donoghue; William H. Sleigh.

Wreck Site

Diving
A fair amount of wreckage, including the engine, exists parallel to the rocks just to the north of Chapel Gullet on Fort Island. The site can only be dived at slack water due to the very strong currents that exist a short distance off the rocks. Expect slack water to occur from an hour before low water to half an hour after.

Bessie

Depth: 15m
Position: 54 03.536 N, 04 36.994 W
Datum: WGS84
Location: Langness
Access: Port St Mary (4.2n.m.) and Douglas (7.4n.m.) slipways at all stages of the tide. Castletown (2.2n.m.) slipway three hours either side of high water.

Vessel

The steel steamship *Bessie*, of Liverpool, (Official Number: 113,455), 177 tons gross, 72 tons net, was completed in 1901 by Scott & Sons, of Bowling. Her machinery was situated aft and she was powered by a compound steam engine built by Ross and Duncan, of Glasgow. She was 95.2ft in length, had a beam of 21.6ft and a draught of 10ft (29m x 6.6m x 3m). The *Bessie* was owned by J.J. Monks & Co. Ltd, of 30 Brunswick Street, Liverpool.

History

The *Bessie*, Captain Joseph Edwards, master, left Preston on Sunday 28 January 1917, with a cargo of 190 tons of coal consigned for the Douglas Gas Co. Ltd in the Isle of Man. Owing to the gale force winds, however, she was unable to make Douglas harbour and sheltered in Castletown Bay until 1.45 p.m. on Monday 29 January, when she again proceeded on her way to Douglas, there being a fresh south-easterly wind.

When the *Bessie* was one mile east of Langness Lighthouse, she lost her rudder. The engines were kept going and the crew tried to steer her using discharging tubs to act as sea anchors. Two of the tubs were fastened to a hawser and one each put on the stern quarters. The mizzen and topsails were hoisted and Captain Edwards steered his ship in an east-north-easterly direction. After an hour the *Bessie* had progressed to about four miles east-north-east of Langness Lighthouse, when Captain Edwards closed down the engine as his vessel had become unmanageable due to rolling heavily and shipping a great quantity of seawater.

Captain Edwards then ordered a distress signal to be hoisted and at 4.00 p.m. he ordered red flares to be fired into the sky to attract attention. No reply was received from any quarter, however, so Captain Edwards decided to abandon ship, especially as night was closing in and they were off a lee shore. He considered releasing the anchors, but thought it highly improbable that they would hold given the weather conditions. The master and his four crewmen took to the ship's lifeboat and rowed towards shore.

Mr T. Forrester, of Port Soderick, observed the lifeboat's predicament in the rough seas and he showed them a light enabling them to navigate safely to make a landing on Port Soderick beach.

The *Bessie* was left to drift with the tides and at 7.00 a.m. the next day she was discovered against rocks opposite the Watch Tower on Langness by the Langness Lighthouse keepers who had been warned by Douglas Coastguard Station to watch out for her. The hatches had been washed off and she was covered at half tide. The *Bessie* became a total wreck and was offered for sale. None of the cargo was salvaged.

On the night of 5 March, during a gale and heavy sea, the *Bessie* disappeared after having remained in the same position from the time she had been driven ashore on 29 January. The *Bessie* was valued at £5,000 and her cargo at £300.

References

Mona's Herald, spool N128 MNH; *Ramsey Courier*, 02.02.1917, 23.02.1917 & 16.03.1917 MNH; World Ship Society, H. Appleyard; Board of Trade Casualty Returns, Guildhall Library; Shipwreck Return Book – Langness Lighthouse (1881-1995); *Monk's Navy*, Fenton; UK Public Records Office CUST104/277.

Wreck of the *Bessie*. (Copyright: John Qualtrough)

Wreck Site

Diving

The boiler and other wreckage have been reported to lie off the rocks opposite the Tower at Langness. The area produces a strong reading on the magnetometer and is assumed to be the wreck of the steamship *Bessie*. Michael and John Corlett, of Laxey, salvaged brass and copper from the *Bessie* in the 1970s. The quoted position of the wreck was located by magnetometer readings.

Citrine

Depth: 13.5m
Position: 54 06.294 N, 04 46.184 W
Datum: WGS84
Location: Just north of Bradda Head at Johnson's Bay
Access: Port St Mary (5.9n.m.) and Peel (8.1n.m.) slipways at all stages of the tide. Port Erin (1.5n.m.) beach launch possible near to the harbour.

Vessel

The steel steamship *Citrine*, of Glasgow, (ex *River Usk*), 582 tons gross, 264 tons net, was built by J. Lewis & Sons Ltd, of Aberdeen, in 1921 for D.R. Llewellyn, Merrett and Price Ltd, of Cardiff. She was 165.2ft in length, had a beam of 27ft and a draught of 11.2 ft (50.4m x 8.2m x 3.4m). The *Citrine* was equipped with a triple-expansion steam engine, built by the shipbuilders, which developed 82hp. During 1925, the *Citrine* was sold to William Robertson, 45 West Nile Street, Glasgow, who owned a large fleet of trading vessels of this class. The *Citrine*, along with her sister ships, frequently traded to and from Douglas.

History

The *Citrine*, Captain John Crawford, master, left Belfast at 4.00 p.m. on Monday 16 March 1931 in ballast. Her first port of call was to be Trevor, North Wales, where she was to be loaded with stones for London. After leaving Belfast, heavy seas were encountered and as the vessel was unable to make any progress in the rough weather, it was decided to shelter just off Bangor, a small port about twelve miles east-north-east of Belfast. She lay at anchor until Tuesday afternoon on 17 March and, as the weather had moderated by that time, she continued her journey and steamed in the direction of the Calf of Man.

Later, on Tuesday evening, she was sailing down the south-west coast of the Isle of Man, when she ran into a thick haze and, according to the statements of the survivors, she was feeling her way towards the Chicken Rock Lighthouse when she hit rocks and foundered. Her normal course to clear the Chicken's was about three miles west of the point where she sank.

From the moment the vessel crashed on to the rocks, to the moment of her final disappearance under the waves, only a few minutes elapsed. The man at the wheel discerned what he thought was an unusually thick bank of fog immediately ahead and almost as soon as he realised it was the face of a precipitous cliff, the terrible impact occurred. Some of the crew were below in their bunks at the time and ran up on deck, scantily clad, to ascertain the cause of the crash. It was quickly apparent that the vessel was doomed and Captain Crawford instructed his crew to lower the lifeboat. Some difficulty was experienced in releasing the boat from its fastenings and so they endeavoured to launch the dinghy on the opposite side of the ship. Before this task could be carried out, the vessel heeled over on her side and sank, leaving the twelve men struggling in the water.

Some of the men must have grabbed lifebelts before they were hurled into the sea, but it was believed that hardly any of them were able to swim, with the exception of the two survivors. Leo Warren and Hugh Morrison struck out for the rocks and, after a terrific struggle against the waves that were dashing against the foot of the cliffs, managed to secure a hold and clambered up the rocks to a point of safety. Here they remained, wet and cold, until daybreak, when they succeeded in scaling the cliffs, and making their way across the fields to the house of Mr Hugh Cowley, of Spaldrick, Port Erin.

Word was then sent to the signalman at Port Erin and he promptly sent out a distress call and the Port Erin Lifeboat crew was quickly mustered under the coxswain, Mr Alfred Cregeen. Survivor Hugh Morrison, despite the awful suffering and hardship he had endured, took his place in the lifeboat when she was launched and guided the coxswain to the place where he had left a lifebelt on the rocks to indicate the spot where the vessel had gone down. A search was made in the vicinity for about three hours, but no trace of wreckage or other survivors could be found.

When the lifeboat returned to Port Erin, the services of a small fishing boat and several men were obtained and both craft returned immediately to the scene of the wreck. A number of men were sent ashore in the small boat and on landing on shore,

Citrine. (Copyright: National Maritime Museum)

Divers on the wreck of the *Citrine*. (Copyright: Phil Hutchinson)

they spread out along the cliffs in search of further survivors. The search resulted in the discovery of the body of a man between forty and fifty years of age. The body was in the water, almost touching the rocks and there was profuse bleeding from the face. The man had apparently been dead but a short time, and it was conceived that he may have struggled on to the rocks, exhausted himself and then fallen back into the sea. This theory was supported by the fact that thirteen or fourteen hours had elapsed from the time he was thrown into the water until the body was discovered. It was also noted that the spot where his body was found was less favourable for climbing than the spot where the survivors had come ashore. When the recovered body was landed at Port Erin, it was identified as that of James Black, of Glasgow, the chief engineer.

In the afternoon, shortly after low water, the lifeboat went out for a third time and quickly located the wreck. The outline of the vessel's lifeboat could be seen four or five fathoms below the surface of the sea and the shadow of a huge dark object deeper still was judged to be the hull of the doomed vessel. The actual spot where she lay was about two hundred yards north of the disused Bradda mine workings and about seventy yards from the rocks.

The following is a complete list of all men on board when the vessel foundered: Captain John Crawford (60), master, Baldwin Avenue, Glasgow, married with children; Paul Cameron, first mate, Percy Road, Boscombe, Bournemouth, married with no children; Dougal McGregor, second mate, Kerrycroy, Buteshire, married with one child; James Black (45), chief engineer, Graham Avenue, Clydebank, Glasgow, married, with children; William Murdoch (55), second engineer, Govan, single; Samuel Stokes, able seaman, Emerald Street, Belfast, single; John Diamond, fireman, Old Mill, Ballygollan, Co. Antrim, single; Robert H. Morrison, fireman, single; John Haggerty, fireman, Main Street, Glenarne, Co. Antrim, married; and Leo Warren, cook, Portland Street, Glasgow, married, with children.

The two survivors were Hugh Morrison (27), of 32 York Street, Ayr; and Leo Warren (17), of 29 North Portland, Townhead, Glasgow.

References

Isle of Man Examiner, 20.03.1931. spool EX26 MNH; World Ship Society, K. O'Donoghue.

Wreck Site

Diving

The wreck of the *Citrine* is situated about 300m north-east of Bradda Stack with the steep cliffs of Bradda Hill looming above. It lies a few metres out from the base of the cliffs in about 13m of water on a sandy seabed and is ideal for novice divers or as a second dive of the day. The wreck is orientated on a north/south axis with the bow facing south.

The boiler and engine stand proud from the remainder of the wreckage, the boiler about 4m in diameter. There are considerable quantities of hull plating lying around the wreck site. Toward the stern, the propeller shaft and stern tube can be observed, both of which appear to be made of bronze. The bow and stern sections are reasonably intact, with railings and chains still visible on the bow. Elsewhere on the wreck are winches and even a spare propeller. The wreck can be dived at most stages of the tide.

Clan MacMaster

Depth: 10-25m
Position: 54 03.734 N, 04 48.110 W
Datum: WGS84
Location: Thousla Rock, Calf Sound
Access: Port St Mary (2.9n.m.) slipway at all stages of the tide. Port Erin (1.8n.m.) beach launch possible.

Vessel

The steel steamship *Clan MacMaster*, of Glasgow, 6,563 tons gross, was built in 1917 by W. Doxford & Sons and was fitted with a triple-expansion steam engine developing 568nhp built by Richardsons, Westgarth & Co. Ltd, of Hartlepool. She measured 420ft in length, had a beam of 54ft and a draught of 34.4ft (128m x 16.5m x 10.5m). The *Clan MacMaster* was owned by Cayzer, Irvine & Co. (the Clan Line), of Glasgow.

History

On Sunday 30 September 1923, during dense fog, the *Clan MacMaster*, Captain Openshaw, master, struck the Thousla Rock in the Calf Sound whilst on a voyage from Glasgow to Liverpool. She was carrying a general cargo of some 3,000 tons consisting mainly of motorcars, sewing machines, machinery, coal and cotton and was only partly laden as the loading of her cargo was to be completed at Liverpool ready for her voyage to the Far East.

When the *Clan MacMaster* struck the rocks, distress signals were fired and the crew took to the boats and landed on the Calf of Man. The crew consisted of nine British officers and seventy-one Lascars. The officers briefly returned to the wrecked ship before being conveyed to Douglas by the salvage boat *Ranger*. The Lascars, however, refused to return to the ship but were also later conveyed to Douglas by motor launch. Both officers and crew left Douglas for Liverpool on the morning of Thursday 4 October aboard the Isle of Man Steam Packet's steamship *Mona*.

The *Clan MacMaster* had run on to a reef of rocks, close to the Thousla Rock, in what is locally known as 'The Blind Sound'. This is not the main channel through the Sound, which is used for navigation of ships, so her wreck did not pose a danger to other shipping. The strong northerly wind and heavy seas on Wednesday

Wreck of the *Clan MacMaster*. (Copyright: Manx National Heritage)

3 October did nothing to aid the *Clan MacMaster*'s position and her stern shifted around and, by high water, all but the bow was submerged. Quantities of the cargo were seen floating around the Calf Sound and the *Ranger* was standing by in the neighbourhood of the wreck.

The *Clan MacMaster* was valued at £100,000 and the cargo about the same value. Over the weeks following her grounding, a large part of her cargo was saved, but the vessel herself became a total wreck. On 16 October, the Liverpool Salvage Association reported that the day before, 1,040 cases of whisky, seventeen cases of beer, 308 drums of paint, thirty-two kegs of lead and a quantity of the ship's gear had been recovered. Three days later, 648 ingots of brass, 231 drums of lubrication oil, thirty-four bags of rivets, two lifeboats and eighteen coils of wire were all recovered. Later still, during November, two motor cars were recovered.

Wreck of the *Clan MacMaster*. (Copyright: Manx National Heritage)

Close up of the wreck of the *Clan MacMaster*. (Copyright: Manx National Heritage)

References

Isle of Man Examiner, spool EX21 MNH; World Ship Society, H. Appleyard; *Ramsey Courier*, 02.10.1923, 19.10.1923, 23.10.1923. & 16.11.1923. spool MN496 MNH.

Wreck Site

Diving

The Thousla Rock sits in the middle of the Sound and is easy to recognise as it has a white navigation tower atop of it. The wreck of the *Clan MacMaster* lies across the Blind Sound i.e. to the west side of the Thousla Rock and facing towards Cow harbour on the Calf of Man.

A considerable quantity of wreckage remains, a substantial proportion of which is composed of the twin boilers and engines. The depth around this part of the wreck is about 10m-15m and the wreckage lies on the bedrock. Some hull plating remains and moving deeper to about 20m, the seabed becomes less rocky and there are patches of sand. Here the propeller shaft can be seen and, finally, marking where the stern would have been is the rudder. The wreck is orientated on north-east/south-west axis and the stern lies at the north-easterly end and closest to the Thousla Rock itself.

Pollack and ballan wrasse are very common on the wreck and watch out for the seals. To finish a dive on the *Clan MacMaster* it is fun to drift dive through the Sound itself.

Expect the slack waters to occur about two and a half hours to one and a half hours before predicted high water, and again from three hours after high water to four hours after high water. On spring tides, expect this window of slack to be of a shorter duration. The flood tide flows from the north-west and the ebb from the south-east.

Crown

Depth: 10m
Position: 54 16.457 N, 04 20.022 W
Datum: WGS84
Location: Traie ny Unaig, Ballafayle, south of Maughold Head
Access: Douglas (9.3n.m.) slipway at all stages of the tide. Laxey (4.0n.m.) slipway three hours either side of high water. Ramsey (4.9n.m.) slipway two hours either side of high water and beach launch possible in front of the Lifeboat House.

Vessel

The steel steam trawler *Crown*, of Grimsby, (Official Number: 122,714), 266 tons gross, 105 tons net, was completed in January 1906 by Earle's Shipbuilding Co., of Hull. She was 130ft in length, had a beam of 22.2ft and a draught of 11.8ft (39.6m x 6.8m x 3.6m). The *Crown* was equipped with a triple-expansion steam engine developing 79rhp, also built by Earle's Shipbuilding Co., of Hull. She was owned by

Messrs Moody and Kelly, of Dock Street, Fleetwood, trading as the Crown Steam Fishing Co. Ltd and she cost £10,000 to build.

History

At 2.30 p.m. on Tuesday 6 November 1906, the *Crown* left Fleetwood bound for a fishing trip off the west coast of Scotland. An hour later, at 3.30 p.m. she reached the Lune Buoy and so a course of north-west was set. One more hour later, the master, Captain John Dier, went below with instructions to the second hand, Lyndhurst, to call him at 6.00 p.m. While Lyndhurst took the wheel and maintained a north-westerly course, the boatswain, Charles Wood, kept lookout. By 6.00 p.m. the master had still not been called by Lyndhurst and, shortly afterwards, Lyndhurst went below leaving Charles Wood in sole charge of the *Crown*.

At 7.45 p.m. she stuck rocks below Ballafayle, near Maughold Head, at a place called Traie ny Unaig. The *Crown* struck twice, each impact being severe, before she settled down on a rock. Charles Wood called the master and crew on deck. It was seen that the steamer was making water, so an effort was made to get clothes and belongings together in readiness for leaving. They stood by until about midnight, when by this time the water had reached the decks, and it was then decided to launch the small boat in order to make land. This was accomplished only with

Wreck of the *Crown*. (Copyright: Maura Mitchell)

Wreck of the *Crown*. (Copyright: Maura Mitchell)

Divers working on the wreck of the *Crown*. (Copyright: John Qualtrough)

Salvage steamer alongside the wreck of the *Crown*. (Copyright: John Qualtrough)

some difficulty and the crew of ten men landed in a creek about twenty to thirty yards from the *Crown*. The beach was tiny and surrounded by high rocks so, as the waves were running up the beach, Captain Dier, sent out a party of men to seek assistance.

The party set off and after a while came across the cottage of Miss Esther Callow, which was situated on the Ballajora (Ramsey) side of where the steam trawler lay. Meanwhile, another party of men came across the cottage of Mr and Mrs Joseph Corteen at Ballacannell, who supplied all the crew with refreshments and shelter for the night. In the morning, Captain Dier and chief engineer King went on the first electric tram to Ramsey to report the wreck to the authorities and seek assistance for a possible salvage operation. They informed Mr Walter Burrows of shipwrights Messrs Yeoward and Burrows. Mr Burrows gave them every possible assistance and the matter was duly reported to Mr Hughes, Collector of Customs, who took the deposition of Captain Dier. The rest of the crew remained by the vessel for the day and then travelled to Ramsey in the evening.

Several unsuccessful attempts were made to try to salvage the *Crown*, but during stormy weather in the middle of February 1907, the hull broke in two and she became a total wreck. Eventually, the wreckage was washed off the rocks into deeper water.

A Board of Trade Inquiry was opened at Liverpool City Magistrates Court on Tuesday 27 November 1906. Mr Stewart, stipendiary magistrate, resided, and was assisted by Commander George Massey, RNR, Captain Kenneth Hore and Mr J. Hallett, as assessor. Mr Paxton conducted the inquiry on behalf of the Board of Trade and Mr Kennedy, barrister, appeared for the master, Captain John Dier. Within two days a verdict was reached; Mr Stewart exonerated all blame from Captain Dier, but suspended Lyndhurst's certificate for three months.

References

Isle of Man Times, spool N26 MNH; *Isle of Man Examiner*, spool EX12 MNH; *The Ramsey Lifeboats*, Seybold; World Ship Society, H. Appleyard; *Ramsey Courier*, Fridays, 09.11.1906. spool MN475 MNH, Friday, 30.11.1906. spool MN475, Tuesday, 19.02.1906. spool MN476 MNH; UK Public Records Office CUST104/233.

Wreck Site

Diving
The wreck site lies about 100m south of Traie ny Unaig. Little remains of the wreck, just a few scattered pieces of indistinguishable metal. Maximum depth of 10m and there is little in the way of tidal current.

Darro

Depth: 10m
Position: 54 03.463 N, 04 47.897 W
Datum: WGS84
Location: The Cletts, Calf of Man near Cow harbour
Access: Port St Mary (2.8n.m.) and Peel (10.9n.m.) slipways at all stages of the tide. Port Erin (2.3n.m.) beach launch possible.

Vessel

The iron steamship *Darro*, of Barrow, (Official Number: 27,210), 325 tons gross, 121 tons net, was built in 1859 by W. Simons & Co., of Glasgow. She was 156.2ft in length, had a beam of 21.2ft and a draught of 12.3ft (47.6m x 6.5m x 3.8m). The *Darro* was originally equipped with a compound steam engine developing 60hp, built by A. & J. Inglis, of Glasgow. In 1879 a new 53hp compound steam engine built by Hall, Russell & Co., of Aberdeen, was fitted. Her owner was Mr J. Mawson, of Barrow, trading as the Darro Steamship Co. Ltd, of Barrow. The *Darro* was schooner-rigged.

History

The *Darro* left Garston on the River Mersey at noon on Wednesday 17 July 1901, bound for Larne, County Antrim, with a cargo of 345 tons of coal and her master, Captain Evan Charles Gawne, who was a native of Peel, reported encountering dense fog at the Bar Light Ship on the entrance of the Mersey at 6.00 p.m. The patent log was put over at this point and a course of north-west steered. At 9.00 p.m. the course was altered to north-west ¼ west, the weather still very foggy and the *Darro* only proceeding at dead slow. The course was further adjusted at 11.00 p.m. to north-west ½ west.

Captain Gawne was of the opinion that his vessel was two to three miles south of the Chicken Rock Lighthouse, so took no depth soundings. No light could be seen and no fog signal heard by those on the steamship.

The *Darro*'s whereabouts remained unknown until 11.30 p.m. the same evening when breakers were seen ahead and immediately Captain Gawne ordered the engine to be put full speed astern, but it was too late and she crashed onto the rocks at the Cletts on the south side of the Calf Sound, not far from Cow harbour on the Calf of Man. Her bow was thrust high on to the rocks with her stern in deep water. When the tide ebbed she slipped back into deeper water.

The crew of ten men, including the chief mate Tomlinson, the second mate Baldshaw and mate Frederick Gawne, having spent some time on the Calf of Man, were able to row in the ship's boat to Port Erin, where they landed safely. From Port Erin they were forwarded to their homes by the local agent of the Shipwreck Mariner's Association on Thursday morning 18 July. Three men proceeded to Barrow, while the others went to Liverpool and Wales.

The *Darro* was valued at £2,000 and her cargo at £175. The mate, Frederick Gawne, was a relative of Captain Gawne and lived in Peel.

References

Isle of Man Times, spool N22 MNH; World Ship Society, G.H. Somner; *Manx Sun*, Saturday, 20.07.1901. spool N76 MNH; *Peel City Guardian*, Saturday, 20.07.1901. spool MN415 MNH; *Isle of Man Examiner*, Saturday, 20.07.1901. spool EX9 MNH; UK Public Records Office CUST104/277.

Wreck Site

Diving

The boiler of the *Darro* is exposed on low waters and can be located between the largest and most northerly of the Cletts Rocks and the Calf of Man itself. Other wreckage extends out northwards from the boiler to a depth of about 10m and is mostly covered in kelp.

Expect the slack water to occur about two hours before predicted low water to about low water itself. On spring tides expect this window of slack to be of a shorter duration. The flood tide flows from the north-west and the ebb from the south-east. Care should be taken as the currents flow strongly around this site at times.

Democrat

Depth: 18m
Position: 54 04.497 N, 0 30.044 W
Datum: WGS84
Location: Little Ness, Marine Drive
Access: Douglas (1.8n.m.) slipway at all stages of the tide.

Vessel

The iron screw steamer *Democrat*, of Liverpool, 1,222 tons gross, 794 tons net, was built by Doxford's at Sunderland in 1872 and later altered in North Shields during 1874. She measured 219.6ft in length, had a beam of 31.9ft and a draught of 16.5ft (67.0m x 9.7m x 5m). The *Democrat* had one deck and four bulkheads and was equipped with two compound surface-condensing steam engines developing 98hp, built by R. Stephenson & Co., of Newcastle. She was capable of carrying 1,550 tons of cargo. Her managing owner was Mr Richard F. Bright, of Liverpool.

History

On Saturday 31 August 1878, the *Democrat* sailed from Lisbon, Portugal, in ballast, bound for Glasgow, with a crew of twenty-two men and one passenger. The journey proceeded well and the South Stack off Anglesey was reached at 9.30 p.m. on Thursday 5 September. The light was distant about eight miles and the master, Captain John Durham Thomson, set a course of north-east ¾ north, the vessel's speed being seven knots. Captain Thomson went below, leaving chief officer George Reeve in command on the bridge. At 2.00 a.m. on Friday 6 September, Captain Thomson went back on deck. The weather was very clear, but haze was evident ahead. There were no lights in sight and he had expected to see the Chicken Rock light or Calf Lights at about 2.00 to 2.30 a.m. At 2.30 a.m. he went down to the chartroom in order to measure up the distance travelled by the *Democrat* from South Stack.

At about this time, the second mate, David Owen, who was now in command, observed a fishing smack anchored up, which quickly disappeared from sight in the thickening haze. He did not report this to the master and the *Democrat* steamed ahead, without reducing speed, into what was now a thick fog. Captain Thomson heard the second mate calling out that there was thick fog bank getting up ahead and he ran onto the bridge, intending to give the order to use the lead. Immediately on gaining the bridge, Captain Thomson spotted land ahead and ordered the helm hard to port. He thought the vessel would clear the rocks, but luck had deserted the *Democrat*, for within five seconds of the command being given, the steamer struck a reef at full speed.

The master ordered the boats to be lowered and dispatched the chief officer in one of the boats to locate a safe place to land. The force of impact had stove in the bow of the steamer and within ten minutes of striking she had heeled over somewhat, but not to the extent as to endanger the lives of the crew still aboard. Luckily, the sea was calm and not long passed before a small fishing boat appeared. Captain Thomson was then able to find out that his vessel had struck the reef at the north end of Port Soderick Bay, known as Little Ness (Langness-beg), about two and a half miles south of Douglas Head.

The fishing boat took Captain Thomson, accompanied by his wife, who was a passenger on the *Democrat*, to Douglas so that he could telegraph the owners the news of the *Democrat*'s grounding. By this time the chief officer had returned to the ship and found the master had gone. He and the rest of the crew stood by the vessel. At 9.30 a.m. Captain Thomson returned, having taken two hours to pull to the wreck against the tide in a small rowing boat. There was nothing the crew could do to help their ship and at 11.00 a.m. they were forced to abandon ship as she heeled over until the masts nearly touched the water. Finally, only a few hours later the steamer parted in the middle with both parts slipping off the rocks into deeper water. Afterwards, only about 30ft of the bow was prominent above the surface at low water.

Mr J. Mylchreest, Lloyd's agent, was immediately contacted by Mr Craige, ship agent, of Douglas and arrived on the scene before the ship sank. Captain Robinson, representing the owners, and Captain Henderson, representing the Glasgow underwriters, where the ship was insured for £19,000, both arrived at the wreck within a short time. A steam tug, which had been dispatched on news of the *Democrat*'s grounding, was soon sent back, as it was quite obvious to the officials that the *Democrat* would become a total wreck, being right on her beam ends in deep water.

The following advert appeared in the *Isle of Man Weekly Times*:

W.J. Craige is instructed to sell by auction, for the benefit of whom it may concern, today, Saturday, 14 September 1878, the whole of the wrecked iron screw steamer Democrat, as she now lies on Langness-beg near Port Soderick and about two miles from Douglas Head, with all her anchors, chains, masts, spars, sails, hawsers, lines, standing and running gear, attached engines, steam winches, windlass, about 300 tons of coal, cabin furniture and stores.

The above steamer which was built in Newcastle in 1872, is of 1550 tons burthen. She now lies on her port side on the rocks, partly under water, and will be sold in one lot, forming a really grand speculation.

An inquiry was instituted by the Board of Trade into the circumstances surrounding the stranding and subsequent loss of the *Democrat*. It was held at the Police Buildings, Dale Street, Liverpool, before Mr Raffles, stipendiary magistrate and Captains Grant RN and Wilson, nautical assessors. The inquiry lasted for three days. Mr Tyndall represented the Board of Trade, Mr Wilson appeared for the owners and Mr W. Pierce for Captain Thomson.

At the conclusion of the evidence, Mr Tyndall charged the master with being the cause of the stranding of the *Democrat* by his wrongful act and default, first in carelessly and negligently navigating his steamship by continuing so long on the same course after passing the South Stack; secondly in neglecting to use the lead and thirdly by not reducing speed on approaching the coast of the Isle of Man. He also charged the second mate, David Owen, with not slowing the engines during foggy weather and in not reporting to the master a fishing boat at anchor that the steamship passed some ten minutes previous to the stranding.

Mr Raffles delivered the judgement, in which the court stated that after careful consideration of the evidence in this case, they were compelled to come to the conclusion that the evidence of the master was unreliable. In the first instance, when giving his account of the disaster to the Receiver of Wrecks at Douglas, the day after the stranding occurred, Captain Thomson had stated that he had passed abeam of the South Stack Light by eight miles, at 9.30 p.m. on 5 September. In giving his evidence before the court, he gave thirteen miles as the distance, admitting he had said eight miles at Douglas and excusing this on the grounds that he had given eight miles in a state of excitement without thinking. The first officer, who was on watch at the time the *Democrat* passed the South Stack and who was himself a certificated master, gave his evidence in a manner that strongly impressed the court. He estimated the distance as being not more than eight miles and other witnesses gave evidence to the same effect. The court found on examining a chart and working the vessel's course according to the evidence that, taking the distance from South Stack at eight miles at 9.30 p.m. on 5 September, she would be carried right on to the Isle of Man to the eastward of the Chicken Rock, without making any allowance for the tide. Tide, which was on the flood on the morning of Friday 6 September, would be sweeping around the Calf of Man to the eastward with great velocity, and this would account for her in fact being where she was wrecked. By no possibility in such weather as prevailed could the vessel have been wrecked where she was, upon the course steered, had she passed the South Stack at thirteen miles distance, as alleged by the master. The court therefore found as a fact that the master had passed the South Stack very much more to the eastward than he expected. He anticipated that he was taking a mid-channel course from the Smalls and that a right course for the Clyde, where he was bound, intending as he did to take the westerly side of the Isle of Man. But finding himself off the South Stack so much more to the eastward than he ought to have been on a mid-channel course, he should have taken a fresh departure from that position.

The master stated that at about 2.00 a.m. on 6 September, he had expected to see the Chicken Light in sufficient time to alter his course to the westward. Up to this point, though the court considered he would have acted more providentially in shaping a more westerly course at 9.30 p.m. when off the South Stack, they would have regarded his not doing so as an error in judgement only. When at 2.00 a.m., however, he did not see the Chicken Light, he assumed, as he had no right to do, that he was too far westward to see it and still continued on the same course. He made no allowance for tide and never used his lead, although the weather, which had been hazy along the horizon all night, developed to a fog. The court therefore felt bound to pronounce him in default of careless navigation, to which they attributed the loss of the ship.

The certificate of Captain Thomson was suspended for six months. With regard to the second mate, the court considered that he was certainly to blame in not reporting to the master a fishing smack said to be at anchor, that circumstance should have at any rate passed a doubt in his mind whether they might have been nearer to land than they supposed; though the second mate seemed to be unaware that it was a circumstance of importance, it might have been regarded as a warning by a certified master. The court, however, found it sufficient to reprimand the second mate and returned his certificate.

References

Mona's Herald, Wednesday, 11.09.1878. spool N101 MNH; *Isle of Man Weekly Times*, 07.09.1878, 14.09.1878 & 28.09.1878. spool N5 MNH; *Lloyd's Register 1873*.

Wreck Site

Diving

The wreck of the *Democrat* lies immediately off the tip of the rocky outcrop at the northern end of Port Soderick Bay, known as Little Ness. It is usually best to enter the water within 10m of the rocks and then dive down the underwater rocky slope until wreckage is encountered. The wreckage is scattered around on the rocky slope and in the small sandy gullies that cut into the rock near to where it meets the seabed at about 18m. Quite a quantity of wreckage survives, including hull plating, ribs, part of the engine, the propeller and the stern tube.

Expect the slack water to occur about an hour before the predicted low water to about low water itself. Slack water before high water occurs about two hours before the predicted high water. On spring tides, expect both windows of slack to be of a shorter duration. The flood tide flows from the south-west and the ebb from the north-east. Care should be taken as the currents flow strongly around this site at times.

Dispatch

Depth: 10m
Position: 54 14.248 N, 04 22.071 W
Datum: WGS84
Location: 'Black Boys' Hole' between the Skerrip and Carrick Roayrt north of Laxey
Access: Douglas (6.9n.m.) slipway at all stages of the tide. Laxey (1.5n.m.) slipway three hours each side of high water. Ramsey (7.3n.m.) slipway two hours each side of high water and beach launch possible in front of the Lifeboat House.

Vessel

The iron steamship *Dispatch*, of Ayr, (Official Number: 79,087), 218 tons gross, 66 tons net, was built in 1878 by R. Dixon & Co., of Middlesborough. She was 129.4ft in length, had a beam of 21ft and a draught of 10.4ft (39.5m x 6.4m x 3.2m). The *Dispatch* was owned by John A. Steele, of South Quay, Ayr and was equipped with a compound steam engine developing 50rhp, built by R. and W. Hawthorn, of Newcastle. For several years she was employed as a fish carrier for Messrs Hewitt & Co., of London.

History

On the evening of Saturday 11 December 1909 at 9.00 p.m., the *Dispatch*, Captain Angus Forsberg, a Dutchman, master, left Liverpool bound for Ayr, with a cargo of 150 tons of principally feeding stuffs, consisting of oil and cotton cakes consigned to her owner, John A. Steele.

At 5.30 a.m. on Sunday 12 December, Captain Forsberg went below for some refreshment, leaving only one man on the bridge, Edward McLaren, who was at the helm and steering the *Dispatch* towards the Point of Ayre, the northernmost tip of the Isle of Man. The night was dark and foggy, but there was only a moderate south-east breeze.

Everything went well until approximately 6.00 a.m., when the *Dispatch* ran on rocks, a short distance south of the Dhoon and opposite Ballamoar Farm, Lonan. The looming cliffs were not seen until it was too late. Her forward sections quickly filled with seawater. Captain Forsberg, on regaining the bridge, ordered the engines to be stopped. He and the six crewmen then took to the steamer's starboard lifeboat. They were unable to find a convenient place to land in the locality, so rowed to Ramsey harbour, arriving there at 9.45 a.m. after an arduous journey, the breeze having freshened from the south-south-east. They were met by the Ramsey harbour master, Captain Clarke. Later, the crew stated that they did not hear any fog signals previous to the vessel going ashore.

Her position was such that no large steamer could get alongside and in a short time the *Dispatch* became a total wreck due to a large hole being made in her starboard side. Through this much of the cargo was washed out of the hold and drifted ashore at Laxey and Douglas. The master attributed her loss to the tidal affect on his vessel, which was only lightly laden.

The crew of the *Dispatch* was: Captain Angus Forsberg, master; S. Brown, mate, of Yarmouth; T. Gale, engineer, of Douglas; Edward McLaren, seaman, of Liverpool; J. Crichton, seaman, of Ayr; F. Karran, seaman, of Castletown; and J. Warren, seaman, of Ayr.

References

Isle of Man Examiner, spool EX14 MNH; *Mona's Herald*, spool N123 MNH; *Ramsey Courier*, 14.12.1909. spool MN113 MNH; World Ship Society, H. Appleyard; UK Public Records Office CUST104/233.

Wreck Site

Diving

The wreck of the *Dispatch* lies up against the base of the cliffs at a place known locally as 'Black Boys' Hole' about two thirds of the way between the Skerrip and Carrick Roayrt, about one and a half miles north-east of Laxey. The site is heavily weeded in summer and wreckage is scattered over a large area and difficult to pick out. The seabed consists of boulders and some of the metal hull plates lie trapped under boulders, showing how the site is battered by winter storms. The maximum depth at high water is about 10m and there is little tidal flow.

Dunrobin

Depth: 10m
Position: 54 13.697 N, 04 22.663 W
Datum: WGS84
Location: 'Flat Rock', between Laxey Head and the Skerrip, north-east of Laxey
Access: Douglas (6.3n.m.) slipway at all stages of the tide. Laxey (0.25n.m.) slipway three hours either side of high water. Ramsey (7.9n.m.) slipway two hours either side of high water and beach launch possible in front of the Lifeboat House.

Vessel

The iron steamship *Dunrobin*, of Glasgow, 340 tons gross, 152 tons net, was launched by Scott & Co., of Bowling, Dumbartonshire in August 1885. She was 160ft in length, had a beam of 23.1ft and a draught of 11ft (48.8m x 7m x 3.4m). The *Dunrobin* was equipped with a compound steam engine developing 70hp, built by Muir and Houston, of Glasgow. She was owned by Mr W.E. Davies, of Glasgow.

History

On the evening of Saturday 21 December 1889, the *Dunrobin*, Captain John McLeod, master, left Barrow bound for Ardrossan and when clear of the port steered a north-west by north course, the wind being south-west. The course was kept and progress went well until about midnight, when it became very dark, rained heavily and a heavy sea commenced to run. No soundings were taken, but the engines were slowed. At about 2.30 a.m. on Sunday 22 December, with a heavy sea running at the time, the *Dunrobin* suddenly ran onto rocks below Skinscoe, north of Laxey, the tide being about half ebb. The master was on the bridge and immediately gave orders for the engines to be stopped and then descended to the hold to see if any damage had been caused to the hull of the vessel. Finding water was rapidly entering the hold, he did not order the engines to be reversed in order to try and back his vessel off, but ordered the boat to be got ready for launching. On going forward, however, it was found there was no necessity to launch the boat, as the crew could easily get ashore over the bows, with the aid of the derrick. Nine of the crew gained the safety of the shore by this method and they remained on the rocks till daylight before they proceeded to Laxey. The captain and mate, however, remained behind on the *Dunrobin*.

Captain McLeod thought that the *Dunrobin* must have gone off course, owing to a variation of the compass, which was most likely caused by the magnetic influence of the 391 tons of pig iron cargo.

At first the *Dunrobin* lay on an even keel with two large holes in her hull, the deck was covered at high water and a portion of the bridge was swept away. During the following week, men were engaged in saving what they could and in removing all the loose sails and materials to a safe place on shore.

Before the storms of 4 January-7 January 1890, the steamship *Lady Loch*, of Douglas was engaged in trying to save the cargo and about 70 tons of pig iron was able to be unloaded and transported to Douglas. At each low water the steamer's bows were beached on the rocks while the stern half was left hanging over the water. Before any more of the cargo could be removed, however, the storms broke her in two, leaving the forepart on the rocks whilst the aft part fell into deep water. One mast vanished, leaving two others still standing. The *Dunrobin* was thus abandoned as a total wreck, but over the next month or so more of the cargo was salvaged.

References

Isle of Man Weekly Times, spool N13 MNH; *Mona's Herald*, spool N109 MNH; *Isle of Man Examiner*, 28.12.1889. spool MN38 MNH; *Manx Sun*, spool N69 MNH; World Ship Society, G.H.0 Somner.

Wreck Site

Diving

The wreck of the *Dunrobin* lies up against the base of the cliffs at a place known locally as 'Flat Rock' about halfway between Laxey Head and the Skerrip, about a quarter of a mile north-east of Laxey. All that remains is a section of her stern and some hull plating. The maximum depth at high water is about 10m and there is little tidal flow. What little tide exists flows from the south-west on the flood tide and the north-east on the ebb tide.

Earl of Carrick

Depth: 12m
Position: 54 09.682 N, 04 44.902 W
Datum: WGS84
Location: Niarbyl
Access: Port St Mary (8.7n.m.) and Peel (4.4n.m.) slipways at all stages of the tide. Port Erin (5.0n.m.) beach launch possible.

Vessel

The iron screw steamer *Earl of Carrick*, of Ayr, (Official Number: 22,812), 214 tons gross, 146 tons net, was built at Glasgow in 1855. She was schooner-rigged with one deck and two masts. The *Earl of Carrick* was 144.3ft in length, had a beam of 19.8ft and a draught of 11ft (44m x 6m x 3.4m). She was owned by the Ayr and Liverpool Steam Packet Co., of Ayr.

History

The *Earl of Carrick*, Captain John Allanbey, master, left Ayr about noon on Saturday 19 December 1857, bound for Liverpool, with a cargo weighing about 280 tons consisting of iron castings, machinery, pig iron, wheat, turnips, potatoes and seed. The sky was clear, the wind south-west and blowing a fresh breeze. At about 4.30 p.m. she was to the west of the Ailsa Craig Rock and by 6.00 p.m. was passing the entrance of Loch Ryan when a rocket was observed coming from the steamship *Caledonia*, Captain Campbell, master, on passage from Ayr to Stranraer. It was thought that this was a signal for the *Earl of Carrick* to shelter in the Loch, because of the imminent arrival of bad weather. Captain Allanbey ignored the advice from his fellow captain, however, and carried on.

    At 12.30 a.m. on Sunday 20 December, a single reef of canvas was set, when the vessel fell off to the south-south-west in a heavy sea and a stiff breeze. At this stage, it was thought that the *Earl of Carrick* was about halfway across the channel towards the Irish coast as the Corswall, Copeland and Portpatrick lights were seen by the watch. Shortly afterwards, all the lights disappeared and the night grew worse. At about

2.00 a.m., the sea, which came over the starboard bow, put out the ship's sidelights and the binnacle light was also extinguished. One of the two seaman on watch, John Watt, went to the cabin to relight it (the other seaman on watch being David Bailey) and found Captain Allanbey looking into the compass that hung at the head of the companion way. John Watt asked him the hour, which he said was 2.30 a.m. John Watt then relieved William Lawson of the wheel, the latter warning the former to take care of himself, as the sea was dashing in over the weather quarter, and blamed Captain Allanbey for having passed Loch Ryan. By this time, John Watt thought the ship's course must have been altered from the last time he was at the wheel. At about 3.30 a.m. the ship took in such a heavy sea that John Watt, still at the helm, thought that she would founder. A quarter of an hour later, the captain took the bearings of a light (which later was realised to be the Calf Lights) over the starboard. The light was barely visible, on account of the rain and it almost seemed like a star each time the ship rose on a wave.

All went well until about 4.30 a.m., when at the relieving of the watch, the mate called to John Watt at the helm, 'Port hard' and so he let the helm fly to port. Immediately after, Captain Allanbey twice called out 'Starboard, hard!' and knowing by the quick orders that there was danger, and looking out, John Watt saw land right above him. He immediately put the helm to starboard to bring the vessel round to the westward. At this moment, several more of the crew rushed up to the helm, but suddenly to their surprise the engine was reversed at full speed and then immediately stopped. Exertions were made to get the mainsail down, but this was only partly accomplished. Who reversed or stopped the engine John Watt did not know, having been at the wheel the whole time, but he is convinced that had it not been done, the vessel would have come round to the westward and got clear of the rocks. In a second or two the vessel struck the rocks and then immediately broke into two parts. He ran to man the lifeboat, but was prevented from reaching it by the vessel breaking up. Then he tried the jolly boat, and, while he was trying to get the tackle clear, the cabin boy suddenly rushed into it before John Watt realised what was happening. The stern tackle being cut, the boat swung to the fore tackle, but the next sea carried both boat and boy away. John Watt then made round by the skylights and met the captain, to whom he said, 'This is a bad job', but the captain did not reply. He then made his way to the after part of the ship, where a number of the crew were holding on and whose cries were heart rendering.

John Watt seized one lifebuoy, while the engineer, Alexander McMullen seized the other, there being only two lifebelts on board the steamer. John Watt prepared himself to dive into the sea, but before he could do so a large wave swept him, Ann Cameron, the stewardess, and Alexander McMullen, off the wreck. Ann Cameron appeared to drown straight away as John Watt passed her corpse when making for the land. Alexander McMullen called pitifully for help and John Watt saw him wave his hand as he went down. After being driven for more than a mile and a half, he was flung ashore by the waves, thankful to be alive. He lay on the shore for some time, half unconscious, before the quacking of a duck awakened him. This made him realise that a farm must be nearby. He staggered through a field of turnips until he reached the Craiglea, Dalby, house of Mr and Mrs Hudgson.

The alarm was raised that a steamer was ashore and a group of local people made their way to Niarbyl, where the wreck of the *Earl of Carrick* lay. Several of the crewmen were still clinging to the wreck and ropes were flung to them, as no boat could be launched in the heavy seas. Only one of them, seaman John Lyon, could be rescued in this manner at about 9.00 a.m. The remainder were drowned in the treacherous seas, thirteen in all out of a crew of fourteen and one passenger.

It was thought afterwards that the pig iron in the cargo caused a deviation to the compass and this caused her to run off course. On her previous voyage from Liverpool to Ayr, John Lyon had remarked to Captain Allanbey that the compass was not steering right and he brought up a second compass to the helm. But it steered no better than the first one. The *Earl of Carrick* became a total wreck, with the bows falling off into deeper water leaving the stern fast on the rocks.

The crew of the *Earl of Carrick* was: Captain John Allanbey, master; James Spencer, mate; James Muir, second mate; Alexander McMullen, chief engineer; Robert Campbell, second engineer; Ezia Moon, donkeyman; William Lawson, seaman; David Bailey, seaman; James Watt, seaman; John Lyon, seaman; James Caddis, fireman; James McCambley, fireman; unnamed cook; and Ann Cameron, stewardess. The sole passenger was Robert Patten, of Ayr.

The bodies of James Caddis (27), of Ayr; Ann Cameron (24), of Glasgow; and Alexander McMullen (60), of Simington near Ayr, were interred at Patrick Churchyard.

References

Mona's Herald, 26.12.1857. spool N90 MNH; *Manx Sun*, 20.02.1858. spool N59 MNH; Lloyd's Register of Shipping; Ayr Register of Shipping Number 7 of 1855, 14.07.1855; Patrick Parish Burial Register 1714-1986; Enquest File Number 3 1858 spool GL778 MNH.

Wreck Site

Diving

A small amount of wreckage from what is thought to be the *Earl of Carrick* can be found at the tip of Niarbyl. I would welcome any further information on the wreck.

Emerald

Depth: 2m
Position: 54 18.850 N, 04 21.400 W
Datum: OGB
Location: The Carrick, Ramsey Bay
Access: Laxey (7.8n.m.) slipway three hours only either side of high water. Ramsey (1n.m.) slipway two hours only either side of high water and beach launch possible in front of the Lifeboat House.

Vessel

The iron screw packet steamship *Emerald*, of Ayr, (Official Number: 1,510), 247 tons gross, 151 tons net, was built in 1855 by Alexander A. Laird. She was schooner-rigged and measured 158ft in length, had a beam of 22.1ft and a draught of 12.8ft (48.2m x 6.7m x 3.9m). The *Emerald* was owned by the Thomas Steele and others, merchants of Ayr trading as the Ayr Steamship Co. (Thomas and William Paton & Co., Liverpool, managers). She was equipped with a compound steam engine developing 80hp. The *Emerald* was valued at £9,000 and was insured for £8,000.

History

The *Emerald* departed from Ayr, in south-west Scotland, at 5.15 p.m. on Monday 22 August 1859 bound for Liverpool with a general cargo which included livestock and a large quantity of pig iron. She carried a crew of fourteen men, including her master, Commander James McLean and twenty-four passengers, but was due to stop at Ramsey in order for additional passengers to embark for the final leg of her journey to Liverpool.

At 5.00 a.m. on Tuesday morning 23 August, the *Emerald* reached Ramsey Bay, but, in consequence of the dense fog that prevailed at the time, missed her course and struck the Carrick in Ramsey Bay and remained fast. As there was no immediate way of getting the *Emerald* off the rocks, the crew and passengers rowed to shore in the ship's boats.

The pig iron portion of her cargo was discharged in preparation to refloat her, although the rock had cut a considerable hole in the forepart of her hull. The little steam boat *Reaper* was engaged to convey casks and materials out to the wreck in preparation to tow her off. A large number of sheep were also landed from the *Emerald*, the greater part of which was bought by Joseph Jefferson, of Bermahague, for his farm at Ballaoates.

The hull of the wrecked steamer was bought at auction on 23 September for £410 by Mr Ellis, of Liverpool, an expert in raising wrecks, but his efforts did not meet with success and the *Emerald* was still lying on the rocks on 1 October of that year.

The Carrick in Ramsey Bay where the *Emerald* ran aground.

References

Manx Sun, Saturdays 20.08.1859, 27.08.1859 & 17.12.1859. spool N60 MNH; Lloyd's Register of Shipping; World Ship Society, G.H. Somner; Parliamentary Papers, Guildhall Library; *Manx Sun*, Saturday, 27.08.1859. spool N60 MNH; UK Public Records Office CUST104/231.

Wreck Site

Diving
Some wreckage from the *Emerald* can be found on the north side of the Carrick Rock in just a few metres of water at low water. There are no tidal currents.

Glendun

Depth: 15m
Position: 54 16.380 N, 04 20.121 W
Datum: WGS84
Location: Below Ballaskeig Farm, Ballafayle to the south of Maughold Head
Access: Douglas (9.3n.m.) slipway at all stages of the tide. Laxey (3.9n.m.) slipway three hours only either side of high water. Ramsey (6.1n.m.) slipway two hours only either side of high water and beach launch possible in front of the Lifeboat House.

Vessel

The steel steamship *Glendun*, of Belfast, (ex *Clareisland*), 633 tons gross, 445 tons net, was launched in September 1915 by Scott & Sons, of Bowling, (Yard Number 257), for A. Guinness, Son & Co. (Dublin) Ltd. During 1931, she was bought by the Antrim Iron Ore Co. Ltd, of Belfast (J. Fisher & Sons Ltd, of Newry, ship managers) and was renamed *Glendun* in place of her original name, *Clareisland*. She was 180.5ft in length, had a beam of 28.6ft and a draught of 10.8ft (55m x 8.7m x 3.3m).

History

At 2.30 p.m. on Thursday 15 February 1940, the *Glendun*, Captain Robert Lockhart, master, left Garston bound for Belfast laden with a cargo of coal. At 10.50 p.m. that same evening, she ran on to rocks below Ballaskeig Farm, Ballafayle, about two miles south of Maughold Head on the north-east coast of the Isle of Man. She was badly holed and soon began to take in water. Distress signals were sent out and the blowing of the ship's siren was heard some time later by William Brearley, of Ballaskeig Farm. He was having a last look round his cattle for the day at the time and it was fortunate for the ten crewmen of the stranded steamer that he was outside in a field near to the cliffs. Brearley immediately telephoned the police at Ramsey.

Word of the *Glendun*'s grounding was quickly passed on by the police to the Ramsey Lifeboat Station, and the Ramsey Lifeboat, under Coxswain Comish, was launched shortly after 1.00 a.m. and set off for the scene of the disaster. Meanwhile, the men on the *Glendun* had fired a line across to the shore and this line was held by William Brearley, members of his family and farm workers.

As the tide rose, a large hole was revealed in the hull of the *Glendun*. This, together with the line being deemed to be too dangerous for an attempt to cross to shore, led Captain Lockhart to order his crew to take to their two small boats. In the heavy seas whipped up by a strong inshore wind and in the darkness, the small boats were close inshore and in dangerous proximity to the rocks. Fortunately, they were soon afterwards picked up by the lifeboat and taken safely to Ramsey.

The crew of the *Glendun* was as follows: Captain Robert Lockhart, of Carrickfergus, master; William McClements, of Portavogie, mate; Patrick McKay, of Newry, chief engineer; Hugh O'Hare, of Carlingford, second engineer; William Adair, of Belfast, lamp trimmer; Archibald Kellett, of Carrickfergus, seaman; Robert McCormack, of Kirkastown, seaman; Thomas McKeig, of Newry, fireman; Owen Crummey, of Newry, fireman; and Thomas Birkmyer, of Larne, cook.

The rescued crewmen were accommodated in Ramsey for the night and during the morning of 16 February, the master, Captain Lockhart, with Mr Jas Ramsay, Lloyd's Agent for the Island, visited the scene of the wreck. It was feared by the two men that the *Glendun* would become a total loss and this became reality over the following weeks.

References

Isle of Man Examiner, spool EX35 MNH; *Isle of Man Weekly Times*, 17.02.1940 MNH; *Sea Breezes*, Page 729, 1980; World Ship Society, K. O'Donoghue; *Ramsey Courier*, Friday, 16.02.1940. spool MN529 MNH.

Wreck of the *Glendun*. (Copyright: Manx National Heritage)

Wreck Site

Diving

The wreck of the *Glendun* is easy to locate at low water as her boiler, which stands on one end, breaks the surface and partly dries. Other wreckage, including the engine, winches, hull plating and ribs, either dries at low water or lies in less than 10m of water. This forward and middle section of the wreck is covered in kelp during the summer. The remains of the stern are located off the rocks and are partly buried in the sand at a depth of 15m. The propeller is visible. Tidal currents pose no problem on this site.

Incentive

Depth: 16m
Position: 54 03.604 N, 04 48.771 W
Datum: WGS84
Location: Gibdale Bay, Calf of Man
Access: Port St Mary (3.4n.m.) and Peel (10.9n.m.) slipways at all stages of the tide. Port Erin (2.4n.m.) beach launch possible.

Vessel

The wooden motor fishing vessel *Incentive*, of Kilkeel (N141), 43.5 tons gross, was built in 1949 by J.G. Forbes, of Sandhaven. She was 66.5ft in length, had a beam of 19.8ft and a draught of 9ft (20.3m x 6m x 2.7m). The *Incentive* was owned by Cecil Trimble and Harry Maginnes, both of Kilkeel.

History

The *Incentive* was on passage from Whitehaven to Kilkeel, when she went aground at Gibdale Bay on the north coast of the Calf of Man at about 6.00 a.m. on Saturday 17 June 1978. The Coastguard telephoned the Honouree Secretary, of Port Erin Lifeboat, Mr Rimington, at 6.15 a.m., to report the casualty. There was a fresh north-easterly wind blowing, with a rough sea, as the Port Erin Lifeboat, *Osman Gabriel*, was launched at 6.35 a.m. and Coxswain Woodworth headed south at full speed.

Thirty minutes later, the crew of the lifeboat found the *Incentive* still ashore, the fishing vessel's port side having been damaged, as a result of which she was taking in water. The lifeboat passed a tow-line to the six men on the fishing vessel and, with her engines going full astern, the lifeboat made three attempts to pull the *Incentive* clear, but without success. With the wind freshening and the tide ebbing, and in view of the amount of water being taken in by the *Incentive*, Coxswain Woodworth decided to take off her crew. There was a heavy swell running, making it a very tricky operation, but all the men got into a life raft, which was pulled out to the Lifeboat. By 8.00 a.m., they were all aboard the *Osman Gabriel*, which landed them at 9.00 a.m. The *Incentive* became a total wreck and broke up.

References

Isle of Man Examiner, spool MN64 MNH; *The Story of the Port Erin Lifeboats 1883-1983*; *Olsen's Fisherman's Nautical Almanac*, 1975; Michael Craine.

Wreck Site

Diving
The broken remains of the *Incentive*, including her engine and winches, lie close inshore towards the edge of the boulders that extend out from the shore at Gibdale Bay, on the northern coast of the Calf of Man. The depth is about 16m and there is little tidal current.

James Crossfield

Depth: 10m
Position: 54 03.238 N, 04 37.362 W
Datum: WGS84
Location: Dreswick Point, Langness
Access: Port St Mary (3.9n.m.) and Douglas (7.9n.m.) slipways at all stages of the tide. Castletown (1.7n.m.) slipway three hours either side of high water.

Vessel

The iron clipper ship *James Crossfield*, of Liverpool, 979 tons gross, was built in 1862 by T. Vernon and Son, of Birkenhead. She was 201ft in length, had a beam of 33ft and a draught of 21ft (61.3m x 10.1m x 6.4m). The *James Crossfield* was owned by Potter Brothers, of Liverpool.

Incentive. (Copyright: Port of Lowestoft Research Society)

History

The *James Crossfield*, Captain Cummins, master, left Calcutta on 15 September 1866, bound for Liverpool and on entering the Irish Sea encountered a severe south-east gale accompanied by heavy snow squalls and a high sea. On Saturday 5 January 1867, she ran aground on rocks at Dreswick Point, Langness, with the thirty crewmen, two passengers and the captain's only son, all perishing. No bodies were recovered; they were all thought to have been carried away by the strong currents that exist off Langness. The vessel quickly became a total wreck, one section lying in deep water and the other visible in a gulley at low water. The *James Crossfield* was insured for £125,000, a quite considerable sum of money for the time.

The following is a complete inventory of the cargo, the total weight of which was 2,000 tons: 2,604 bags of saltpetre; 5,161 bags of linseed; 2,000 pockets of indigo; 3,505 bags of bapeseed; forty-five bales of cowhides; 1,796 bales of cotton; 1,078 bales of jute; eighty-five bales of silk cocoons; and one bale of manufactured goods.

In addition to her main cargo, she was also carrying a large amount of specie of an unknown type or exact amount and at the time it was doubted that any of it would be recovered.

Part of the crew list was later ascertained from Captain Cummins' papers, which were washed ashore. It was as follows: D. Marcay, John Lamb, L. Antonis, Natty Antonis, T. Watson, William Murray, J. Wishard, J. Herti, E. Winser, W. Johnson, D. Grashaw, J. Crosby, E.F. Kinsman, D. Cumming, F. Schmidt, W.W. Stowell, – Williamson, – McDowell, C.A. Gustafern, Robert Mitchell, J. McIntyre, – Lewis, – McNair.

References

Dictionary of Disasters at Sea, Hocking; *Manx Sun*, spool N62 MNH; *Mona's Herald*, Wednesday, 09.01.1867. spool N94 MNH.

Wreck Site

Diving
The site of the wreck of the *James Crossfield*, which consists of scattered hull plates etc., was identified in the summer of 1994 by a diver who recovered the ship's bell from a gulley close to Dreswick Point and near to the foghorn.

Madge Wildfire

Depth: 15m
Position: 54 04.155 N, 04 36.610 W
Datum: WGS84
Location: Claberry, Langness
Access: Port St Mary (3.9n.m.) and Douglas (7.9n.m.) slipways at all stages of the tide. Castletown (1.7n.m.) slipway three hours either side of high water.

Vessel

The steel steamship *Madge Wildfire*, of Liverpool, (ex *Jerfalcon*), 348 tons gross, 136 tons net, was completed in December 1905 by the Ardrossan Dry Dock and Shipbuilding Co. Ltd, (Yard Number 202). She was 146.7ft in length, had a beam of 23.6ft and a draught of 9.8ft (44.7m x 7.2m x 3m). The *Madge Wildfire* was powered by single-ended manually stoked boiler raising steam pressure of 130psi feeding a compound steam engine built by McKie and Baxter, of Glasgow, developing 65hp. She was owned by Gilchrist's Traders (Steamships) Ltd, of Liverpool, at the time of her loss.

History

On 1 March 1941, the *Madge Wildfire*, Captain John Fairclough, master, sailed from Liverpool bound for Glasgow carrying a cargo of flour and soap. At 2.30 a.m. on 2 March, during good visibility but with heavy rain, she struck the north-east side of Langness, just south-east of the Golf Links Hotel adjacent to Claberry Rock.

Moments before the steamer hit the rocks, the order was given to put her engine full a stern in an attempt to keep her off the rocks. It was too late however, as she ran on the rocks shearing off all the blades from her propeller in the process. Once grounded, the sea was calm enough to allow the eleven crewmen to leave the ship by the seaward starboard lifeboat. They rowed to a suitable landing place and then proceeded on foot to nearby Castletown.

The cargo was later salvaged and large parts of the wreck were cut up for scrap.

References

Sea Breezes, 1986; World Ship Society, K. O'Donoghue; William H. Sleigh; Shipwreck Return Book – Langness Lighthouse (1881 – 1995) MNH.

Madge Wildfire leaving Bristol Docks in May 1936. (Copyright: William H. Sleigh)

Above: Wreck of the *Madge Wildfire*. (Copyright: William H. Sleigh)

Left: Wreck of the *Madge Wildfire* from the bow. (Copyright: William H. Sleigh)

Below: The engine room control platform of the wreck of the *Madge Wildfire*. (Copyright: William H. Sleigh)

Wreck Site

Diving

The wreck of the *Madge Wildfire* lies adjacent to the rocks at Claberry on the northeast coast of Langness not far from the Golf Links Hotel. The salvage contractor's concrete plinth is still on the rocks and at low water, the compound engine cylinder block is visible. Further wreckage lies scattered about the gulley parallel to the rocks. Maximum depth is about 15m and there is little in the way of tidal currents close into the rocks.

Mary Barrow

Depth: 16m
Position: 54 03.612 N, 04 48.784 W
Datum: WGS84
Location: Gibdale Bay, Calf of Man
Access: Port St Mary (3.4n.m.) and Peel (10.9n.m.) slipways at all stages of the tide. Port Erin (2.4n.m.) beach launch possible.

Vessel

The three-masted auxiliary schooner *Mary Barrow*, of Truro, 168 tons gross, 133 tons net, was completed in October 1891 by William Henry Lean of Falmouth and was constructed of wood. She was 103ft in length, had a beam of 24ft and a draught of 10.8ft (31.4m x 7.3m x 3.3m). She was fitted with a two-cylinder, four-stroke SA oil engine (made and fitted 1934) on the starboard side and a four-cylinder paraffin motor made in 1918 by Bergins Co. Ltd, of Glasgow, on the port side. Each engine drove a separate screw.

History

The *Mary Barrow*, William Mortenson, master, left Ayr on Tuesday 26 September 1938 with a cargo of 230 tons of coal, bound for Truro in Cornwall. At 4.00 a.m. on Wednesday morning of 27 September, during thick fog, she ran aground on a reef of rocks near Gibdale Bay on the Calf of Man. The mate was on watch at the time of the impact, with visibility down to twenty or thirty yards and a calm sea. The vessel was going very slowly and no fog signals from the Calf of Man were heard. After impact, the schooner made a considerable quantity of water, so the crew of five men launched the two lifeboats.

They left the schooner's navigation lights switched on and kept close to the stern of the ship till daybreak. While it was still dark, the mate returned to the ship and recovered some of their belongings. On being able to determine their position at daybreak, they rowed round to Port Erin and when they left the vessel the water was up to the engine room.

The master had about a three quarters share in ownership of the vessel, a product of his life savings. The remaining quarter was owned by a Scotsman in Tynemouth. The *Mary Barrow* was well found and in excellent condition and was worth approximately £2,000 at the time of her loss, but was only insured for £1,000.

Lloyd's agent, Mr Clugston, of Port St Mary, later visited the scene and feared that the vessel would soon afterwards become a total wreck.

The crew of the *Mary Barrow* was: William Mortenson, master; Joseph Jeffery, mate; Peter Woods, deckhand; William Job, deckhand; and William Andrew, deckhand.

Above: *Mary Barrow* (Copyright: National Maritime Museum)

Wreck of the *Mary Barrow*. (Copyright: John Qualtrough)

References

Isle of Man Examiner, 30.09.1938. spool EX33 MNH; *World Ship Society*, K. O'Donoghue; World Ship Society, M. Benn.

Wreck Site

Diving

The very broken remains of the *Mary Barrow* lie on the sand and gravel seabed at the edge of the boulders that extend out from the shore at Gibdale Bay, on the northern coast of the Calf of Man. The depth is about 16m and there is little tidal current.

Mary Heeley

Depth: 12.5m
Position: 54 10.076 N, 04 25.937 W
Datum: WGS84
Location: 'Brither Clip Gut', Bank's Howe, Onchan
Access: Douglas (2.1n.m.) slipway at all stages of the tide. Laxey (3.6n.m.) slipway three hours either side of high water.

Vessel

The steel steam trawler *Mary Heeley*, of Lowestoft, 162 tons gross, sixty tons net, was built in 1937 by the Goole Steam Boat and Repairing Co. Ltd, of Goole and her engines were built by Crabtree (1931) Ltd. She was 101.2ft in length, had a beam of 21.2ft and a draught of 10.3ft (30.9m x 6.5m x 3.1m). The *Mary Heeley* was owned by the Vigilant Fishing Co., of Lowestoft, and managed by D.F. Cartwright.

History

The *Mary Heeley*, Arthur Long, master, left Fleetwood on Thursday 27 April 1950 to trawl in the Irish Sea. One of the crewmen, Victor Long, sustained a bad cut on his head after falling and hitting the winch, however, so the master decided to put into Douglas so that his namesake, the injured man, could receive attention. Subsequently, Dr MacPherson stitched the wound.

This duty completed, the *Mary Heeley* left Douglas at 11.30 p.m. on Saturday 29 April, in thick mist and steamed on an east-north-east course which should have taken her clear of the coast to the north of Douglas. The skipper had just left the bridge when she ran on the rocks. As the propeller had sheared off she must have hit a submerged rock shortly before grounding. An 'SOS' was put out on the radio and this was received by Mr Colby Cubbin, an amateur radio enthusiast living at Strathallan Crescent at the northern end of Douglas promenade. He alerted the Douglas police by telephone who told him that the Douglas Lifeboat, Robert Lee, coxswain, had already been launched and the Coast Life Saving Corps had been called out.

Mr Cubbin then resumed contact with the trawler's skipper, told him that help was on the way and advised him to keep blowing the ship's whistle as a guide to his rescuers. He also warned him against any attempt by the crew to climb the cliffs.

The alarm had first been raised by Mr R.C. Pickford, of Thallooyn-ny-Cree, King Edward Road, who first heard the trawler's whistle when the vessel was steaming through the fog and then heard an 'SOS' message on the whistle after she had run aground. He notified the police, the harbourmaster on duty and Mr A.E. Kitto, the secretary of the Douglas branch of the Royal National Lifeboat Institution, that there was a vessel in distress below the Far End. He then saw flares fired by the crew of the *Mary Heeley*.

In the inky darkness and swirling fog, members of the Coast Life Saving Corps made an extensive search of the cliffs before locating the vessel and the life-saving

Part of the wreck of the *Mary Heeley*.

equipment was about to be brought into use when the *Mary Heeley* was located by the Douglas Lifeboat just north of Onchan harbour. At the second attempt, they took off the ten crewmen. They were given food and accommodation in the Claremont Hotel on Douglas Promenade, Mr William Harrison, proprietor, under the supervision of Mr Leonard Callow of the Shipwrecked Mariner's Society.

After resting for three hours, the skipper and harbour officials went out to the stranded vessel in the hope of being able to refloat her, but she was badly holed and became flooded at high water. The high winds and stormy seas of the next forty eight hours completed the tale of destruction and the *Mary Heeley* became a total loss. An attempt to float the *Mary Heeley* off failed and the vessel was partly salvaged where she lay.

References

Isle of Man Examiner, 05.05.1950. spool MN150 MNH; Lloyd's Register of Shipping; *Isle of Man Weekly Times*, 06.05.1950. spool MN356 MNH.

Wreck Site

Diving

A surprising amount of wreckage still lies in the numerous kelp-rich gullies close under the cliffs. The boiler is the largest piece of wreckage, with many other pieces of her shattered hull scattered around over a large area. A couple of pieces of wreckage dry on the rocks adjacent to the site at low water. Expect a maximum depth of about 12.5m at high water.

Evidence of past salvage activities, in the form of a plinth and rusted steel cables, can be found on the rocks overlooking the wreck site by following the footpath down from King Edward Road to the rocks below the last house. Despite this, copper and lead are quite common finds on this site.

Mayfield

Depth: 16m
Position: 54 10.174 N, 04 44.634 W
Datum: WGS84
Location: Lhoob Doo near Dalby Point
Access: Peel (3.6n.m.) slipway at all stages of the tide. Port Erin (5.3n.m.) beach launch possible.

Vessel

The steel steamship *Mayfield*, of London, 2,632 tons gross, 1,725 tons net, was built in 1890 by the Bute Steamboat and Engineering Co., of Cardiff. She was equipped with a triple-expansion steam engine capable of producing 245nhp built by W. Kemp, of Glasgow. She was 300ft in length, had a beam of 39ft and a draught of 20.5ft (91.5m x 11.9m x 6.3m). The *Mayfield* was owned by Messrs Woods, Taylor and Brown trading as the Woodfield Steam Shipping Co. Ltd, 44 Leadenhall Street, London.

History

At 9.00 a.m. on Friday morning 24 September 1909, the *Mayfield*, Captain Sampson, master, left Glasgow bound for Savona, a port in Italy, laden with 3,300 tons of coal consigned by Mr W.S. Millar, of Glasgow.

The weather was very thick and hazy all the way. The last light seen was that of Ailsa Craig. The fog was so heavy that the officers thought they were close to the Irish coast. They heard a signal and imagined that it was Black Head, Ireland, but it must have been in fact the siren at the Mull of Galloway Lighthouse.

At 3.00 a.m. on Saturday 25 September, the first mate was on the bridge and Captain Sampson was below in the chartroom resting. Suddenly, the *Mayfield* struck on a jutting reef of sharp rock known as Lhoob Doo situated between Niarbyl and Dalby Points and remained ashore. Very thick fog prevailed at the time and it was impossible for the master and his crew to see land. The *Mayfield* struck at an angle of about forty-five degrees and, as subsequent examination disclosed, ripped a great seam in her hull and in the bulkhead between the main hold and the boilers, a fatal spot for any ship of her type.

Upon the steamer striking, distress signals were made on the ship's whistle and, as the neighbourhood was fairly populous at the time, many people soon gathered along the adjacent cliffs. Some excitement prevailed among the crew due to two outbreaks of fire, probably resulting from the drawing of the furnaces. It was feared by the sailors and firemen that an explosion in the engine room would result and there was a rush for the boats. Discipline, however, prevailed and the fires were quickly subdued.

It was evident that the vessel was in serious danger and the crew removed their clothes and other portable property to the shore by means of the steamer's boats. The

Wreck of the *Mayfield* with the salvage steamer *Ranger* in the background. (Copyright: Maura Mitchell)

Wreck of the *Mayfield* at high water. (Copyright: Manx National Heritage)

first mate proceeded to Peel and Mr Jas Morrison, Lloyd's agent for Peel and Customs Officer Mr G. Cooper, at once journeyed to the wreck. It was so foggy at the time that the coastguards on Peel Hill could not see the wreck.

Telegrams were then dispatched to the owners and Lloyd's Agent, Mr D.T. Callow, of Castletown (deputy for Mr J. Mylchreest, Chief Lloyd's agent), notifying them of the situation. A wire was subsequently sent requesting a salvage steamer from Liverpool. Later on Saturday afternoon three Peel nobbies, the *True Love*, *Cushag* and *Water Lily*, returning to Peel from Port St Mary, sighted the wreck and their services were secured for the salvaging of compasses and other instruments. They also assisted in saving such gear as was of particular value and moveable. The nobbies landed the salvaged gear at 11.00 p.m. on Saturday night.

During Sunday 26 September, the *Mayfield*'s watertight bulkheads were evidently giving away before the seawater and the stern end of the vessel began to sink during the afternoon, and then progressively into deeper water. By Monday night nothing, apart from the funnel, could be seen above water.

The salvage steamer *Ranger*, of Liverpool, arrived early on Sunday morning and stood by the *Mayfield*. Soundings were taken and a diver went down to examine the hull. By the morning of Tuesday 28 September all hopes of getting the vessel off the reef were abandoned. A second salvage steamer, the *Duke of Edinburgh*, of Hull, arrived, but she was no more successful than the *Ranger*. The *Mayfield*'s crew were accordingly paid off and left for their homes in England. The hull of the *Mayfield* later slipped back into the sea and sank in deeper water.

A magnetic storm was at full force as the *Mayfield* steamed down from the Mull of Galloway and it was thought at the time that this may have deviated her compasses leading to an incorrect course being steered.

The *Mayfield* had a crew of twenty-four men, comprising: Captain Sampson, master; J. McDonald, first mate; J. Ferguson, second mate; F.W. Plumb, steward; D. Simpson, mess room steward; L. Goodall, cook; H. Pertzsch, boatswain; W.H. Nisbet, able seaman; S. Carlsen, able seaman; T. Boomadooff, able seaman; V. Baister, able seaman; A. Sandison, able seaman; J. Beaton, able seaman; Thomas Browell, chief engineer; H. Gifford, second engineer; R. Morley, third engineer; N. Petersen, donkeyman; F. Jansen; R. Butchart; J. Kelly; J. Keenan; T. Brogan; J. Stewart; and J. Dowie.

References

Dictionary of Disasters At Sea During the Age of Steam, Hocking; *Isle of Man Examiner*, EX15 MNH; *World Ship Society*, H. Appleyard; Board of Trade Casualty Returns, Guildhall Library; *Peel City Guardian*, Saturday, 02.10.1909. spool MN422 MNH.

Wreck Site

Diving

The wreck of the *Mayfield* lies just off the point of rocks at Lhoob Doo near Dalby in about 16m of water. Large amounts of wreckage remain, with the bow still embedded in the rocks. The midships and stern sections of the wreck stretch out from the rocks onto the sand. The two boilers lie in the middle of the wreck. One boiler stands upright and rises to about 4m from the seabed while the other is flat on the seabed. Quantities of the cargo of coal can still be located scattered around the wreck. The tidal current does not pose too much of a problem when diving this site.

Merisia

Depth: 10m
Position: 54 14.662 N, 04 22.061 W
Datum: WGS84
Location: Bulgham Bay, north of Laxey
Access: Douglas (7.3n.m.) slipway at all stages of the tide. Laxey (1.7n.m.) slipway three hours either side of high water. Ramsey (6.8n.m.) slipway two hours either side of high water and beach launch possible in front of the Lifeboat House.

Vessel

The steel steam trawler *Merisia*, of Fleetwood (FD153), 286 tons gross, was built in 1912 by Cochrane & Sons, of Selby, and the triple-expansion engine was built by Amos and Smith Ltd, of Hull. She was 130ft in length, had a beam of 23.5ft and a draught of 12.5ft (39.6m x 7.2m x 3.8m). At the time of her loss she was owned by the Fleetwood Steam Fishing Co. Ltd.

History

The *Merisia* left Fleetwood at 2.15 p.m. on 21 January 1940 for a deep sea fishing trip in home waters. Only the day before, Captain Edgar Neave and the crew of the *Merisia* had received awards and testimonials from the owners of the Dutch ship *Sliedrecht*, lost the previous November due to enemy action, five of whose crew the *Merisia* had rescued after being in a small boat for several days.

That night the *Merisia* was caught in a south-east gale accompanied by a snowstorm and ran aground on rocks in Bulgham Bay, it being low water at the time. First news of the wreck was received in Ramsey through villagers who had heard the trawler's hull grating on the rocks and hurried down to the shore to locate the vessel. The villagers were in communication with the *Merisia*'s crew and soon learned of the crew's serious position.

At Ramsey Lifeboat house it was decided that it was impossible to launch the lifeboat because of the stormy sea generated by the onshore wind. The Douglas Lifeboat was out of commission and so the Port St Mary Lifeboat was launched soon after receiving communication at 8.30 p.m. It took the Port St Mary Lifeboat two hours to reach the scene, but Coxswain George Kelly could see nothing of the wreck in the darkness and he deemed it too risky to approach too close to the rocks in the dreadful weather conditions. Later, it was generally considered that no lifeboat could have made contact with the trawler because of her position on the rocks.

Meanwhile, Ramsey Rocket Brigade, with district officer P. Kershane in charge, proceeded by road, and, upon arrival, it was seen at once the great difficulty they would have in trying to effect a rescue. Members of the Brigade would have to be lowered down the cliff face to a position from which they could work and then their apparatus would have to be sent down separately.

Meanwhile, the tide was rising and the decks of the *Merisia* were awash and huge seas were breaking over her. She was badly holed and quickly filled with water on the rising tide. The crew of twelve men, in their desperate plight, climbed up the rigging and desperately hung on, but continued to be swept by huge waves.

Mr Crummey, of the Ramsey Coastguard, led his team down the 600ft high cliff face with part of the light saving gear weighing about seventy pounds. When about halfway down, the line box, containing the line and rocket pistol, broke away and rolled down the cliffs to where it could not be found until the next day.

From the bottom of the cliffs Mr Crummey signalled to Mr Keshane at the top for the heavy apparatus to be sent down. The fog was very thick and prevented the signal from being seen. Mr Crummey, therefore, had to send a messenger to the top of the cliff. This was at 10.00 p.m. and in the meantime an attempt had been made to send a line from the top of the cliffs. A rocket was fired, but the wind was so strong that the line was blown back.

It was 11.45 p.m. by the time the heavy gear was brought down to the bottom and a rocket was fired. At this time, visibility was only ten yards and in firing the rocket, Mr Crummey had to be guided by shouts from the men on the trawler. After firing the line it was found that the trawler men had not secured it and the line was pulled back in.

At 12.45 a.m. on 22 January, visibility was slightly clearer to the south-west and Mr Crummey scrambled along the foot of the cliffs to the north-west with the object of silhouetting the vessel against the skyline. He was able then to make out the vessel, at least to discern one of the masts and part of the funnel. He returned to the firing position and another rocket was fired at 1.15 a.m. At that time there was still one man on the mast. The line was shot across the vessel, between the foremast and funnel, but yet again was not secured to the vessel and was washed back to shore by the waves.

By 2.30 a.m., the man on the mast was calling only faintly and Mr Crummey was preparing a third rocket, but the man disappeared into the sea before it was sent. At 2.45 a.m. he signalled to Mr Keshane at the top that all the men had been swept off the *Merisia* and drowned. The men at the cliff face then searched along the shore,

Merisia. (Copyright: Jim Porter)

but could find no one who had been washed ashore. At 3.20 a.m., they started to collect their gear and return home.

Seven of the men who were lost left widows, and many children were left fatherless. The crew of the *Merisia* was Edgar Neave (50), master, 47 Abercomby Road, Fleetwood; Hector Neave (20), 19 Elm Street, Fleetwood; George Neave (45), mate, 19 Elm Street, Fleetwood; William Hannon (36), 4 Shed Street, Oswaldtwistle; Edward Crellin (31), 118 Radcliffe Road, Fleetwood; James Mountford (45), Seaman's Mission, Fleetwood; Charles Mansell (18), Seaman's Mission, Fleetwood; Thomas Harrison (29), boatswain, 32 Belmont Road, Fleetwood; Richard Bennett (37), 80 Beach Road, Fleetwood; James Dryer (44), 52 Mowbray Road, Fleetwood; Bernhard Hearty (41), chief engineer, 137 Shakespeare Road, Fleetwood; John Millet (39), second engineer, 13 Church Street, Fleetwood. The bodies of Edgar Neave, Hector Neave, Edward Crellin, Charles Mansell, James Mountford and William Hannon were found washed up on the shoreline the following day.

References

Isle of Man Examiner, spool EX34 MNH; *Fleetwood's Fishing Industry*, Horsley and Hirst; *Isle of Man Times*, 03.02.1940. MNH; *Ramsey Courier*, Friday, 02.02.1940; World Ship Society, K. O'Donoghue.

Wreck Site

Diving

The wreck of the *Merisia* lies in 10m or less of water at the bottom of the high cliffs at Bulgham Bay. The seabed is mostly rocky with gullies criss-crossing the site. The boiler and engine lie at the centre of the wreckage and are relatively intact. Large amounts of hull plating lie around the site, along with winches, bollards and chains. There are also a couple of portholes still securely fixed into metal plating. Over the last ten years, items such as the ship's brass steam whistle and compass have been located.

North British

Depth: 15m
Position: 54 11.869 N, 04 23.225 W
Datum: WGS84
Location: Clay Head
Access: Douglas (4.5n.m.) slipway at all stages of the tide. Laxey (1.6n.m.) slipway three hours either side of high water.

Vessel

The iron schooner-rigged steamship *North British*, of Ardrossan, (Official Number: 67,492), 526 tons gross, 319 tons net, was built by Barclay at Glasgow in 1871. She was 201.5ft in length, had a beam of 26.1ft and a draught of 13.1ft (61.4m x 8m x 4m). The *North British* was owned by the Ardrossan Shipping Co. whose shareholders were Mr Robert Henderson and Mr Moffat. The *North British* had been built for them to replace their former steamer *Countess of Eglinton*, which had been lost on Langness on 14 July 1871. The *North British* was fitted with two vertical compound engines, developing 72hp that gave her a top speed of twelve knots. She had a main bridge, on which was located the wheelhouse and a few feet above it was located the monkey bridge. She also had a wheel aft, but she was invariably steered from the wheel amidships.

History

The *North British* was normally employed in carrying passengers and goods between Silloth and Dublin, calling at Whitehaven and Douglas on the way, and had a certificate to that effect from the Board of Trade.

The vessel left Silloth on the night of Saturday 19 July 1879 at about 10.20 p.m., with a crew of twenty-three hands. She had about forty passengers and a general cargo, bound for Dublin. The cargo included about seventy-five sheep, a quantity of malt and 30 tons of Plaster of Paris. The tide was then at flood and there was a gentle breeze from the south. The weather was described as 'exceedingly fine'.

She proceeded safely on her voyage and called at Whitehaven about 12.50 a.m. on Sunday morning 20 July, where she took board on three more passengers. The course to be steered was given by the ship's master, Captain Brodie, as south-west by west ½ west and that course was maintained under the master's own direction until the time of the casualty. When the vessel left Whitehaven, she proceeded at full speed. The weather soon seemed to have become somewhat thick with fog, but the sea was exceedingly calm. No land was visible almost from the time they left Whitehaven.

At 4.00 a.m. on Sunday 20 July, the fog increased and became so dense that the master directed the engines to be slowed. The vessel's speed was thus reduced to between three and four knots. A little after 4.00 a.m. the master appears to have considered that he was about two miles from land. This was mere conjecture, because he seemed to have taken no means to verify the position of the ship either then or afterwards. In the midst of the dense fog and in the knowledge of the master of the *North British* being so near to the land, the vessel was kept going at her reduced speed. The lead was not used then, or during the morning at any time. It was the chief mate Mr Douglas' watch from the time of passing the Solway Lightship to the time of the casualty and that officer was on the deck the whole time. At the same time, the course was given and continued and the vessel's speed was personally regulated by the master.

About 4.15 a.m., land was suddenly observed on the starboard bow of the helm. By the master's orders, the *North British* was put hard to starboard and the engines were reversed full speed. Before an appreciable way could be taken off the vessel, she went on the rocks at Clay Head, remained fast and suffered considerable damage to her hull. She rapidly commenced filling with water after stranding, but the passengers and luggage were got ashore safely and nearly all the livestock was saved.

Mr Robert Henderson, the registered managing owner of the vessel, deponed at the Board of Trade Inquiry at Glasgow on 11 August that at the time she left on her last voyage she was in thoroughly good condition and was well found. She had been overhauled the previous May. Her last valuation was a private valuation and was given as £15,000. She was insured for £12,000. The value of her cargo was estimated at £3,500. Captain Brodie had been in service of the company since 1873 as a second mate, chief mate and master. He was, in the opinion of the directors of the company, a steady, sober and careful man.

Captain Brodie was examined next and gave evidence in line with Mr Douglas' statement. He considered the crew of twenty-four hands quite sufficient for the correct handling of the vessel. There were about forty passengers, but she was licensed for nearly four hundred. About 4.00 a.m., in the midst of dense fog, when he slowed the engines, he had no positive idea where the vessel was, but he believed he was about two miles from the land when his vessel went on the rocks. He did all in his power to save the *North British* and remained on board until compelled to leave by the rising water.

The following account was taken from the *Mona's Herald* newspaper on 20 August:

North British. This vessel has virtually become a total wreck. On Wednesday morning last, by the action of the sea, she was forced off the rocks where she had been stuck fast for several weeks, and fell back into deeper water. She now lies on her side, and only the tops of masts and about 20ft of her bow bulwarks are visible at low water spring tides. There is little or no chance of her being saved now, the stiff inshore breeze will in all probability be her destruction. A quantity of her cargo still remains in the lower holds, only that in the top holds having been got out.

References

Mona's Herald, spool N102 MNH; *Isle of Man Times,* spool N6 MNH; World Ship Society, G.H. Somner; *Lloyd's Register 1873.*

Wreck Site

Diving

The wreck of the *North British* lies in 15m of water just off the tip of Clay Head at the southern end of Laxey Bay. The seabed is composed of rocks and boulders and the tides can be quite strong at times. It is best to dive the wreck at the slack water periods, which occur about half an hour either side of high and low waters. The wreckage is mainly composed of various pieces of hull plating, ribs and stone blocks. One notable piece of wreckage, which was presumably from her cargo, is a carved sandstone block about 4m in length, 1.5m high and about 1m wide.

Prince Alfred

Depth: 17.5m
Position: 54 16.598 N, 04 19.712 W
Datum: WGS84
Location: Below Ballafayle, one mile south of Maughold Head
Access: Douglas (9.5n.m.) slipway at all stages of the tide. Laxey (3.8n.m.) slipway three hours either side of high water. Ramsey (4.9n.m.) slipway two hours either side of high water and beach launch possible in front of Lifeboat House.

Vessel

The iron paddle steamship *Prince Alfred*, of Fleetwood, (Official Number: 27,320), 745 tons gross, 548 tons burthen, was built at Glasgow in 1861. The schooner-rigged steamship was 227.2ft in length, had a beam of 28.2ft and a draught of 15.7ft (69.3m x 8.6m x 4.8m). The *Prince Alfred* was owned by Frederick Kemp and others, of Fleetwood, trading as the North Lancashire Steam Navigation Co. and was operated on the company's Fleetwood to Belfast route.

History

On Friday 22 January 1869, the *Prince Alfred*, Captain Peter McKellar, master, left Fleetwood at 7.47 p.m. with a crew of thirty-one and thirty-eight passengers, twenty-three of whom were steerage and the remainder saloon passengers. She was also carrying a general cargo consisting of such things as linen and tea, consigned for Messrs Henderson and Son, of Belfast. In addition, she had a deck cargo of between twelve and sixteen tons of angle iron.

The *Prince Alfred* proceeded at her regular speed of thirteen knots in very hazy conditions bound for Belfast. After leaving Fleetwood, the steamer steered various courses between west-north-west and north-west till 8.30 p.m. when Captain McKellar shaped a course north-west by north ½ north by the bridge compass, which had a deviation of one quarter of a point to the westerly. The weather was still hazy with a light breeze from the south-south-east. At 11.30 p.m. the master was heard to exclaim, 'We have been away from Fleetwood three and a half hours!' Captain McKellar didn't take his usual precautions of slowing the engine and taking soundings with the lead, however, precautions he always used when poor visibility prevented him from seeing the lights and they were approaching the shallow waters of the Bahama Bank. On this occasion, no such order was given and the vessel blindly continued on at full speed.

At low water at 11.35 p.m. during fog, rain and a fresh south-south-east wind, the men on the bridge saw land, very close ahead and the captain called out, '*Port!*' The bell sounded and the engines were reversed, but shortly afterwards the steamer struck the rocks beneath the farmstead of Ballacannell at Ballafayle near Port Mooar, one mile south of Maughold Head, a position fifteen miles away from her normal course. So great was the force of the collision that the bows of the steamer ran up on a ledge of rock, her bottom was broken in the forward part and, within a moment, there was 8-9ft of seawater in the hold.

For a time, great alarm prevailed among the passengers, but fortunately sea conditions were kind enough to allow all passengers and crew to be saved. Captain McKellar, seeing there was no hope of saving his vessel, and that the lives of those in his charge would be jeopardised by remaining much longer on board, gave orders to lower the boats immediately. Two boats were lowered under direction of the first mate, Mr Cross. Into one boat climbed eight passengers and five crewmen. This boat tried to make Ramsey, but lost sight of Maughold Head in the fog. They then saw the lights of a steamer in the distance, which turned out to be that of the steamship *Magnetic*, of Liverpool, Captain Dixon, master. All of the passengers boarded the *Magnetic*, together with some of the crewmen from the *Prince Alfred*. Several of the crewmen decided to continue to row their boat to Ramsey, then a distance of eight miles. The *Magnetic* waited around for the second lifeboat from the *Prince Alfred*, but met with no success.

The second boat had, in fact, made its way around Maughold Head to Ramsey, arriving there at between 3.00 a.m. and 4.00 a.m. on the Saturday morning 23 January. Its occupants were thankful for the calm seas in making the six-mile journey. There was no opportunity of saving any property. One lady passenger lost her luggage, gold watch and £200 in cash.

The *Prince Alfred* remained held on the rocks, stern in the water, until the next morning, when she slid off the rocks into deeper water. Several days later, only the funnel and part of the stern could be seen above the surface of the water. The *Prince Alfred* later broke completely into two sections. Divers were only able to salvage part of the cargo. The ship was insured, but the cargo was not.

A Board of Trade inquiry was held at the Whitworth Institute, Fleetwood, before Reverend R. Moore and J. Eden, Justices of Peace, together with the nautical assessors Captain Baker and Staff Commander Mayes, RN, of the compass department of the Admiralty, as to the cause of the loss of the paddle steamer. Mr O'Dowd conducted the investigation on behalf of the Board of Trade. Mr Bateson, solicitor, of Liverpool, represented the North Lancashire Steam Navigation Co. and Mr Edelston, of Preston, appeared for Captain McKellar. After the evidence was given, it was decided that the cause of the *Prince Alfred* going aground was the deviation of the two compasses due to the deck cargo of angle iron. Captain McKellar had made over three thousand trips across the Irish Channel without mishap, but on this occasion his error of judgement in not slowing the engines or taking soundings with the lead was found to be unpardonable and his certificate was suspended for six months.

References

Mona's Herald, Wednesdays, 27.01.1869. & 03.02.1869. spool N95 MNH; *Isle of Man Times*, spool N1 MNH; *Manx Sun*, spool N63 MNH; *Sea Breezes*, Page 642 1966; World Ship Society, G.H. Somner; Parliamentary Papers Volume 60 1870 – Inquiries; UK Public Records Office CUST104/231.

Wreck Site

Diving

The wreck of the *Prince Alfred* lies in up to 18m of water off a point of rock at Ballafayle. The wreck is well broken up and scattered over a large area either on the rock slope or on the sand in deeper water further out. The engine and boiler still lie on the sloping rocks. The wreckage on the sand is largely buried. There is never much of a tidal current at this site.

Racehorse

Depth: 10m
Position: 54 03.145 N, 04 38.000 W
Datum: WGS84
Location: Dreswick Point, Langness
Access: Port St Mary (3.6n.m.) and Douglas (8.1n.m.) slipways at all stages of the tide. Castletown (1.5n.m.) slipway three hours only either side of high water.

Vessel

The Royal Naval brig *Racehorse*, 385 tons burthen, was constructed of wood and armed with eighteen guns. She was built by Hamilton and Breed, of Hastings and was launched on 17 February 1806.

History

The *Racehorse*, under the command of Captain William B. Suckling, left Milford Haven on 14 December 1822, bound for Douglas to pick up the crew of the cutter *Vigilant*, which had been badly damaged on Conister Rock on 6 October that year. She made the Calf Lights at 5.00 p.m., with another light being distinguished shortly afterwards, which the pilot concluded to be that on Douglas pier head.

Captain Suckling gave orders to haul windward and reef the topsails, with the brig's head offshore, but before the command could be executed, she struck upon a rock, which they would later find out was adjacent to the Skerranes, at Langness Point. It was dark and cloudy, the sea was running high, and the *Racehorse* was thrown violently against the rocks. Difficulty was experienced in getting the cutter out and every effort used to get the stream anchor into it, in order to carry it out, but the breakers rendered the idea impracticable. It was at this moment that the commander and officers became certain that the ship was badly holed and would not survive.

The cutter was filled with men and, under the command of Lieutenant Mallock, was directed to reach shore to seek assistance. The galley, also, was dispatched, manned by Mr Curtis, the purser, Mr Edwards, a midshipman and seventeen men. At 11.30 p.m.

the galley was rowed into a gulley at Fort Island, from where the men could land and they proceeded immediately to Castletown. At 1.00 a.m. the cutter also reached land.

In the time it took the two boats to reach shore, the flood tide continued to rise and heavy seas began to sweep right over the brig. All hopes of saving the brig gone, the officers concentrated on saving the crew. By now the party from the galley had reached Castletown and help was launched in the form of five local boats. The seas were unfortunately too rough for all but one of the boats. This boat broke through the breakers and bravely headed for Langness Point, where the *Racehorse* lay stranded.

Despite the rough seas, the boat made several journeys to and from the brig, succeeding in getting all the crew off the wreck of the *Racehorse*. On the final journey back to Castletown, however, a large wave swamped the boat drowning eight men, three of them local. The five crewmen from the *Racehorse* who drowned were: John Grundy; William Thomas Bone (24), mate, of London; Charles Caggett; James White; and William Stewart. The three local men who drowned were Norris Bridson, Thomas Hall and Robert Quayle. William Millett, boy, had been drowned earlier while attempting to get into one of the boats.

Amongst the last to be saved were Captain Suckling and Lieutenant Faulkner, both considerably bruised and experiencing a state of shock at the loss of their vessel.

Court martial proceedings enquiring into the loss of the *Racehorse* were held aboard HMS *Superb* on Wednesday 12 February 1823. The following witnesses were called: First Lieutenant Faulkner; Lieutenant John Mallock; Charles Gouch, boatswain; John Curtis, purser; William Brown, seaman; Quarter master Ferguson; and Alfred Cranley, midshipman.

First Lieutenant Faulkner's statement confirmed that given by Captain Suckling, but both statements did not reveal the exact cause of the navigational error, which had led them both to believe that the lights they observed were that of Douglas harbour when in fact they were those of Castletown harbour.

Lieutenant John Mallock's statement finally made sense of the error. He stated that he relieved the late William Bone at 4.00 p.m. The master, William Hodder, and pilot, William Edwards, were on deck discussing the ship's course, with the master saying they had better alter course one point to starboard. The pilot hesitated, saying there was no need to alter course, then changed his mind and altered the ship's course easterly by half a point. After the vessel struck the rocks, the pilot stated that the ship must have struck Clay Head (more than nine miles away).

The master related that the pilot had told him that they were well to the eastward of the Isle of Man as the Calf Light had been bearing north-north-west when sighted. In fact, the *Racehorse* had sailed straight into Castletown Bay from the south and was not to the east of Langness as thought.

William Edwards appears to have anticipated the Court's ruling and had previously submitted a letter pleading his cause and giving various explanations for his uncertainty about the exact position of the *Racehorse* prior to her hitting the rocks:

To the Honourable Gentlemen Comprising of the Members of this Court Martial,
I trust this court will be pleased to notice the following statement of facts and take it into their serious consideration.

I have been upwards of seventeen years acting as Master and Pilot, and never did any accident happen to any vessel put under my charge before – on 14 December 1822 at 3.40 made the Isle of Man (with the wind southwest) but not very distinctly, the weather being very hazy all the afternoon, at 4.10 saw Douglas Head bearing NNE ½ E – at 4.25 turned up the watch and took in studding sails – at 4.40 turned up the hands to reef topsails, and foresail, when the man stationed on the cat head to look out, was without my knowledge, sent aloft, without another being sent to relieve him, in consequence of which the land was not discovered as soon as might other ways have been done. It became about this time very thick and dark when I stated to the master that I thought it would be better to haul the Brig offshore, and go around the Calf to have the channel open, during this time the topsails had been reefed, and hoisted and were lowered down to be hoisted a second time, when Mr Gouch, the boatswain, discovered breakers on the starboard bow, I immediately ordered the helm to starboard when in a few minutes the Brig struck.

I beg leave to observe that the light which deceived me, was right over Langness Point and is called Scarlett House, the Gentleman who occupied it (a Captain Thompson) died on that day so the house was well lighted up which occasioned me to take it for Douglas Pier Light, and on account of the haziness of the weather I took that light to be a greater distance – I further beg leave to state that, that light has before deceived many, and have been the occasion of several vessels being lost.

I have stated before the length of time I have acted as Master and Pilot, and having a Wife and seven children depending on my endeavours, I humbly hope this court will take their distressed state and my case into their consideration.
William Edwards.

The enquiry found that no blame could be attached to Captain Suckling or to his officers, but the master, William Hodder, and the pilot, William Edwards, were to blame through navigational error and were reprimanded.

References

Manks Advertiser, spool N46 MNH; *British Warship Losses In The Age Of Sail*, Hepper; *Lloyd's List*, Tuesday, 24.12.1822; Malew Parish Burial Register Book 1.

Wreck Site

Diving

A search by divers led by Brian King was commenced in June 1968 for the wreck of the *Racehorse*. An area of sea was searched between Dreswick Point and the Skerranes rocks over a week-long period but only one large copper rivet was located. On the last day of the search, however, two smaller rivets were recovered from a position much closer to the Skerranes.

Later that summer, local salvers brothers Michael and John Corlett, accompanied by Brian Stigant, conducted a more thorough search of the seabed around the Skerranes and quickly located wreckage consisting of some ballast and many nails. They were also reported to have found cannon balls, musket balls and one cannon.

Further dives by Brian King and his team of divers, under the supervision of the Manx Museum, recovered many vulnerable items from gullies around the Skerranes. Many artefacts were marked with the Admiralty arrow or 'crow's foot', firmly establishing the wreck's ownership as that of the Admiralty.

The greater amount of wreckage lies away from the Skerranes in a gulley situated about 30m south of the Skerranes and on an east/west axis. The depth of water in the gulley is about 10m at low water, while the rocks around the gulley rise to within a couple of metres of the surface.

The tidal currents are a major feature of this site and the flood tide travels through the gulley from a westerly direction at two to three knots and more on spring tides. The tide is slack on the site during the ebb tide, except for the first hour of the ebb when it runs strongly in a southerly direction.

The gulley is heavily weeded with kelp and the bottom of the gulley is composed of stones and pebbles, intermixed with the debris from the wreck, much of it concreted together.

Many of the artefacts recovered from the site have been conserved and are now housed in the Manx Museum in Douglas. The Isle of Man Sub-Aqua Club purchased the wreck from the Admiralty in 1969 and it is now a protected wreck site under Manx law. Diving is restricted within a radius of 350m from position 54 03. 120 N, 04 37.730 W and permission must have been granted for divers to visit the site.

Sarah Latham

Depth: 30m
Position: 54 03.100 N, 04 37.600 W
Datum: WGS84
Location: Dreswick Point, Langness
Access: Port St Mary (3.6n.m.) and Douglas (7.9n.m.) slipways at all stages of the tide. Castletown (1.2n.m.) slipway three hours either side of high water.

Vessel

The wooden auxiliary ketch *Sarah Latham*, of Chester, (Official Number: 104,478), 87 tons gross, 63 tons net, was built at Connah's Quay in 1903 and was owned by Jones, of Connah's Quay.

History

On Monday 19 July 1948, the *Sarah Latham*, Ralph Ashton, master, was bound from Mostyn in North Wales for Belfast, with a cargo of 117 tons of bricks and tiles. Her voyage originally commenced in Connah's Quay, but she was forced to shelter at Mostyn from strong winds until the morning of Sunday 18 July, when she recommenced her voyage.

She was in the vicinity of the Isle of Man at 12.30 a.m. on Monday 19 July in thick fog and with visibility practically nil, when a force seven west-south-west wind suddenly sprang up. Two sails were blown away and the mizzen mast sprung. The crew found themselves close to Langness, so an effort was made to stand out to sea again using the auxiliary motor, but it broke down at a critical moment.

Ralph Ashton later recalled that:

Seas were sweeping green over the whole ship, and she began to take water badly. The heavy seas made it almost impossible to stand to work the pumps, and in half an hour the ship was down to the bulwarks. Everything was awash. I aimed at drifting to Castletown Bay in the hope of beaching on the sand, but found the ship was going on towards the rocks so we dropped an anchor as a last resort. Luckily we found bottom and the anchor held the ship within a few yards of a submerged reef on which we would have broken up quickly.

The crew then sent up distress signals. The Langness Lighthouse keeper, William Christie reported in the Lighthouse Shipwreck Return logbook, 'At 4.20 a.m. when fog cleared I saw flares about three miles to south-southwest. I immediately communicated with coastguards who called out the lifeboat and lifesaving apparatus.' The Port St Mary Lifeboat was launched and the Castletown Rocket Brigade went out to Langness, as it was thought that the ship would be carried on to the rocks. One report indicates that she hit the 'Skenes' Rock. When the lifeboat reached the vessel, about thirty minutes after the distress signals had been given, the *Sarah Latham* had shipped a great deal of water and was in imminent danger of sinking. Manoeuvring on the lee side, Coxswain George Kelly brought the lifeboat up to the vessel. The crew of the ketch managed to scramble aboard the lifeboat whilst the captain's wife was thrown bodily aboard.

Some reports suggest that the *Sarah Latham* dragged her anchor for up to a mile towards Castletown before foundering at 9.10 a.m. in the bay. Other reports state that she sank within one quarter of a mile of Langness Lighthouse, not far from Dreswick Point.

The *Sarah Latham* a short while before she foundered. (Copyright: John Qualtrough)

The crew of the *Sarah Latham* was Ralph Ashton, master and owner, of 16 Lakemay Street, Blackpool; Mary Ashton, wife of master; Thomas Hanley, mate, of 145 Peter Street, Blackpool; Ralph Gell, deckhand, of 56 Raffles Road, Birkenhead; and Roman Jaworski, cabin boy, of 509 Old Chester Road, Rock Ferry.

References

Isle of Man Examiner, 23.07.1948. spool MN148 MNH; Port St Mary Lifeboat Service Records; World Ship Society, M. Benn; *Isle of Man Weekly Times*, 24.07.1948. spool MN 354 MNH; *Mona's Herald*, 20.07.1948. MNH; Shipwreck Return Book – Langness Light (1881-1995) MNH.

Wreck Site

Diving

The wreck of the *Sarah Latham* lies in about 30m of water off Dreswick Point, Langness. Her exact location still remains a mystery. During 1999, divers conducting a drift dive in the very strong tidal currents off Dreswick Point stumbled across anchors and chains, on the seabed. Following the chains they located the wreck of the *Sarah Latham*, which now composes mainly of a mound of her cargo of bricks and tiles.

Useful

Depth: 15m
Position: 54 05.995 N, 04 33.315 W
Datum: WGS84
Location: Near the Baltic Rock, Santon Head
Access: Douglas (4.1n.m.) slipway at all stages of the tide. Castletown (5.6n.m.) slipway three hours either side of high water.

Vessel

The two-masted auxiliary schooner *Useful*, of Chester, 99 tons gross, 68 tons net, was built of wood in 1879 by Ashburner, of Barrow. She was 89.3ft in length, had a beam of 21.3ft and a draught of 9.1ft (27.2m x 6.5m x 2.8m). The *Useful* was owned by John Wynne, 112 Church Street, Connah's Quay, Flintshire.

History

The *Useful*, Captain John Wynne, master, of Connah's Quay, left Mostyn, North Wales, on Sunday morning 19 January 1947 with a cargo of slates, bricks and tiles, weighing 120 tons, bound for Belfast. She had hardly left the harbour when she ran into a bank of fog and visibility became practically zero. Captain Wynne proceeded down the coast for forty miles until he picked up the North West

Lightship, and then steamed on looking for the Langness and Chicken Rock Lighthouses.

Although there was now half a gale blowing from the south-east, there was no sign of the fog lifting and the schooner was beginning to roll badly. Captain Wynne went to the stern to check the log and found that the line was streaming. Hauling on it, he discovered that the line was broken and that the log registered forty-five miles. He immediately sent his only crewman and son, James Wynne, aloft to keep a watch for lights, but he reported being unable to see anything in very poor visibility.

There was a heavy sea running and Captain Wynne could see no guiding light until land suddenly loomed up on the starboard side of the *Useful*. Straight away the ship struck rocks near the Baltic Rock at Santon Head and heeled over. A large hole was stove in her side and she settled on the rocks within three minutes of striking.

Captain Wynne and his son fired all the distress rockets carried on board in an effort to attract attention on the shore and also poured petrol on the galley and set it alight. The flames roared as high as the masts, but there was still no reply from the shore. Not long afterwards, waves breaking over the schooner quickly put the fire out.

The ship had gone on the rocks at 11.00 p.m. and by 3.00 a.m. there was still no sign of assistance, so Captain Wynne and his son decided to endeavour to reach the safety of shore by themselves. This they successfully accomplished by climbing the high cliffs. They lay exhausted on a grassy refuge until the first signs of dawn, when they searched for a house and finally reached Meary Vooar farmhouse where they were given hot food and clothing by the occupants, Mr and Mrs Christian. They rested all morning at the farmhouse and then travelled to Douglas in the afternoon.

Captain Wynne returned to the scene of the disaster with a Coastguard representative on Monday afternoon on 20 January and found the *Useful* to be a total wreck. None of the cargo was saved whilst the vessel's hull disintegrated the following day. The only item that they managed to save from the wreck was Captain Wynne's Scotch terrier dog.

References

Isle of Man Examiner, 24.01.1947. MNH; World Ship Society, K. O'Donoghue; World Ship Society; Shipwreck Return Book – Langness Lighthouse (1881-1995) MNH; *Isle of Man Weekly Times*, Saturday, 25.01.1947. spool MN353 MNH.

Wreck Site

Diving

Immediately east of the Baltic Rock at Santon lies a gulley where bricks from the cargo of the *Useful* can be found in a maximum depth of 15m.

William Hanbury

Depth: 5m
Position: 54 05.755 N, 04 35.315 W
Datum: WGS84
Location: 300m north-east of Port Soldrick, Santon
Access: Douglas (5.7n.m.) slipway at all stages of the tide. Castletown (4.5n.m.) slipway three hours either side of high water.

Vessel

The steel steam trawler *William Hanbury*, of Grimsby, 204 tons gross, 82 tons net, was completed in September 1918 by Hawthorns & Co. Ltd, of Leith. She was equipped with a triple-expansion engine, rated at 57hp, built by the shipbuilder. The owners were the Boston Deep Sea Fishing and Ice Co. Ltd, of Grimsby (B.A. Parkes, manager). She was 115.4ft in length, had a beam of 22.2ft and a draught of 12.1ft (35.2m x 6.8m x 3.7m).

History

At about 10.00 p.m. on 20 January 1942, the *William Hanbury*, Thomas Wade, master, bound from Fleetwood for the fishing grounds off the west of Scotland, became stranded on rocks at Santon Head. There was a force eight south-east gale blowing with showers of sleet and rain.

At 10.20 p.m. Coastguards at Castletown reported to Port St Mary Lifeboat Station that flares had been sighted off Santon Head and they were told to stand-by. Finally, at 11.10 p.m., the signal was received by telegraph for the lifeboat to leave. The lifeboat proceeded under engine through the heavy seas, not reaching the area off Santon until 1.00 a.m. the next day. All twelve men came ashore on the ship's raft as the Port St Mary Lifeboat was reluctant to get too close inshore because of the very rocky nature of the coast at the spot where the trawler had run aground. The lifeboat returned to Port St Mary at 3.30 a.m. on 21 January.

The crew were taken to the nearby farmhouse at Arragon Veg and were given something to eat and drink. Later, they were taken to a church room for the remainder of the night. About 3.10 a.m., the master Thomas Wade was suddenly taken ill. Dr Stephen was called, but Thomas Wade was dead when the doctor arrived soon afterwards.

It was later reported that the *William Hanbury* became a total wreck.

References

Port St Mary Lifeboat Service Records; World Ship Society, K. O'Donoghue; *Ramsey Courier*, Friday, 23.01.1942. spool MN532 MNH; Shipwreck Return Book – Langness Lighthouse (1881-1995) MNH.

Wreck Site

Diving

The wreck of the *William Hanbury* lies in a gulley about 300m north-east of Port Solderick, Santon, in about 5m of water. The gulley is characterised by a rock at its head with an 'eye' through it. Amongst the kelp, a jumble of ribs and plates can still be seen. At the entrance to the gulley lies the large boiler and triple-expansion steam engine. Tidal currents do not impose a problem at this site.

Above: Wreck of the *William Hanbury* showing the bow section. (Copyright: William H. Sleigh)

Right: Wreck of the *William Hanbury* looking towards the stern from the bow. Photograph taken in August 1944. (Copyright: William H. Sleigh)

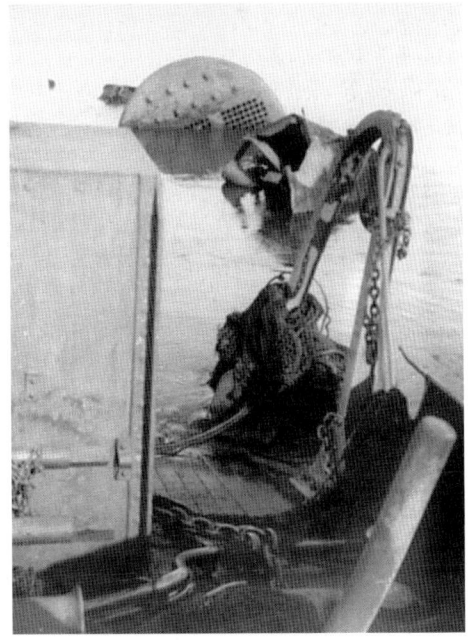

Wrecks on the Shore

1	*Capella*	7	Unknown	12	*Girl Mary*
2	*Cevic*	8	*Provider*	13	*Agnes*
3	*Thorne*	9	*John Fairfield*	14	*Passages*
4	*Grietje*	10	*Lily*	15	*Austrums*
5	*Argo*	11	*Jeune*		
6	*Manx Maid*		*St Charles*		

Wrecks on the Shore

Agnes

Position: 54 19.835 N, 04 33.914 W
Datum: WGS84
Map Reference: SC 330 957
Location: Ballakeig, half a mile south of the Cronk, Ballaugh
Access: From the car park at the Cronk, Ballaugh, turn left and head in a southerly direction for about 500m.

Vessel

The Norwegian barque *Agnes*, of Frederickshavn, 813 tons gross, 752 tons net, was built of wood in 1862 by Johann Lange, Vegesack, Germany. Her owner at the time of loss was F. Ohlsen, of Laurvig. She was 159.5ft in length, had a beam of 34.7ft and a draught of 21.3ft (48.6m x 10.6m x 6.5m).

History

The *Agnes* was three days out of Fleetwood bound for Salpo, Hyrland, Georgia, in the United States, in ballast, after discharging timber at Fleetwood, when she was caught by the fearful storm of 21-22 December 1894 when off the south-western coast of the Isle of Man. On Friday 21 December, the sails of the *Agnes* were torn to rags and the crew attempted to anchor, but this proved quite useless in the hurricane force west-north-west wind and the *Agnes* was swept up onto Ballaugh beach at Ballakeig just after midnight on Saturday 22 December.

    The crew of thirteen men were unable to get ashore. The mate, Karl L. Johanson, made a valiant attempt to reach shore in a small boat, but this upturned. Only with great difficulty did he finally manage to swim ashore with a rope. If it were not for the aid of Messrs T.S. Keig and C.S. Mundell, who, with ropes fastened around them, bravely rushed out into the surf to his assistance, it is doubtful whether he would have succeeded in reaching the safety of the shore. The remainder of the crew could not use the rope to get ashore, however, because of the heavy seas that were sweeping around the vessel.

Capstan from the *Agnes* lies on the shore.

The Ramsey Rocket Brigade tried to get a line on board the *Agnes*, but failed with every attempt and exhausted their supply of rockets. The Peel and Ramsey Lifeboats were launched, the Peel Lifeboat arriving on the scene first and the Ramsey Lifeboat setting out immediately after returning from Laxey, where they had landed the crew of another wrecked vessel.

It was not until 3.00 a.m. on Sunday 23 December that the Peel Lifeboat was able to take the remaining twelve men off the stranded barque, twenty-four hours after beaching. The crew were taken to the Alexandra Temperance Hotel in Ramsey. The *Agnes* became a total wreck and the crew returned to her the following day in order to recover personal possessions.

References

Mona's Herald, spool N112 MNH; *Isle of Man Times*, spool N17 MNH; World Ship Society, G.H. Somner; Board of Trade Casualty Returns, Guildhall Library; *Ramsey Courier*, Friday, 28.12.1894. spool MN106 MNH.

Wreck Site

The main portion of the wreck of the *Agnes,* consisting of her keel and ribs, lies in a few metres of water about 50m–80m from the low water mark. This part of the wreck has been dived by a local diver who has recovered several interesting items from the wreck. Wreckage, which was swept off the vessel as she broke up, lies around the low water mark. The most obvious piece is the ship's large capstan, about 5m in length. Most other pieces of wreck are now buried in the sand.

Argo

Position: 54 06.100 N, 04 32.700 W
Datum: OGB
Map Reference: SC 333 702
Location: Meary Vooar, Santon
Access: Car park at Port Grenaugh, then following public footpath northwards.

Vessel

The steel steamship *Argo*, of Glasgow, (Official Number: 113,918), 675 tons gross, 159 tons net, was built in 1900 at Irvine Shipbuilding and Engineering Co. Ltd, of Irvine. She was powered by a triple-expansion steam engine built by Muir and Houston Ltd, of Glasgow. Her owner was Messrs J. and P. Hutchinson, of Glasgow. She was 190.1ft in length, had a beam of 28.5ft and a draught of 11.7ft (58m x 8.7m x 3.6m).

History

The *Argo* left Bordeaux for Glasgow at about 2.00 p.m. on Friday afternoon 22 December 1905. She had 450 tons of arsenic ore on board, together with a large quantity of wine and spirits. She called at Saint Nazaire and took on board two boilers, which had just been removed from a wrecked vessel. She again proceeded on her voyage to Glasgow on Monday afternoon 25 December.

The Bardsey Lighthouse was passed at 4.00 p.m. on Wednesday afternoon on 27 December, at a distance of five miles and a course of north-north-east was set. At 7.35 p.m. she passed the South Stack Lighthouse at a distance of eleven miles. After the log had read forty miles, her master, Captain James Masson, was expecting to pick up the Chicken's Light, so he altered her course to north by east (magnetic).

Within thirty minutes of the new day beginning on Thursday 28 December, the *Argo* struck rocks below Meary Vooar Farm, near Santon Head. Visibility was poor and neither the Lighthouse on Douglas Head nor that on Langness could be seen. When the cliffs at Santon Head loomed directly ahead, the *Argo*'s engines were hastily reversed in the hope of averting disaster, but it was too late and, at a speed of two knots, she ran into a bight in the rocks and became fast. This was within a few minutes of the top of a spring tide.

There was a heavy sea running at the time driven by a force six south-south-east wind. The waves dashed clean over the vessel so that it was impossible to stand on the forecastle and the main deck was awash with breaking waves.

An attempt was made to launch one of the boats, but it was smashed in against the hull of the *Argo* by the rough seas. The crew of fourteen men, finding escape impossible, remained on the vessel until 5.00 a.m. when the tide had receded far enough to allow them to climb down a ladder onto the rocks and to the safety of the shore. They then had time to remove their spare clothes and some of the smaller articles of value belonging to the steamer.

It was clear that the steamer was seriously damaged and that it would be impossible to refloat her as she lay. The sounding pipes had been forced through the deck and the engine room and cabins were flooded. The fact that the water was strongly

Above: Wreck of the *Argo*. (Copyright: Maura Mitchell)

Left: Wreck of the *Argo*. (Copyright: Manx National Heritage)

Below: Bow section of the *Argo* after she completely broke up. (Copyright: Manx National Heritage)

discoloured showed that the ore, which formed part of her cargo, was escaping through the gash in the bottom of her hull.

Upon getting ashore the crew climbed the cliff and made a fire under the shelter of a hedge. When daylight came they could see Meary Vooar farmhouse a short distance off, so they made their way to it and were hospitably received. Later on, they boarded the steamer again and salved a large quantity of loose material. At the next high water, around noon, heavy seas again swept the *Argo*. The crew made their way to Santon Railway Station and, in due course, the master and chief engineer went to Douglas where they wired the owner for assistance.

Captain Batchelor, of the Liverpool Salvage Association, Captain Dawson, of London and Mr Nicholls, superintendent of the owners, arrived on the Isle of Man on Friday 29 December by the steamer *Fenella* and on Saturday visited the wreck. Nothing had been done to save the cargo, which included a quantity of wine valued at £800. A brig, hired on behalf of the owners, arrived on Saturday 30 December, but even with improved weather, it was impossible to do anything to to save the vessel. The *Argo* was valued at £9,000 and her cargo £8,000.

Later, the *Argo* broke up into three pieces. Her forepart remained above the water, whilst the other two parts fell back into deeper water. Many barrels of wine were seen to dash to pieces against the cliff. Her boilers were eventually salvaged.

The cause of running aground was concluded to be a twenty-seven ton boiler on the fore hatch deflecting her compass, so sending her off her intended course.

The crew of the *Argo* consisted of: Captain James Masson, of Findhorn, Scotland, master; Mr W. Robertson, of Nairn, first officer; Mr Hanasty, steward; Cardwell, of Glasgow, cook; McGuinness, of Larne, seaman; McGaskell, of Scotland, seaman; Jackson, of Glasgow, seaman; Keins, a Greek, seaman; Carr, of Waterford, first engineer; Flowers, of Garston, second engineer; Alvaro Toplo, donkeyman; Lindsay, of Glasgow, fireman; and Galloway, of Glasgow, fireman.

References

Isle of Man Examiner, spool EX12 MNH; World Ship Society, H. Appleyard; Board of Trade Casualty Returns, Guildhall Library; *Mona's Herald*, Wednesday, 03.01.1906. spool N120 MNH; *Isle of Man Weekly Times*, Saturday, 30.12.1905. spool N25 MNH; *Ramsey Courier*, Friday, 29.12.1905. spool MN474 MNH; UK Public Records Office CUST104/277.

Wreck Site

Wreckage from the *Argo* is reported to lie on the shore next to Santon Head, but, as yet, I have been unable to locate it.

Austrums

Position:	54 24.018 N, 04 27.562 W
Datum:	WGS84
Map Reference:	NX 405 034
Location:	Knock-e-Dooney, Andreas
Access:	Park at Smeale car park/turning area and walk down the beach to the left for about 500m.

Vessel

The wooden barquentine *Austrums*, of Riga, Latvia, 390 tons register, was owned by Messrs Buer & Co., of Riga. She was 142ft in length and had a beam of 31ft (43.3m x 9.5m).

History

On Thursday 20 January 1927, the *Austrums* left Runcorn bound for Valencia, in Spain, with a cargo of pitch. The wind in the channel kept changing direction and, after tacking about for a couple of days, the master of the *Austrums*, Karl Berhsin, decided to shelter in Ramsey Bay, arriving there on Saturday 22 January.

All went well until Wednesday 26 January when the wind went around to the south-east. When the rockets signalling the launch of Ramsey Lifeboat went off early in the morning, Karl Bershin thought it was a signal for him to move his vessel out of the bay. This he did, but only after losing an anchor and a length of chain, the result of a hurried move from amongst a cluster of fishing boats. The sea was sheltered around the western side of the Point of Ayre. The *Austrums*' problems were only just beginning. Soon the south-east wind increased in strength and blew away some of the sails. The ship could still be steered, but finally the wind increased to such an extent that all the remaining sails were blown away as well. The *Austrums* trembled all over and the master feared the masts would go over the side at any moment. The order was given to drop anchor and this was done in six fathoms of water between Jurby Head and the Point of Ayre. The *Austrums* was safe, but only for a short time for the wind soon veered to the north-west bringing mountainous seas sweeping over her. The capstan was smashed and the cable broke, leaving the crew powerless to prevent the *Austrums* from running aground on the beach at Knock-e-Dooney, Andreas.

A message was received at Ramsey Coastguard Station to the effect that a large vessel was ashore. Coincidentally, the Ramsey Rocket Corps had just finished a practice session and they were immediately ready to proceed to Knock-e-Dooney with the help of a requisitioned motor wagon to tow the carriage containing the rocket apparatus. The party was commanded by Lieutenant Pennington-Lay, with Division Officer Lace and Officers Hurrell and Sayle also in attendance. For the last stretch over the rough Ayres, the carriage had to be manhandled to the beach. No

Above: Wreck of the *Austrums*. (Copyright: Manx National Heritage)

Right: Ballast blocks and other wreckage from the *Austrums* still lie on the shore near Rue Point.

time was lost in fixing up the necessary equipment and soon communication was established with the distressed ship. One by one the nine crewmen took their turn in the breeches buoy and eventually all were landed safely.

The crew of the *Austrums* was: Karl Berhsin, master, of Riga; Alexander Berhsin, mate, (son of the master), of Riga; Karl Tomasonos, of Windau; August Ulbert, of Riga; Ferdinand Purit, of Riga; Indrik Langer, of Talsen; James Pole, of Windau; Serjey Bols, of Riga; and Eungen Kasak, of Riga.

Soon after the *Austrums* ran aground, she lay on her starboard side with the keel imbedded 6-10ft in the sand. The master reckoned there was no hope of refloating her as the bottom was smashed in. The work of salvaging her cargo began. The steam lighter *Dragon*, of Glasgow, was used to convey 300 tons of pitch to Peel in the first week and in all over 500 tons was salvaged. The pitch was then shipped to Valencia in a Norwegian steamer.

References

Isle of Man Examiner, spool EX23 MNH; *Ramsey Courier*, 04.02.1927, 25.02.1927. & 13.05.1927. MNH.

Wreck Site

Little remains of the *Austrums* today. A number of large ballast blocks mark the position on the beach where she broke up. There is some associated wreckage made of steel, one piece in particular being a spoked wheel about 1m in diameter, and another piece being a long pipe. The most recognisable piece of wreckage is the ship's steel capstan. Lying slightly away from the ballast blocks, it is about 5m in length and about 0.75m at its widest point.

Capella

Position: 54 21.714 N, 04 22.621 W
Datum: WGS84
Map Reference: SG 458 990
Location: Between Ballavair and Shellag Point, north of Ramsey
Access: Join the 'Raad ny Foillan' at the Dog Mills and walk northwards for about a mile.

Vessel

The wooden motor fishing vessel *Capella*, of Ramsey, formerly a well-known local yacht, which had for some time been engaged in the fishing trade, had taken part in

Above: The *Capella* in Ramsey harbour. (Copyright: Manx National Heritage)

Right: Remains of the *Capella*'s keel on the shore. (Copyright: John Qualtrough)

many a cross-channel race and had a proud record. She was owned by William George Cooper, of Ramsey. The *Capella* was more than forty years old when wrecked.

History

The fine weather on Friday 4 March 1949 enabled the *Capella*, crewed by William Cooper and Eric Lyall jnr., to reach the fishing grounds in the vicinity of the Bahama Bank from her homeport in Ramsey. Later in the day, the fishermen were returning home with their catch in a fresh south-east breeze when the engine broke down and it was impossible to get it started again. As the mainsail was inoperative, the *Capella* could not make headway and was in grave danger of being driven ashore in the heavy swell despite two anchors being put out.

By this time darkness had set in and the fishermen, in view of the worsening conditions, sent up distress flares. At 10.15 p.m. a watchman in Ramsey reported seeing a red light off Shellag Point, three miles north of Ramsey. The Coastguard Station Officer was called to the Harbour Lookout and he made the light out to be flares burning close inshore. The Ramsey Lifeboat was requested to launch and the Rocket Brigade Auxiliary were summoned. The mast light of the *Capella* was noted about a mile beyond the Dog Mills, on the Ramsey side of Ballavair, and was judged to be between three hundred and four hundred yards from the beach.

The Rocket Brigade wagon drove through a ploughed field to get to a point at the top of the cliff overlooking the spot. The men, under the direction of the District Officer of the Coastguards Mr Pardoe, took the apparatus down the brows to the shore and lost no time in getting to work with a view of firing a line across the *Capella*. A rocket was then fired from the shore and the line passed over the vessel, but no signals were received from the *Capella* and the whip line was not hauled out. A second rocket was therefore fired, but proved very erratic and only made one hundred yards before hitting the sea and carrying on at right angles to the line of fire. The rocket line then parted.

The Ramsey Lifeboat, *Thomas Corbett*, under Coxswain Ernest Starkey, was in the neighbourhood and her powerful searchlight swept over the wreck scene continually. Sometimes the yacht would be caught in the beam and two figures could be discerned near to the mast. The lifeboat circled around several more times before Coxswain Starkey decided to risk the shallow water and heavy seas which were running inshore from the strong south-south-east wind and got alongside the distressed boat. At 12.25 a.m. on 5 March the *Capella*'s crew of two men, George Cooper and Eric Lyall, jumped aboard the lifeboat, together with the boat's cat 'Joe', and they were safely returned to Ramsey before 1.00 a.m. Watching on shore was Eric Lyall's father, a member of the Rocket Brigade, who must have experienced great emotions watching the lifeboat rescue his eldest son.

The *Capella* was left anchored in about three and a half fathoms of water and when George Cooper came away he was hopeful that the anchors would hold and, if the weather moderated, that his vessel would be saved. His hopes were not realised for the day after the *Capella* grounded, she broke up. The main hulk lay fairly close inshore and another large piece of wreckage was thrown high and dry on the beach. Gone with the *Capella* were George Cooper's livelihood and his occasional home.

References

The Ramsey Lifeboats 1829-1991, Seybold; *Isle of Man Weekly Times*, Saturday, 12.03.1949. spool MN355 MNH; *Ramsey Courier*, Friday, 11.03.1949. spool MN539 MNH.

Wreck Site

All that remains of the *Capella* is the keel imbedded in the sand just below the shingle line at the top of the beach. The remains are about 7m in length. Some wood remains and what appear to be stone ballast blocks fixed to the top of the keel. Even in the last ten years the remains have deteriorated considerably and have become more buried in the sand of the beach.

Cevic

Position:	54 18.724 N, 04 21.759 W
Datum:	WGS84
Map Reference:	SC 462 934
Location:	Below Ballure, South Beach, Ramsey
Access:	The steps by the Iron Pier, Ramsey, or though Ballure Glen and along the beach.

Vessel

The iron steam trawler *Cevic*, of Fleetwood (FD 186), 151 tons gross, 59 tons net, was built by Edwards Brothers, of North Shields, in 1895 and was equipped with a 50rhp triple-expansion engine built by the North Eastern Marine Engineering Co. Ltd, of Sunderland. At the time of her loss she was owned by the Devon Steam Trawler Co. and was managed by the Cevic Steam Fishing Co. She was 106ft in length, had a beam of 20.6ft and a draught of 11ft (32.3m x 6.3m x 3.4m).

History

The *Cevic* came into Ramsey Bay on the Saturday afternoon of 25 June 1927 and in the evening her master, Captain Richard Collinson, along with the mate, boatswain and chief engineer, went ashore leaving seven men on board. They had intended to return to the *Cevic* at around midnight, but the weather worsened, with a gale springing up from the north, preventing the small boat from setting off from the *Cevic* to take them back from Ramsey to the trawler. At daybreak the remaining men on board the trawler decided to try again to get the small boat ashore. So, at 3.00 a.m.

on Sunday 26 June, the second engineer, John Dick, got into the small boat moored alongside the vessel and was bailing it out, with a view to rowing ashore, when the painter attaching it to the trawler snapped and he was cast adrift. It was feared by his crew mates that he soon would be in great danger given the weather conditions. The remainder of the crew, seeing him in difficulties, weighed anchor and attempted to reach the small boat, but failed and the *Cevic* ran aground on rocks below Ballure on Ramsey South Beach.

At 4.40 a.m. the signal for the Ramsey Lifeboat was given and large numbers of people gathered around the Lifeboat House. The lifeboat crew mustered smartly, with coxswain Garrett in charge and John Christian as second coxswain. The very low tide and lack of haul-off warp on the slipway meant that there was no possibility of launching the main lifeboat. Under the direction of Chief Launcher Oscar Corlett, the reserve lifeboat, the *Matthew Simpson*, was run on to the beach and willing hands abounded to haul her towards the Queen's Pier and make the best of the situation. The haul-off warp on the Queen's Pier was normally kept on the north side of the structure and had to be moved to the opposite side of the pier given the northerly wind. Much difficulty was experienced in the launch and it was fortunate that such a large body of willing helpers had turned out to haul the warp. Finally, the *Matthew Simpson* was away and headed towards the wrecked steam trawler at Ballure.

The lifeboat gradually dropped down on the *Cevic*. The seas were now washing over the stern of the trawler and men could be seen on the deck, apparently anxious to get off their vessel. With the sea coming in from a northerly direction, it made the going difficult for the lifeboat, but in no time at all the *Matthew Simpson* had the six men from the *Cevic* on board and was heading back to Ramsey harbour.

The wreck of the *Cevic*. (Copyright: Manx National Heritage)

Scenes of excitement at the wreck of the *Cevic*. (Copyright: Manx National Heritage)

The remains of the *Cevic* today.

Remains of the engine and engine bed.

Meanwhile, John Dick in the small boat narrowly missed being wrecked on the Carrick in Ramsey Bay and landed at Port Lewaigue. He took some hours to walk along the beach and find his way back to Ramsey.

All the crewmen of the *Cevic* came from Fleetwood. They were Richard Collinson, master; J.E. Bywater, mate; E. Salthouse, boatswain; J. Hobb, chief engineer; John Dick, second engineer; R. Sims, fireman; T. Holden, fireman; J. Hitchens, deckhand; T. Harrison, deckhand; G. Whiteside, deckhand; and P. Corrigan, cook.

The crew of the Ramsey Lifeboat was: J. Garrett, coxswain; J. Christian, acting second coxswain; E. Starkey; W. Gawne; E. Kinnin; D. Evans; E.B. Kinnin; L. Martin; J. Kinnin, F. Corlett; and W. Garrett.

During the morning, the weather conditions did not improve and the *Cevic* was driven up further on to the bottom of the cliffs at Mon-y-Don. She lay wedged between rugged rocks and large boulders, with a list to port. On the starboard side were two large holes and other damage. Attempts were made to save her and much of the gear was salvaged. The *Cevic* was not to be saved and, eventually, she became a total wreck.

References

Isle of Man Examiner, spool EX26 MNH; *Ramsey Courier*, 01.07.1927; *Fleetwood's Fishing Industry*, Horsley and Hirst; World Ship Society, H Appleyard; *Ramsey Courier*, Friday, 01.07.1927. spool MN504 MNH.

Wreck Site

The wreck of the *Cevic* lies on the beach adjacent to the cliff at a promontory of rock about 300m south of where Ballure Glen meets the beach. The wreckage is orientated north-east/south-west and is accessible at all low waters. The wreckage extends for 32m, is 9m wide and 1.5m at the highest point. The keel remains in situ, as are the engine beds, crankshaft, boiler brackets, propeller shaft and rudderpost. The whole of this part of the wreck is angled to what would have been her port side. A large section of curved hull plating lies to the starboard side amidships. Remains of the concrete ballast can be seen in the forward bilge sections.

Girl Mary

Position:	54 09.681 N, 04 44.316 W
Datum:	WGS84
Map Reference:	SC 213 774
Location:	Traie Vrish, south of Niarbyl
Access:	Car park at Niarbyl beach and follow the public footpath south-westwards

Girl Mary. (Copyright: Michael Craine)

Wreck of the *Girl Mary*.

Vessel

The wooden motor fishing vessel *Girl Mary*, of Peel (PL45), twelve tons register, was built in 1946 by Tyrells, of Arklow. At the time of her loss she was owned by Maynard Campbell, of Peel. She was 49ft in length, had a beam of 15ft and a draught of 5ft (14.9m x 4.6m x 1.5m).

History

At 1.05 a.m. on Friday 1 May 1992, David O'Connell, skipper of the *Girl Mary*, radioed coastguards at Liverpool that she had run aground on a falling tide and was taking in water. Port Erin Lifeboat was launched at 1.34 a.m. and Peel and Port Erin coastguard rescue companies attended the scene at Elby Point near Niarbyl. A successful rescue operation was effected despite the onshore force-six north-westerly winds. The crewman, Frank Christian, was taken off the trawler by an inflatable launched from the lifeboat and the skipper was helped ashore over the rocks. The cause of the grounding was uncertain, but the crew had thought they were three miles off land when in fact they must have been nearer to a quarter of a mile off the rocks at Niarbyl.

It was hoped that they could salvage the vessel at high water the same day, but she drifted off the rocks and ran shore again about five-hundred yards across the bay towards Eairy Cushlin at Traie Vrish, where she sustained extensive structural damage and became a total wreck.

References

Manx Independent, Tuesday, 05.05.1992; *Isle of Man Examiner*, Tuesday, 05.05.1992; Michael Craine 14.02.1996; *The History of the Port Erin Lifeboats*, Morris.

Wreck Site

The remains of the *Girl Mary* lie scattered on the boulder-strewn beach at Traie Vrish. The winch is discernible together with the propeller shaft, gearbox and part of the engine. The rest of the metal parts on the beach come from the gantries etc. The top of the wheelhouse, which was also steel, lies around the rocks in a separate gulley.

Grietje

Position: 54 07.657 N, 04 30.752 W
Datum: WGS84
Map Reference: SC 360 731
Location: Keristal, near Port Soderick
Access: Not recommended except by boat landing on the shingle beach.

Vessel

The steel motor vessel *Grietje* (ex *Amasus Fluvius*), of Groningen, 296 tons gross, 170 tons net, was launched on 22 September 1949 by Sebr-Coops-Scheeps. She was equipped with a four cylinder oil engine by Appingedammer Brons. At the time of her loss she was owned Rederi 'M.S. Hans' (N.V. Ritmeester, of Groningen, managers). She was 130.3ft in length, had a beam of 22.8ft and a draught of 8.8ft (39.7m x 7.0m x 2.7m).

History

The *Grietje*, Captain Zorn Boersma, master, laden with 200 tons of coal, left Garston on 4 February 1963, but soon encountered a 60mph south-east wind and blinding blizzard as she headed for Douglas. At 4.00 a.m. on 5 February, the watch could see nothing through the blizzard, but knew they were being blown steadily towards the rocks on the east coast of the Isle of Man. The *Grietje* struck suddenly on rocks at Keristal, about three miles south-west of Douglas.

The eight crewmen stayed on board, too fearful of the heavy seas to attempt the short journey to the shore in a life-raft. A mayday message was broadcast on the ship's radio and was received immediately by coastguards. The Rocket Brigade and police were on the scene within thirty minutes of the distress call. They made their way from the road part of the way down the high cliffs.

From a tiny platform above the sheer cliff drop to the rocky beach near Little Ness, the Rocket Brigade fired ropes aboard the ship as it crushed between jagged rocks a few yards from the shore. The breeches buoy was then set up, but they had to wait until daybreak to rescue the crew of the *Grietje*.

Coastguard Ronald Weston was lowered to the beach as the wind bounced him against the rock face. He later said:

Above: Wreck of the *Grietje*.
(Copyright: Manx National Heritage)

Left: Bow of *Grietje* today.

When I got to the beach I shouted to the men that we could start hauling them up the breeches buoy. But they did not like the idea and I don't blame them. So we rigged up a cliff ladder for them. Six of them launched a life raft and got to the beach but the skipper and mate decided to stay aboard. It was then just about daylight, so we sent the first one up. We got six of them up by about 9.00 a.m. It took nearly twenty minutes each.

Coastguard District Officer David McGarrie, in charge of the rescue party, defied the wind to climb part of the way down the cliff to help the soaked and weary men the last few yards of the steep and exhausting climb. While the six Dutch crewmen, four of them teenage youths, were taken to a Douglas hotel for food, whisky, and a bath, Captain Boersma and the mate, D.G. Jager, stayed aboard the *Grietje*. 'They shouted to me that they would wait for low water to see if the ship could be floated off,' said Coastguard Weston. 'There was a tug from Liverpool standing by. We got the ship's papers off and sent them to the top.'

For over six hours the two men stayed aboard the ship. Then, with holes torn in the hull and the continual battering against the rocks, she started to flood and settle in the water. The two men then decided to come off and were hauled up the cliff by the breeches buoy. In the same hotel as his crewmen, a weary Captain Boersma said later, 'I don't feel like saying much, except that I'm thankful to be back on shore.'

The *Grietje* became a total wreck and gradually broke up over the subsequent years.

References

Isle of Man Examiner, MNH; *Isle of Man Times*, 08.02.1963 MNH; World Ship Society, B. Lawley.

Wreck Site

The rusty bow section, complete with winch, of the *Grietje* lies on a shingle beach below the cliffs at Keristal. The site is inaccessible except from a boat. Other parts of the *Grietje* are believed to lie below the low water mark.

Jeune St Charles

Position: 54 03.829 N, 04 47.605 W
Datum: WGS84
Map Reference: SC 173 667
Location: Calf Sound
Access: Car park at Calf Sound.

Vessel

The French coastal schooner *Jeune St Charles* of Pontrieux, 69 tons gross, was built at Flecamp in Normandy in 1852, and in 1857 was acquired by a Paimpol ship owner.

History

On 28 March 1858, at the small river port of Pontriex on the River Trieux, the *Jeune St Charles*, Captain Joseph Jegou, master, had completed her loading of flour for transport to Londonderry in Northern Ireland. Shortly afterwards, she was issued with her certificate of sea worthiness by the port authorities. On 29 March, she left Pontrieux on her voyage and was expected there five days later, with favourable winds.

For two days she stayed in the mouth of the River Trieux, before setting off in a stiff south-easterly breeze. They had variable winds up to 4 April, then they were caught in a south-easterly gale. Forty miles north of the Longships off the coast of Cornwall, they were forced to heave to, being unable to hold course because of the wind and heavy swell.

At 10.00 a.m. on 5 April they took a heavy sea, which stove in the hatch over the accommodation and flooded it. The following day, as the weather moderated, her original course was resumed. At 2.00 a.m. the strap on the mainsheet block parted and the mizzen boom broke, so Captain Jegou gave the order to set the sail and run before the wind, hoping to repair the damage. At 4.00 a.m. they resumed course in a full south-easterly gale and blinding rain.

They were sailing under main sail and storm jib when, at 10.00 p.m., the weather cleared briefly. They saw the Calf Lights, but to the westwards. Judging his position to be too close to the Isle of Man, he decided to luff up and weather it. Shortly afterwards, the mate, Yves Lemsur, gave a cry of alarm as land was sighted at a distance of about one cable ahead. Immediately they dropped the two bow anchors and were held by these at one ship's length from the land. The sea was washing over the ship from stem to stern. The sails were furled and the pumps were manned in a desperate attempt by the crew to keep the ship afloat.

At 8.00 a.m. the next day the anchor chains parted and she began to drift along the coast. Desperately, the storm jib was hoisted as they were driven along, about three fathoms from the cliffs, and, as her head could not be got out to sea, they dropped their one remaining anchor in the Calf Sound. It held the ship just long enough for the crew to launch their small boat for immediately afterwards, it parted.

The Thousla Cross monument to the wreck of the *Jeune St Charles*.

It was obvious that the ship would be swept onto the rocks and wrecked, so the crew abandoned her, taking a few personal belongings and the ship's papers. The wind and currents were so strong that the small boat was driven on a rock in the middle of the channel.

The first wave took away their oars, the second capsized the boat and all six crewmen were left clinging perilously to the rocks. One minute later, the two ship's boys were swept away and drowned. The captain, mate and two crewmen were left clinging to the rocks in terrible anguish.

At first light, the dangerous position of the French schooner had been noticed by farmers on the hillside over looking the Sound and word of the shipwreck, and the plight of the sailors on the Thousla Rock, quickly spread to the nearby harbour of Port St Mary.

A boat was launched from the Sound, crewed by Henry Qualtrough, Thomas Taubman, John Maddrell, Edward Fargher and Thomas Keig, but it could not reach the wreck due to the tide and weather.

A second boat was carried from Port St Mary. It was this boat, crewed by Thomas Harrison, Joseph Harrison, John Watterson, Daniel Lace and John Karran, that succeeded in battling against the odds to the wreck. The cries of the sailors could be heard clearly from the shore. Their ordeal had lasted for three hours, their hope apparently disappearing as the first rescue boat was swept by. Straining on the oars, the second boat was swept towards them and they were grasped with willing hands and taken aboard, to be driven by the strong current to the safety of the Calf of Man. There they were given aid by the lighthouse keepers.

The rescue of the survivors was officially reported by Mr J. McMeikan, Honouree Agent, Shipwrecked Fishermen's and Mariners Royal Benevolent Society. He consulted M. Fleury, the French consul in Liverpool, to commend the rescuers to the authorities in France.

So it was that on 7 December 1858, the five crewmen of the second boat were awarded the Silver Medal of Honour. A beacon was later erected on the Thousla Rock.

References

Mona's Herald, spool N90 MNH; *The Thousla Cross*, Clucas.

Wreck Site

About 50m to the west of the car park at the Calf Sound is situated the Thousla Cross monument to the wreck of the *Jeune St Charles*.

John Fairfield

Position: 54 04.135 N, 04 40.897 W
Datum: WGS84
Map Reference: SC 246 670

Location: Poyll Vaaish side of Scarlett, near Close ny Chollagh Point
Access: Follow the public footpath from Poyll Vaaish around to just past the earthwork at Close ny Chollagh.

Vessel

The wooden brig *John Fairfield*, of Liverpool, 247 tons old measurement, Captain Winby, master, was built at Poole in 1834 and was owned by Fairfield.

History

The *John Fairfield*, Captain W. Winby, master, began loading the cargo for her maiden voyage on 11 September 1834 and was cleared for sailing on 5 October.

She sailed from Liverpool for Havana in Cuba, on Monday 3 November at about 1.00 p.m. and, after passing the Floating-light, with the wind at south-west, stood to the north-west. During the night it began to blow hard and she kept between the Skerries and the Calf of Man till Thursday morning. Losing ground on every tack, Captain Winby decided to take shelter in Ramsey Bay and accordingly the vessel arrived there at 3.00 p.m. Finding the wind had gone round to the north-east and with every appearance of a strengthening of the wind from that quarter, he weighed the anchor the same evening. Owing to the lightness of the wind and the strong inshore currents around Maughold Head, the *John Fairfield* only just managed to pass the headland with difficulty. After running some fifteen miles south, Captain Winby bore a direct course for the Skerries, with the wind at south-east by east.

At 2.00 a.m. on Friday morning on 7 November, the breeze freshened and, at 4.00 a.m., the chief mate was called to the watch and he found it blowing a brisk gale, with the vessel bearing a press of canvas. In his anxiety to reduce the quantity of sail, the chief mate was unaware of the close proximity of the vessel to the Skerries. When the *John Fairfield* was within a mile or so of the rocks, Captain Winby came on deck. He immediately realised the danger the ship was in and wore the ship with only a cable's length to spare, making another short reach to the northward. When sail was taken in and reduced to the reefed topsails, the ship's course was resumed down the channel. The wind moved more to the south from which direction it increased to a severe gale. Captain Winby kept his vessel beating in the hope that the gale would abate or veer round to the north. At this point the foretopsail sheets gave way and it came to blow a perfect hurricane from the south. He then wore the ship with a view of passing through the North Channel. The crew saw the lights on the Calf of Man at about 6.00 p.m. and with the wind now from the south-west, Captain Winby decided to run for the shelter of Ramsey Bay for a second time.

At about 7.00 p.m., fancying himself to the leeward of Langness, he hove to with the supposed light of Douglas harbour and those on the Calf of Man on full view. Again the captain wore the ship, but could not weather and in less than ten minutes she struck beam on and her topmasts went overboard. The anchor was let go, which caused her stern to swing around inshore. At this point the waves broke over her bow, engulfing the cabin and half deck. Eventually, the bow was driven by a surge onto a rock ledge where she held fast and fell over to windward at the Poyll Vaaish side of Scarlett.

Fortunately for the eighteen crew and passengers, the tide was on the ebb and the hull held together, allowing the crew time to launch the jolly boat. But as this was immediately swamped, it was decided to reach shore by lashing a studding sail-boom to the bowsprit to allow each person to climb far enough ashore to drop onto the rocks between waves.

The cargo had an estimated value of £40,000-£50,000 and consisted of bales of calicoes, stuffs, broad cloths, webs of linen, blankets, hundreds of fouling pieces, lamps and scotch caps, strewn over a two-mile stretch of the coast. Mr Brine, the agent to Lloyd's and the Custom-house officers, used every exertion to save the property. Much of the cargo was saved, but there were still instances of stealing from the site even with soldiers from the garrison at Castle Rushen being on guard duty.

The *Mona's Herald* newspaper on Friday 14 November provided a vivid account of the scenes that attended the wreck in the week after the loss of the brig:

…Some men of the garrison were ordered out, and special constables sworn in for the protection of wreck property, but a most daring system of plunder was, not withstanding, carried on; which, it would appear, could not be checked.

The scene was a singular one when viewed from the higher ground. —To the left lay the brig with a great part of her bottom out and nearly cut in two, and the angry waves beating over her. In the midst of all dozens of men were actively engaged in rescuing from her bottomless hold, all their hands could grasp; parties of workmen, under the superintendence of the constabulary force, were seen all along the line amongst the rocks, some engaged in dragging from the sea long pieces of floating calicoes and linens, others heavily laden, slowly and cautiously treading back their tangle and slippery way, and depositing their respective burdens on the already collecting masses. In the field above, carts were seen moving in all directions, conveying the property to the appointed store houses; but in spite of the watchful care on one side, and the animated exertions and energies displayed on the other by the constabulary for the protection of wrecked goods, vast quantities were, not withstanding, boldly carried off by many daring plunders, but some of these were seized and made to disgorge, and others were sent to cool their heels in Castle Rushen. Nearly a cart load of property was discovered in Kirk Arbory village by Mr Chesterman, and ill-gotten spoils were brought back by him to the encampment.

One of the stores belonging to the Lloyd's agent, Mr Brine, was even broken into and its contents stolen. The inability of the authorities to maintain law and order clearly embarrassed them and the governor himself felt it necessary to write to London to explain the circumstances. In particular, he was keen to defend the Water Bailiff, who was accused by some of colluding in the looting. In addition, the governor made pains to explain why it had not proved possible to convict any of the fifty-two individuals who were caught for looting and arrested. The situation worsened further by the case of the accidental shooting of a fourteen-year-old-boy, John McHutchin. He was at the wreck site in a small boat with some other men, when he was shot by one of the soldiers guarding the site who had mistaken the men in the boat for looters.

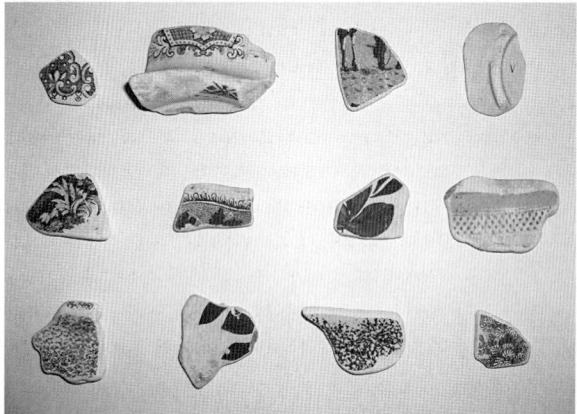

Above: The rocky beach where evidence of the wreck of the *John Fairfield* lies.

Left: Selection of pottery shards from the site of the wreck of the *John Fairfield*.

Below: Two musket flints from the site of the wreck of the *John Fairfield*.

References

Mona's Herald, spool N81 MNH; World Ship Society, M. Benn; Parliamentary Papers – Shipping Safety Volume 2 1836-39, Queens University, Belfast; *Manx Sun*, Friday, 21.11.1834. spool N52 MNH; *Lloyds List*, Tuesday, 18.11.1834.

Wreck Site

The wreck itself is no longer visible (as far as it is known). The wreck site, however, is indicated by the large deposits of pottery sherds, pieces of glass and gunflints present in the beach sediment. Artefacts have been found all the way from the ford, which crosses the track just to the east of Poyll Vaaish farm, to some of the shingle beaches located to the south-east of Close ny Chollagh.

Professor Peter J. Davey, in his study published in 1999, *A nineteenth-century export ceramic assemblage from Poyll Vaaish*, has provided a valuable insight into the six types of ceramics which make up the sherds.

The commonest sherds are white and undecorated plain ware. Some of the pieces include the knobs of lids and tureen handles, and as a group are more bulky than sherds from the other groups.

The next most frequently encountered group is that of the red transfer printed wares. Davey identified the sherds as coming from known transfers used, normally in blue, by William Adams, of Liverpool. Four designs 'Garden Sports', 'Grecian Font' and two completely different representations of 'Andalucia' can be identified. Davey further estimated that perhaps half of the sherds are from plates on which such patterns were applied. Many of the pieces of the plain ware are likely to have been part of plates, tureens, meat dishes and jugs, which were red transfer printed.

Three groups, namely dipped wares, spongewares and painted wares compose approximately a third of the sherds. A wide range of dipped wares are represented. Mocha is common, as is slip trailing, slip marbling, common cabling decoration and cat's eyes. Most of the sherds appear to be from jugs. All were probably made in Staffordshire. Spongeware was a speciality of Scottish potteries. All the Poyll Vaaish sherds are in rainbow spatter and appear to come from bowls with internal decoration. Like the transfer wares, the painted wares were thought by Davey to have been made by William Adams, but in his Staffordshire factories.

Shell-edged wares occur with blue, green, red and yellow colouration with scalloped edges. They all appear to be from plates on pearlware and are likely to have also been made in Staffordshire. The smallest group of sherds is derived from moulded spot edged wares.

The majority of the gunflints found at the site are of the 'platform' type and would have been intended for use with muskets and carbines.

Lily

Position: 54 03.764 N, 04 47.596 W
Datum: WGS84
Map Reference: SC 173 665
Location: Calf Sound
Access: Car park at Calf Sound

Vessel

The wooden brig *Lily*, of Liverpool, 196 tons burden, was owned by Hatten and Cookson, of Liverpool.

History

The *Lily*, John Owens, master, bound from Liverpool for Ambrazo, south-west Africa, with a general cargo, including twenty puncheons of rum, fire-arms, and fifty tons of gunpowder, was caught off the Calf of Man in the storm of Monday 27 December 1852. The sea was mountainous, and, despite the efforts of the crew, she was driven ashore at Kitterland in the Calf Sound at 11.00 a.m. The crew of thirteen men desperately tried to reach the rocks by means of the boats, but huge waves carried off the master, the cook and two lads. All of them drowned. In addition, one of the masts fell upon the carpenter killing him immediately.

The survivors were taken off the rocks by men from Port St Mary and a guard of policemen was left beside the wreck. Early on Tuesday morning 28 December 1852, Mr Enos Lace, grocer and ship broker of Port St Mary, being sub-agent for Lloyd's, proceeded with a party of men to the wreck to see what could be saved. They started work on the vessel, but at approximately 8.00 a.m. smoke was observed coming from the middle of the hold. Several carpenters were then employed in cutting a hole in the deck for the purpose of throwing water on the fire to extinguish it. As soon as the air entered the hold spontaneous combustion caused a huge explosion, killing all on the isle, apart from James Kelly, who miraculously survived albeit with severe facial injuries, despite standing only ten yards from the wreck when the explosion occurred. He recollected nothing of the incident, only finding himself gaining consciousness and sitting on a rock washing himself in his own blood. He later recounted under oath at the inquest that he saw a flash of fire from the deck and saw the head of a companion flying in the air.

So violent was the explosion that at the Level Mines, Colby, about three miles off, all the miners in the level thirty-five fathoms deep, were instantly thrown on their backs and the lights extinguished. Large and small pieces of timber and other wreckage, including human remains, were scattered all over the Parish of Rushen as far as Balladoole and even Red Gap, just outside of Castletown. Part of a mast or spar was found embedded in a field near the Howe near Port St Mary. Eyewitnesses to the explosion thought that an earthquake had occurred.

The following twenty-nine salvers were killed, all but four from Port St Mary: John Fell, mariner; William Cowley, mariner; William Kermode, labourer; Edward Gale, publican; Henry Gale, mariner; John Gale, labourer; Thomas Witted, mariner; John Cubbon, mariner; William Lawson, master mariner; Thomas Callister, mariner; William Taubman, blockmaker; John Callister, mariner; Samuel Callister, carpenter; John Callister, mariner; Thomas Turnbull, carpenter; George Costain, roper; William Watterson, mariner; Thomas Nelson, mariner; Charles Clugston, labourer; Enos Lace, shopkeeper and roper; Robert Callister, baker and mariner;

The plaque commemorating the 150th anniversary of the wreck of the brig *Lily*.

Edward Qualtrough, assistant tide waiter; William Watterson, mariner; William Cone, mariner; John Hudgeon, mariner; Edward Watterson, fisherman; John Watterson, carpenter; John Craigs, chief constable; and John Wright, constable.

References

Mona's Herald spool N88 MNH; *Dictionary of Disasters at Sea*, Hocking.

Wreck Site

Nothing of the wreck of the brig *Lily* is known to survive to this day, but a stone plaque commemorating the 150th anniversary of the disaster in 2002 lies about 150m south-west of the Sound car park and is set into the rock.

Manx Maid

Position: 54 06.071 N, 04 33.462 W
Datum: WGS84
Map Reference: SC 329 703

Location:	Meary Vooar, near Santon Head
Access:	Car park at Port Grenaugh, then follow the coastal footpath northwards. After Meary Vooar Farm, a cove with a stream is reached. The site lies on the rocky shore.

Vessel

The steamship *Manx Maid*, of Ramsey, (Official Number: 87,581), 49 tons register, was launched on Tuesday 1 October 1890 from Mr Parr's cement yard at the corner of Derby Road and the Big Bridge in Ramsey. The naming ceremony was performed by Miss Burrows, daughter of her owner, Mr George Burrows. The vessel was built by Mr James Duggan and was of a composite build i.e. an iron frame with wooden planking. She was towed to Douglas to be fitted with a boiler and engine by Messrs Knox. The *Manx Maid* was 78ft in length, had a beam of 18ft and a draught of 9ft (23.8m x 5.5m x 2.7m) and was schooner-rigged.

History

The *Manx Maid*, under the command of Captain Leslie Burrows, son of the owner, departed from the Point of Ayr in North Wales at 11.30 a.m. on Saturday 19 March 1904, bound for Laxey with a cargo of 100 tons of coal consigned for the Laxey Co-operative Society.

As she approached the Manx coast, a dense fog came on and Captain Burrows slowed her speed to below three knots. At approximately 9.30 p.m., he took a sounding which measured nine fathoms and he erroneously estimated that his ship was a little to the north of Douglas and about a mile from land.

Not long after taking the sounding, Captain Burrows thought it was time to put the steamer's head to sea and heave her to. Accordingly, just as the vessel was turning around, she struck on a beach of rock and boulders under Meary Vooar, near Santon Head at 9.50 p.m. At the time of stranding, the tide was half flood and a considerable rent was made in the hull of the vessel, allowing seawater to enter.

The crew of six men found it impossible to refloat the steamer and so decided to launch her small boat, but as a heavy onshore sea was running they experienced great difficulty in climbing into the boat. They eventually managed to safely get into the small boat and rowed around to the beach at Port Soderick. However, their troubles were not over and the small boat was dashed to pieces on the beach throwing the men into the water. Luckily, all six men managed to stagger safely to shore at 2.30 a.m. From Port Soderick they made their way by steam train to Douglas, to relay the news of the stranding to the owner, Mr George Burrows.

On later inspection, it was found that the vessel would become a total wreck and both the hull and cargo were put up for sale, although the owner's loss was partly covered by insurance. The *Manx Maid* was valued at £1,400 but insured for £600. Her cargo was valued at £70.

Above: The wreck of the *Manx Maid*. (Copyright: Mannin Collections Archive)

Right: The *Manx Maid*'s boiler still lies on the shore at Santon.

References

Isle of Man Examiner, spool EX11 MNH; *Manx Sun*, spool N77 MNH; *Mona's Herald*, Wednesday, 08.10.1890. spool N109 MNH; *Ramsey Courier*, Saturday, 23.11.1889. spool MN102 MNH; Board of Trade Casualty Returns, Guildhall Library; *Ramsey Courier*, Friday, 25.03.1904. spool MN111 MNH; *Mona's Herald*, 23.03.1904. spool N119 MNH; UK Public Records Office CUST104/297.

Wreck Site

All that remains of the *Manx Maid* is her boiler, lying on the rocky beach near to the Baltic Rock at Santon Head. It is a 'scotch' boiler, about 2.25m long and about 2m in diameter. The two furnaces can still be clearly seen along with the fifty-six tubes above the furnaces which allowed the water to be heated by the fires. A hole in the side of the boiler allows the girder plates to be seen. The boiler is fitted with three steel stays and the dome can still be seen on the top of the boiler.

Passages

Position: 54 21.332 N, 04 33.007 W
Datum: WGS84
Map Reference: SC 342 982
Location: Jurby Head
Access: Car park at the Cronk, Ballaugh. Wreck lies about two miles to the north along the beach, below Jurby Head.

Vessel

The steel steam trawler *Passages*, of Fleetwood (FD119), 271 tons gross, 123 tons net, was built by the Dominion Steam Boat Co. Ltd, of Toronto, Canada, in 1917. She was equipped with engines developing 62hp, which were built by the National Steam Boat Co. Ltd, of Goderich, Ontario, Canada. At the time of her loss, her owner was the Boston Deep Sea Fishing and Ice Co., of Grimsby and she was managed by Mr Basil A. Parkes of Fleetwood. She was 125.6ft in length, had a beam of 23.4ft and a draught of 12.6ft (38.3m x 7.1m x 3.8m).

History

During Wednesday 2 December 1931 and into the early hours of 3 December, a south-south-west gale of intense severity swept over the Isle of Man, and in the course of the night the *Passages*, which was returning from fishing grounds off the north-west of Ireland after a successful trip for herring, experienced a terrible buffeting. In the pitch darkness and in blinding rain, with huge seas sweeping the vessel from stem to stern, the skipper, W. James (37), of Fleetwood, was proceeding very cautiously, when suddenly the trawler stopped dead with a grating noise and it was realised she had run aground. The engines were immediately put full astern, but the vessel was held fast in soft sand and in an extremely dangerous position. It was 6.00 a.m. and skipper James had been on the bridge for six hours without a break.

Distress rockets were immediately fired and were observed from the shore enabling the Ramsey Rocket Brigade, under the command of District Officer Lace, to be mobilised. When the Brigade reached Jurby, they found the *Passages* aground in the shadow of the steep headland near the church. In order to reach the beach, the rescuers had to drag and carry their apparatus through waterlogged fields and make a perilous descent of the headland.

As soon as communication was established with the stranded vessel, Norman Platt, of Fleetwood, the cook on board the *Passages*, plunged overboard into the mountainous seas and succeeded in reaching the shore with a light line, which was then used to swing up the life-saving apparatus and the remainder of the thirteen crew were hauled to safety in the breeches buoy.

The Peel Rocket Brigade and the Peel and Ramsey Lifeboats were also called out at about 8.30 a.m. and the two boats experienced a gruelling time as they made their

The *Passages* shortly after running aground. (Copyright: Manx National Heritage)

Locals inspect the *Passages*. (Copyright: John Qualtrough)

respective ways to Jurby. Both boats were in sight of the trawler, when signals were fired to indicate that a rescue had been affected. The Peel Lifeboat was unable to return to her station due to the adverse weather conditions and accompanied the Ramsey Lifeboat back to the shelter of Ramsey Bay.

The mate, Richard Collinson, also of Fleetwood, praised skipper James's devotion to duty and attempts to get the *Passages* off the beach.

The *Passages* sank deeply into the sandy beach and became a total wreck. The cargo of herring, valued at £600, had to be dumped overboard.

References

Isle of Man Examiner, Friday, 04.12.1931. spool EX27 MNH; *Ramsey Courier*, 04.12.1931. MNH; Lloyd's Register of Shipping.

The wreck of the *Passages* as it appears today.

Wreck Site

The wreck of the *Passages* lies on the sandy beach below the cliffs at Jurby Head. For the non-diver she provides a good example of what a wreck may look like underwater. The wreck is about 40m in length and about 8m in width. It is orientated on a north-east/south-west axis with the bow facing north-east.

Most of the hull plating has vanished, but the general outline of the vessel can still be seen in the sand. The stern area is still reasonably intact and the sand is scoured out around the rudder. The highest part of the wreck is the triple-expansion engine standing proud above the beach. Ahead of the engine are the remains of her boiler and ahead of her boiler the fish hold can be still be made out. The bow area however, is much less distinct. Pieces of wreckage lie around the beach away from the main wreck.

Provider

Position: 54 03.689 N, 04 37.010 W
Datum: WGS84
Map Reference: SC 288 660
Location: Langness
Access: Car park at Langness. Walk across Langness to the eastern side, passing by the old explosives house. Upon reaching the end of the stone wall, turn left and walk about 200m to the north-east. There is a bench immediately above the site.

Vessel

The wooden schooner *Provider*, of Plymouth, 89 tons net, was built by Shilstons, of Plymouth in 1845. She was a two-masted topsail schooner, rigged fore and aft. The *Provider* was owned at the time of her loss by John Shilston, shipbuilder; John Wilcocks, mariner; Mr Cope, coal merchant; Edward Davies, sailmaker; John Putt, blacksmith; Mr Best, master mariner; and John Ellis, ropemaker. As well as being her master, John Wilcocks also managed the vessel.

History

The *Provider*, John Wilcocks, master, arrived at Liverpool from Morlaix, Brittany, on 16 March 1853, where she took on board a cargo of salt and left Liverpool at 3.00 p.m. on Thursday afternoon 31 March, bound for Glasgow. Later that evening, a severe easterly gale blew up and the *Provider* was driven on rocks on the outside of Langness at 1.30 a.m. on Friday 1 April. She went down almost immediately.

One man, James Boom, twenty-four years of age, who had joined the ship in June 1852, succeeded in getting onto the rocks and in so doing saved his life. John Wilcocks, master, of Plymouth; John Drew (60), mate, of Brixham; George Eddy (19), seaman, of Exmouth; Henry Stephens (16), seaman, of Devon; and Joseph Thomas (16), seaman, of Plymouth, however, all perished.

References

Manx Sun, spool N58 MNH; *Lloyd's Register 1852*; Article in *Manx Life*, Chris Pickard.

The *Provider* stone at Langness.

Wreck Site

A large slab of stone, believed to be a natural outcrop, marks the spot above the gulley where the *Provider* was lost. It provides a poignant symbol, reminding us today, over 150 years later, of the fate of the *Provider* and the unfortunate men who drowned on her. The stone is inscribed with the name 'Provider' on the left-hand side, with the letters running vertically. To the right are the words 'All lost' and the date '1853'. Flowers are sometimes placed at the stone. It is believed that the grief-stricken James Boom carved the original words on the stone, which have been re-carved over the years.

Thorne

Position:	54 09.922 N, 04 27.008 W
Datum:	WGS84
Map Reference:	SC 401 772
Location:	Port Jack, Onchan
Access:	Port Jack, Onchan

Vessel

The iron barque *Thorne*, of Liverpool, 905 tons gross, 877 tons net, was built in 1878 by James Thompson of Sunderland and was owned by Mr James Dowie & Co., of Liverpool. She was 194.3ft in length, had a beam of 33ft and a draught of 19ft (59.2m x 10.1m x 5.8m).

History

The *Thorne* left Liverpool on Monday 13 January 1890, Captain James Francis W. Glazebrook, master, bound for Adelaide in Australia, her crew consisting of a first mate, Stanley Taggart, formerly of Douglas, a second mate, a boatswain, a carpenter, eleven able seamen, two apprentices and a ship's boy. There were also two passengers.

Strong head winds thwarted two of her attempts to get down the Irish Channel, and the furthest she reached was opposite Bardsey Island. The wind then swung to the north-west and strengthened further, forcing the *Thorne* to shelter in Douglas Bay. Here she lay at anchor for some days before the wind strengthened to gale force from the south-west on Friday 24 January.

Many times in the past, ships have sheltered in Douglas Bay during a north-westerly or westerly wind, forgetting that the temporary sanctuary of the bay soon turns into an exposed and dangerous coastline in the south or south-westerly gales which are so prominent around the Isle of Man in the autumn or winter months.

The *Thorne* began to drag her anchor sometime between 11.00 p.m. and 12.00 a.m. on 24 January, and the crew were called to give more chain at 1.30 a.m. on Saturday 25 January.

The wreck of the *Thorne*. (Copyright: Manx National Heritage)

At about 2.30 a.m., the *Thorne* was observed from the shore to be drifting towards the rocks at the northern end of Douglas Bay. The predicament of the *Thorne* was reported to harbourmaster Kelly and customs officer John Corkill by the captain of the steam tug *Manx King*, who had sighted a blue light burning towards Onchan Head. At 2.45 a.m., the signals for the Douglas Lifeboat and Rocket Brigade were fired off. The two crews soon reported to their stations, the lifeboat house at that time being located on Douglas promenade near to the site of the Villa Marina shopping arcade, and the lifeboat reached the *Thorne* not long after 3.00 a.m. By the time the lifeboat reached her, the *Thorne* was lying aground on a reef, with her stern towards the land and heavy seas sweeping over her motionless hull.

The lifeboat hailed the stranded barque, but received no answer. The lifeboat crew then observed a faint light lying some distance away close to shore. They made for this light and found the crew and passengers of the *Thorne* in their boat a couple of hundred yards off Port Jack. Great difficulty was experienced in approaching the boat, because of the sea driving the lifeboat towards the rocks; considerable skill and care was needed by coxswain John Kelly to manoeuvre the Lifeboat into position by means of her anchor. The crew of the *Thorne* were successfully transferred to the lifeboat, but this was not the end of their troubles. In the meantime, the wind and sea had increased in severity, putting the lifeboat in distress. Captain Kelly, the superintendent coxswain, had fortunately requested the *Manx King* to steam out into the bay and tow the lifeboat back into harbour. This was accomplished and all involved landed safely. Meanwhile, the Rocket Brigade had taken several hours to hike over rough terrain to reach the rocks opposite the stranded vessel. Not knowing the *Thorne*'s crew had already departed the doomed vessel, the Rocket Brigade managed to fire a line over the wreck.

Over the next day or two, the heavy seas burst open the main hatch, and a quantity of the cargo, comprising cases of spirits and casks of liquor amongst other items, floated out of the vessel. The police and customs officials were at hand to try and prevent pilfering and misappropriation of goods, but many individuals still managed

One of the anchors from the *Thorne* can be seen at Laxey harbour.

to obtain large quantities of spirits, leading to amazing scenes of public drunkenness. Serious consideration was given to sending to Castletown for the military at the garrison there, and at one stage a customs official fired his pistol to disperse the crowd.

The cargo, which was insured for between £40,000 and £50,000, comprised of the following: several hundred cases of spirits, totalling 9,800 gallons, Roderick Dhu whisky and brandy, a quantity of bar iron, a great number of grinding stones, crates of crockery, linen, blankets, flannels, silks, a large number of tins of cured fish, coils of barbed wire and reels of paper for web printing machines. Captain Young, of the Liverpool Salvage Association, arrived in Douglas the same day as the grounding of the *Thorne* and the company's steamer *Mallard* reached Douglas on the night of Monday 27 January. The *Mallard* had several divers on board and all the necessary specialist equipment for salvage operations. The powerful gang of men on board the salvage steamer were reinforced by a number of men usually employed in discharging the steamers at the quay and the work of stripping the vessel of her gear and saving the spars began at once. Divers went down and examined the ship's bottom. It was found that there was a large hole knocked in her underneath the mainmast and another further aft. The small steamship *Lady Loch*, of Douglas, was engaged to assist in saving the cargo and this work carried on day and night for a week.

The cargo, on being landed, was conveyed to the Victoria and Battery Piers. The cases of spirits and other dutiable goods were stored in the bonded warehouse and a large part of the other cargo was stored in Duff's warehouse on the South Quay. On Friday 31 January 1890, the steamer *W.S. Caine* sailed for Liverpool with a large portion of the salvage, including spirits, beer and bale goods. Later, when the tide permitted, the *W.S. Caine* moored alongside the *Thorne* and goods were loaded directly from the wrecked vessel into the streamer.

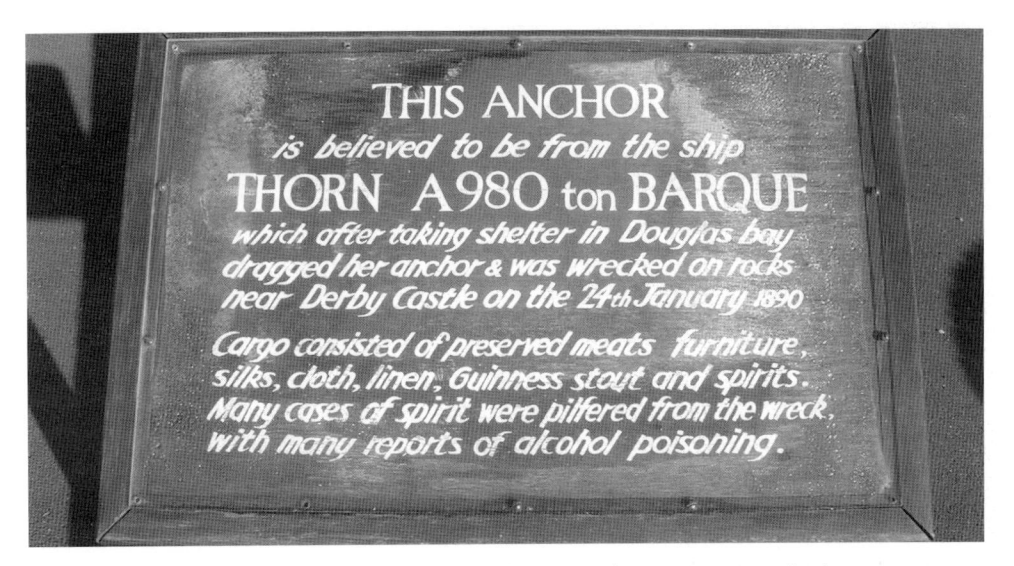

> **THIS ANCHOR** is believed to be from the ship **THORN A 980 ton BARQUE** which after taking shelter in Douglas bay dragged her anchor & was wrecked on rocks near Derby Castle on the 24th January 1890. Cargo consisted of preserved meats, furniture, silks, cloth, linen, Guinness stout and spirits. Many cases of spirit were pilfered from the wreck, with many reports of alcohol poisoning.

The plaque commemorating the wreck of the *Thorne* can be seen at Laxey harbour.

The Board of Trade Inquiry at Liverpool gave the following judgement as to the cause of the loss of the *Thorne*. The master was justified in putting into Douglas Bay and remaining there so long. He made an attempt to leave when the weather moderated and engaged a tug to assist in getting underway, but on heaving up the port anchor, it was found to be foul of the starboard chain. To clear the tangle took the crew of the barque the whole of the following day. The master was justified at riding at one anchor with ninety fathoms of cable out in twelve fathoms of water, the second anchor being ready to let go. Sufficient cable was paid out to the port anchor. Had he used more cable, then there would have been greater risk of fouling the anchor. A proper anchor watch was set. Gilbert Morice, the apprentice, who had been in charge from 10.00 p.m. to 1.00 a.m. on 25 January, had served three and a half years and appeared to the court to be fully competent. All reasonable precautions were taken to ascertain whether the vessel was dragging, by the bearings of landmarks on the shore and by the use of the lead. Although the master left full and proper instructions, he was on and off deck all during the night and always ready for a call. After stranding, it was noticed that the starboard cable was hanging up and down, and the port cable, on which seventy-five fathoms had been veered and was straight out. From this, it was apparent that the starboard cable must have parted and the port anchor was possibly fouled. At any rate, it failed to hold. The master was in no way in default and could not be held to blame for the loss of the *Thorne*.

References

Mona's Herald, spool N109 MNH; *Isle of Man Examiner*, 25.01.1890, 01.02.1890. & 15.02.1890. spool MN39 MNH; *Isle of Man Examiner*, Tuesday, 21.04.1992; World Ship Society, G.H. Somner.

The keel and ribs are all that are left of the *Thorne*.

Wreck Site

The remnants of the *Thorne* lie on the rocky beach at Port Jack close to the sewer outfall. The wreck only shows at the lowest astronomical tides in the spring and autumn. It consists of about 12m of the iron keel protruding above the surface with an unknown length continuing to run underwater towards the stern. At right angles to the keel are the iron ribs, spaced about 2ft apart. The width of the wreckage is about 7m. As would be expected with the vessel running bow first into the rock, the keel is orientated north/south with the stern end pointing towards Douglas Head Lighthouse. A large girder about 6m in length lies on the starboard side of the forward end of the keel.

One of the anchors from the *Thorne* can be found on display at Laxey harbour next to the entrance to the boat park. The anchor was trawled up in Douglas Bay and is believed to come from the *Thorne*. There is also a plaque commemorating her loss. A second anchor was trawled up in the 1980s and was on display on the South Quay in Douglas until recently.

Unknown

Position: 54 05.406 N, 04 36.208 W
Datum: WGS84
Map Reference: SC 298 692

Location:	Santon Gorge
Access:	Car park at Ronaldsway side of Derbyhaven near to the Flying Club, and then along the public footpath 'Raad ny Foillan' to Santon Gorge.

Vessel

No details are available.

History

It is likely, given the style of the cross, that the shipwreck most likely occurred pre-1800. This theory is supported by the historical evidence. I have accumulated a database of shipwrecks, numbering over 1,220 individual wrecks since 1644. The sequence is as complete as can be achieved since 1800. Between 1644 and 1799, not all wrecks were recorded, or no reference remains in the few records that now exist from that period. I have no shipwreck recorded at this location with the loss of thirteen lives, however – assuming that each cross carved on the rock represents one crewman or passenger lost.

Wreck Site

The crosses are carved on a slab of bedrock just above the high-water mark at the southern side of the entrance to Santon Gorge. The plane of the rock is angled at forty-five degrees and faces to the south.

The thirteen crosses carved on the rock at Santon Gorge.

INDEX OF WRECKS

Wrecks in Open Water

Wreck	Page	Wreck	Page
Adgillus,	25	Lady Louisa Pennant,	98
Afton,	28	Lembas,	100
Albatross,	30	Limesfield,	102
Amber Rose,	33	Liverpool,	104
Ardbeg,	37	Lucy,	107
Ballina,	39	Manchester,	109
Ben Rein,	43	Mhari-L,	111
Ben Veg,	46	Octavia,	113
Blue Star,	48	Oona Hall,	115
Briar,	50	Opal,	117
Cardea,	51	Paddle Wheel,	118
Carmelite,	54	Peveril,	119
Clwyd,	56	Polarlight,	123
Dawn Waters,	59	PT1,	126
Don Bosco,	61	Queen of the Isles,	128
Dundalk,	64	Rian,	131
Empress Eugenie,	66	Ringwall,	132
Fenella Ann,	69	Robert Dee,	134
Fire King,	73	Romeo,	136
Float,	76	Rostrevor,	139
Florence,	77	Skerries,	140
Flying Meteor,	80	Sustain,	142
Girl May,	82	Teasel,	144
Glenmaroon,	83	Thracian,	147
Grinder,	85	Tuskar,	149
Hibernian,	87	U246,	152
Inkosi,	91	Vivid,	153
Joseph Hodgkins,	94	Westburn,	156
Lady Louisa,	96		

Index of Wrecks

Wrecks on the Coast

Wreck	Page	Wreck	Page
Alyn,	159	James Crossfield,	189
Bessie,	162	Madge Wildfire,	190
Citrine,	164	Mary Barrow,	193
Clan MacMaster,	167	Mary Heeley,	195
Crown,	170	Mayfield,	197
Darro,	174	Merisia,	200
Democrat,	175	North British,	202
Dispatch,	179	Prince Alfred,	205
Dunrobin,	180	Racehorse,	207
Earl of Carrick,	182	Sarah Latham,	210
Emerald,	184	Useful,	212
Glendun,	186	William Hanbury,	214
Incentive,	188		

Wrecks on the Shore

Wreck	Page	Wreck	Page
Agnes,	217	John Fairfield,	235
Argo,	219	Lily,	239
Austrums,	222	Manx Maid,	241
Capella,	224	Passages,	244
Cevic,	226	Provider,	246
Girl Mary,	229	Thorne,	248
Grietje,	231	Unknown,	252
Jeune St Charles,	233		

Other titles published by Tempus

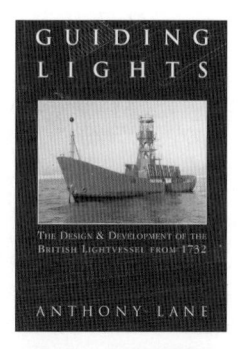

Guiding Lights The Design and Development of the British Lightvessel from 1732
ANTHONY LANE

Guiding Lights is the story of the light vessels that have protected our coast since 1732 and the variety of innovative engineering that has gone into their development; from the first lighthouses and lightships, to the replacement of the bell and gong by poweful air foghorns, this book charts the methods of safeguarding vessels around the British coast.
07524 2115 8

Isle of Man Shipping The Twilight Years
IAN COLLARD

The Isle of Man has had a long tradition of seafaring; the Island has been connected to both Britain and Ireland by sea since pre-Viking times. This book covers the period from the 1960s to the present day, reflecting on the advances in technology and changes that have occurred across this period, through the author's extensive collection of photographs, tickets and other memorabilia.
07524 2131 X

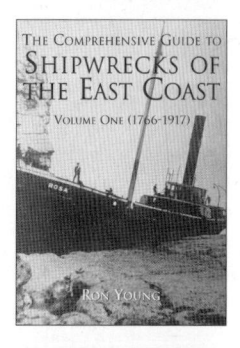

A Comprehensive Guide to Shipwrecks of the East Coast
RON YOUNG

This is the story of just some of the disasters that have occurred along the east coast, from Robin Hood's Bay in Yorkshire to Lincolnshire. This book assesses the numerous wrecks as diving and boat angling sites, as well as describing the marine life and wrecks to be found on the seabed along this busy and treacherous stretch of coastline.
07524 2764 4

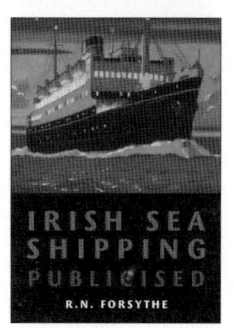

Irish Sea Shipping Publicised
R.N. FORSYTH

The companies that operated across the Irish Sea have been using posters, pamphlets, brochures and guides for over two hundred years in an effort to attract custom, whether passenger or freight. This book considers Irish Sea trade from Swansea in Wales to Campbeltown in the west of Scotland and from Cork to Londonderry, using original guide books, posters and pamphlets and photographs.
0 7524 2355 X

**To discover more Tempus titles please visit us at:
www.tempus-publishing.com**